Safeguarding Adults
Under the Care Act 2014

of related interest

Safeguarding Adults and the Law
Michael Mandelstam
ISBN 978 1 84905 300 6
eISBN 978 0 85700 626 4

Good Practice in Safeguarding Adults
Working Effectively in Adult Protection
Edited by Jacki Pritchard
ISBN 978 1 84310 699 9
eISBN 978 1 84642 825 8
Part of the Good Practice in Health, Social Care and Criminal Justice series

Good Practice in Safeguarding Children
Working Effectively in Child Protection
Edited by Liz Hughes and Hilary Owen
ISBN 978 1 84310 945 7
eISBN 978 1 84642 894 4
Part of the Good Practice in Health, Social Care and Criminal Justice series

Recording Skills in Safeguarding Adults
Best Practice and Evidential Requirements
Jacki Pritchard with Simon Leslie
ISBN 978 1 84905 112 5
eISBN 978 0 85700 229 7

Safeguarding Children Across Services
Messages from Research
Carolyn Davies and Harriet Ward
ISBN 978 1 84905 124 8
eISBN 978 0 85700 290 7
Part of the Safeguarding Children Across Services series

Safeguarding Black Children
Good Practice in Child Protection
Edited by Claudia Bernard and Perlita Harris
ISBN 978 1 84905 569 7
eISBN 978 1 78450 011 5

Safeguarding Adults Under the Care Act 2014

Understanding Good Practice

Edited by **Adi Cooper OBE** and **Emily White**

Foreword by **Lyn Romeo**

Jessica Kingsley *Publishers*
London and Philadelphia

Figure 11.1 reprinted with permission of the
Domestic Abuse Intervention Project

First published in 2017
by Jessica Kingsley Publishers
73 Collier Street
London N1 9BE, UK
and
400 Market Street, Suite 400
Philadelphia, PA 19106, USA

www.jkp.com

Library of Congress Cataloging in Publication Data
A CIP catalog record for this book is available from the Library of Congress

British Library Cataloguing in Publication Data
A CIP catalogue record for this book is available from the British Library

ISBN 978 1 78592 094 3
eISBN 978 1 78450 358 1

Printed and bound in Great Britain

Dedication

This book is dedicated to John Gunner who died suddenly during its preparation. We want to commemorate his significant contribution to the world of mediation and restorative justice.

Acknowledgements

We would like to thank: Lyn Romeo for 'volunteering' us to edit this book; Stephen Jones and colleagues at JKP for their advice and help; Lindsey Pike at RiPfA and all their associates who reviewed chapter drafts; Christine Cocker for her support and advice on editing; Michael Preston-Shoot, Suzy Braye and Fiona Bateman for their legal expertise and commentary on the Appendix; the Cheshire East Safeguarding Adults Board Service User Sub-group; and of course all of the chapter authors for their fantastic contributions and commitment to our common ambition of improving safeguarding adult practice.

Contents

Section 3: Current Issues for Practitioners

Foreword

Lyn Romeo

I am very pleased to welcome this book as an important contribution to support all practitioners working with people who are experiencing abuse or neglect, or are at risk of these, in their lives. In particular, I think that social workers, social work students and social work leaders, as well as practitioners in all agencies and organisations working to safeguarding adults, will benefit from the range of insights, knowledge and reflections by the contributors in this challenging and critically important area of practice.

Adult safeguarding practice is on an exciting journey, with research and evidence informing changes in the way we work with people. Making Safeguarding Personal, supported by the Care Act (2014) statutory guidance, promotes a person-centred and outcome-focused approach, complementing the strengths- or asset-based practice. This approach encompasses some key features: human rights informing our value base for working with people; and relationship-based working informing how practitioners support people to manage a range of risks in their lives. As I said in my annual report: 'Social work practice with adults which is focused on personalisation and co-production, promoting choice, independence and best outcomes, is consolidating the principles of social justice, human rights and respect for diversities. These are central to social work and contribute to developing a broader definition of social work practice and the contexts within which it can make a positive difference to people's lives' (Romeo 2016, p.6). I am pleased to see that these approaches and themes recur throughout the chapters covering the considerable range of topics within adult safeguarding practice that are featured in this book.

Continuing practice development is one of my highest priorities and, in this book, the authors offer considerable insights that will assist all practitioners in their learning and reflection on their practice. We need to understand what works in current social work practice so that we can understand the effectiveness of social work models of intervention and develop an evidence base for our work and do the right thing. Authors of the different chapters in this book have brought considerable research and knowledge that provide this evidence base for working in this area. These will benefit all practitioners, assist them to improve their safeguarding practices and contribute to their ongoing learning. Enhancing and valuing legal literacy and its application in practice is key, and I am pleased to see this woven through the chapters of the book for readers to access and be informed by the experts in these areas. Listening to and learning from people who experience social work services in this context is also of vital importance if we really are going to shape and develop social work practice that chimes with their needs and aspirations for better lives. Helpfully this book also makes a welcome contribution to co-producing improvements in safeguarding practice.

Lyn Romeo,
Chief Social Worker for Adults

Reference

Romeo, L. (2016) *Annual Report by the Chief Social Worker for Adults 2015–16.* London: Department of Health.

Introduction

Adi Cooper and Emily White

They say it doesn't happen

They say I'm 'different'
They say I'm 'the weird guy'
They say I'm 'not right'
They say I don't fight back

They say it's kind of funny
to take my money
They say that I should work harder
They say they'll pay in experience

They say to do my chores
They ask for more
To give more, to do more,
I'm told
To give this, and do this,
I'm told
They'll take this and do this
I'm told
To be ignored
And never say a word
and words can hurt
I've been hit with names spat in my face
While they say the same old phrase
About sticks and stones
but I know the power of words
because all of mine are silent

If I could say one thing to you
Don't.
Don't see an opportunity to take
Don't excuse the hate
like 'this doesn't happen to adults anyway'
don't sweep this away
don't say borrow when you mean steal
don't say sorry when you don't feel it
don't say help when you mean use
don't say that this is not abuse

instead
just say

hey how are you today?
Say hey you're looking good today?
You're looking like you should today
And I've got something I want to say

I just want to dance with my friends
I want a cruise ship that never ends
I want to travel on my own
And watch with pride as my kids grow

I want to tie the knot
Not be forgot when you're making plans
I don't want to meet demands
I want my life in my own hands
My heart beating fast

I want friends who make me laugh
And lend a little help
Who make me feel proud of myself
To help improve my health
I know that all I need to do is say

and they
will believe me
will relieve me
and free me from silence
They say 'I'm different' and that's alright

Speak up, speak out
There is no excuse
Help stop adult abuse[1]

11

These words are written and spoken by people with learning disabilities about some of their experiences and remind us why safeguarding is important. We are all people, with needs and dreams, and we all deserve respect and to be safe. We are reminded time and time again to listen to what people with care and support needs tell us about their experience of abuse and their experience of safeguarding from abuse. They say that they want to be listened to, believed and trusted, informed and involved, so able to make decisions, and they want support from confident practitioners and not to be judged.

> 'Never give up on us. If you walk away, the person isn't going to have a very nice life.'[2]

This book aims to help practitioners to do what people want and need, so that they can deliver good safeguarding practice, in order that people can keep themselves safe. We must listen to what people tell us about their lives and experiences if we are to fulfil our safeguarding responsibilities successfully.

The term 'safeguarding' is used to describe a wide mix of duties, powers and measures across the criminal justice, health, housing and social care sectors. Authors use the term to describe both adult protection functions of public bodies to enquire and intervene to protect an adult, unable to protect themselves from abuse and neglect or the risk of it, and the range of proactive measures expected to be taken by those responsible for providing safe standards of care, support or treatment to prevent the risk of abuse or neglect. This book sets out the principles behind working in adult safeguarding, describes core skills and knowledge that support practice in this area, and covers areas that present challenges for practitioners where specific skills or knowledge may apply.

---

1   Copyright. Reprinted by permission of the Cheshire East Safeguarding Adults Board. Thank you to the Service User Sub Group who produced the material with support from Annette Lomas, Cheshire East Council & Manchester Metropolitan University. Permission is granted for this material to be shared for non-commercial, educational purposes, provided that this copyright statement appears and that the recorded piece is not edited in any way and is always shown in its entirety. For feedback, comments or queries, please visit www.stopadultabuse.org.uk. See the audio-visual version Stop Adult Abuse: Cheshire East Service User's Spoken Word at www.stopadultabuse.org.uk/home. aspx.

2   Interviews with people with care and support needs, with experience of adult safeguarding, in Cheshire East, facilitated by the Cheshire Centre for Independent Living, undertaken for this book. They were asked questions about what works well in adult safeguarding and what they wanted to say to practitioners reading this book.

Why this book now? Adult safeguarding practice continues to develop and evolve. The Care Act (2014) made safeguarding adults a statutory responsibility, and the accompanying detailed guidance sets out expectations of practice. This book aims to bring this to life, relate it to experience and knowledge, in order to help practitioners and inform their practice. Chapter 14 of the *Care and Support Statutory Guidance* (Department of Health [DH] 2016), also referred to as the Care Act (2014) statutory guidance, is core and essential reading for all practitioners in this field, not only because it is statutory guidance, but also because it is hugely helpful and informative in defining what is expected of practitioners. The authors in this book present perspectives and insight into some of the complexities and dilemmas when applying the guidance to support people through the difficulties and challenges in their lives. They offer a range of different ways of working with people experiencing, or at risk of, abuse or neglect. They provide evidence from research and practice, explore issues and themes, and offer a range of models and methods. They aim to promote good and innovative safeguarding practice, encouraging readers to learn from current knowledge and evidence, for practitioners to consider how to apply this learning in their work. Adult safeguarding practice is a journey; there is still a long way to go and a lot to learn. As it evolves there are new challenges, and the authors address a range of practice issues, including some where there may be more questions than answers.

The term 'practitioner' is used as an inclusive term to refer to anyone working with adults who are at risk of experiencing abuse or neglect, and the people around them. This is because the good practice described in this book can be adopted by people working in different sectors, in various roles and in a range of circumstances: anyone offering support to people who need it. This book is intended for all practitioners encountering people at risk of abuse or neglect, for example those working in social care, housing, policing, health, care provision, and the voluntary and community sector, who wish to develop their understanding of adult safeguarding, as well as students learning about adult safeguarding, as well as practitioners in all agencies and organisations working to safeguard adults. The authors themselves come from a wide range of backgrounds, deliberately reflecting the spectrum of people who can write about good practice in adult safeguarding: social workers, people working in community and voluntary sectors, academics and lawyers. We wanted to present a variety of approaches based on a broad range of evidence and experience.

There are two core themes that run through the book which are essential for good practice in adult safeguarding: a person-centred and outcome-focused approach to safeguarding, also known as Making Safeguarding Personal (MSP); and knowing the law and how it applies to adult safeguarding practice – that is, legal literacy.

Making Safeguarding Personal is a national programme promoting a shift in culture and practice to make adult safeguarding more effective from the perspective of the person being safeguarded. It was developed because previous approaches to safeguarding practice were not meeting people's safeguarding needs – they were no longer fit for purpose (see Chapter 1). This personalised approach is essential to working with people, whether using a 'signs of safety' model or working with people who are victims of scamming. It involves listening to and talking with people to understand what outcomes they want and how best to achieve them. The Care Act (2014) guidance supports this approach as recommended practice (DH 2016, para.14.15). Evidence of its effectiveness is emerging as it is implemented and embedded (Cooper *et al.* 2016). The MSP approach further stimulates a productive debate around challenges, such as how best to support and empower people being coerced, or those without the mental capacity to make decisions about their own safety, or who say that they don't want help (see Chapters 7, 9 and 10).

Improving legal literacy or 'making safeguarding legal' (Mandelstam 2017) runs throughout the book. Not only the Care Act (2014) but also a wide range of legislation and evolving case law is referred to in different chapters, as well as being the focus of the Appendix. Authors reinforce the importance of practitioners: being aware of relevant legislation and the legal frameworks within which they practise; knowing how to work within the boundaries of the law; using legislation pro-actively to support people to keep themselves safe and prevent further abuse or neglect; and also knowing when to ask for specialist support and advice, given the complexity of some safeguarding practice challenges.

The book is structured in three sections, which reflect different aspects of safeguarding practice: how to work with people; how to apply the range of legal tools at our disposal; and how to engage with the newer areas of adult safeguarding activity. Chapters in each section include contributions from different practitioners and expert authors who provide: case studies to illustrate good practice; checklists, top tips or key messages for their specific area of practice; and signposts to other resources, as relevant. The Appendix provides an overview of the relevant core legal frameworks for all safeguarding adults practice, although authors cite further statutory guidance where more specialist areas apply.

Section 1: Making Safeguarding Personal: Approaches to Practice

In Chapter 1, 'The "Making Safeguarding Personal" Approach to Practice', Jane Lawson explains how to practise a person-centred and outcome-focused approach to safeguarding adults. This is fundamentally about having conversations with people about what they want to achieve, how to improve and achieve safety, wellbeing, resolution and recovery, and addresses risk.

In Chapter 2, 'Working More Reflexively with Risk: Holding "Signs of Safety and Wellbeing" in Mind', Tony Stanley discusses this 'asset-based' approach to practice. He describes the tools for assessment and person-centred planning, decision making and engaging adults and their family networks, using appreciative inquiry to help people achieve goals of empowerment, and improvement in their wellbeing.

Marilyn Taylor and Linda Tapper describe how family group conferencing is used in adult safeguarding to bring together people closest to the person concerned to formulate a plan to promote their safety and protection in Chapter 3, 'Participative Practice and Family Group Conferencing'.

In Chapter 4, 'Working towards Recovery and Resolution, including Mediation and Restorative Justice', John Gunner explores how these approaches, developed from outside social care, are consistent with Care Act (2014) principles and have applicability and learning for adults with care and support needs at risk from abuse or neglect.

Trish Hafford-Letchfield and Sarah Carr, in Chapter 5, 'Promoting Safeguarding: Self-Determination, Involvement and Engagement in Adult Safeguarding', look at how people who use services can be involved in adult safeguarding, using narrative techniques to communicate and redefine them, and their issues and problems.

Section 2: Working with Risk and Using the Law

Section 2 aims to identify the fundamental skills and knowledge that practitioners working in adult safeguarding need. In Chapter 6, 'Assessing and Responding to Risk', Emily White discusses different approaches to working with risk, recognising that balancing risk and protection is an inherent tension in adult safeguarding. People can make unwise decisions or cope with some level of risk, and this is core to a personalised approach to practice. She provides tools and ideas for effective risk assessment, positive risk enablement and management.

In Chapter 7, 'Mental Capacity Act and Adult Safeguarding', Dan Baker explores issues arising from working with people who lack mental capacity in safeguarding situations, as this presents specific challenges. He describes how practitioners undertake best-interests decision making, and the need to work to empower people to address safeguarding concerns.

In Chapter 8, 'Using the Law to Support Adult Safeguarding Interventions', Fiona Bateman discusses the underlying principles of the law that apply to adult safeguarding as a foundation for practice, as well as relevant statutory guidance, using case law examples. Knowing about the legal basis of adult safeguarding is fundamental because the law defines the extent and limits of what can be done to enable people to be safe.

Jill Manthorpe, Rebecca Johnson, Stephen Martineau and Caroline Norrie, in Chapter 9, 'Managing Difficult Encounters with Family Members', discuss what helps and hinders engagement with adults at risk of abuse or neglect, citing Safeguarding Adults Reviews and Serious Case Reviews.

Section 3: Current Issues for Practitioners

The third section of the book provides chapters that cover newer areas of adult safeguarding practice that were not always previously seen as such, and were included in the Care Act (2014) statutory guidance (DH 2016). The principles and approaches described elsewhere in the book are woven through these chapters: person-centred and outcome-focused approaches; legal literacy; and mental capacity and working with risk.

In Chapter 10, 'Self-Neglect and Hoarding', Suzy Braye, David Orr and Michael Preston-Shoot discuss the wide range of literacies which inform practice in this area. Citing evidence from Safeguarding Adults Reviews and Serious Case Reviews, they indicate practices that are more likely to be helpful with people who hoard or self-neglect.

In Chapter 11, 'Domestic Abuse and Adult Safeguarding', Lindsey Pike and Nicki Norman make connections between these areas of practice focusing on adults with a range of care and support needs, providing guidance for practitioners working with survivors.

In Chapter 12, 'Palermo to Croydon', Antony Botting, Tish Elliott and Sean Olivier discuss this new area of safeguarding to support practitioners to develop their understanding, and to be able to recognise and respond when they identify people with care and support needs who may be the victims of modern slavery.

Chapter 13 looks at 'Safeguarding Adults at Risk of Financial Scamming'. Sally Lee, Rebecca Johnson, Lee-Ann Fenge and Keith Brown provide an overview of what scamming is, who might be vulnerable and why, and how to undertake safeguarding in this area.

In the Conclusion, Adi Cooper draws together some key messages for good practice in adult safeguarding.

We are pleased that we have been able to bring together contemporary expertise into one volume to address the current challenges and tensions faced by practitioners and we hope that you find this volume useful for practice.

References

Cooper, A., Briggs, M., Lawson, J., Hodson, B., and Wilson, M. (2016) *Making Safeguarding Personal Temperature Check*. London: ADASS.

Department of Health (2016) *Care and Support Statutory Guidance*. London: DH.

Mandelstam, M. (2017) *Care Act 2014: An A–Z of Law and Practice* (forthcoming). London: Jessica Kingsley Publishers.

MAKING SAFEGUARDING PERSONAL: APPROACHES TO PRACTICE

Chapter 1

The 'Making Safeguarding Personal' Approach to Practice

Jane Lawson

Introduction and context

This chapter examines developments leading to the explicit inclusion of Making Safeguarding Personal (MSP) within the statutory guidance and what we can take from this for current practice. It emphasises that putting core principles into practice and using these as a measure of effectiveness must be at the heart of safeguarding adults. It underlines and gives practice examples of central aspects of an MSP approach to practice. These are explored in greater depth in this chapter.

MSP began as a national programme in 2009. The work continues to be supported by the Association of Directors of Adult Social Services (ADASS), the Local Government Association (LGA) and the Department of Health (DH). The programme gathered pace, and in 2014/15 all local authorities in England were engaged in progressing MSP. Resources linked to findings of councils that participated in the programme are referenced below. They offer helpful practice advice and are available on the LGA website.[1]

What is safeguarding adults?
What is Making Safeguarding Personal?

The definition of safeguarding adults is set out in the *Care and Support Statutory Guidance*:

> Safeguarding means protecting an adult's right to live in safety, free from abuse and neglect. It is about people and organisations working

---

1   See www.local.gov.uk/adult-social-care/-/journal_content/56/10180/6074789/
     ARTICLE and www.stopadultabuse.org.uk

together to prevent and stop both the risks and experience of abuse or neglect, while at the same time making sure that the adult's wellbeing is promoted including, where appropriate, having regard to their views, wishes, feelings and beliefs in deciding on any action. This must recognise that adults sometimes have complex interpersonal relationships and may be ambivalent, unclear or unrealistic about their personal circumstances... People have complex lives and being safe is only one of the things they want for themselves. Professionals should work with the adult to establish what being safe means to them and how that can be best achieved. (DH 2016, paras.14.7–14.8)

This emphasises the person's involvement, the balancing of wellbeing with safety, and prevention. Expectations set out in the guidance in respect of MSP add value to this approach:

Making safeguarding personal means it should be person-led and outcome-focussed. It engages the person in a conversation about how best to respond to their safeguarding situation in a way that enhances involvement, choice and control as well as improving quality of life, wellbeing and safety. (DH 2016, para.14.15)

The guidance makes it clear that MSP is not only for local authority professionals, but it is for everyone: 'Making safeguarding personal... underpins all healthcare delivery in relation to safeguarding, with a focus on the person not the process' (DH 2016, para.14.207).

Policies and procedures across organisations 'should assist those working with adults on how to develop swift and personalised safeguarding responses and how to involve adults in this decision making' (DH 2016, para.14.52).

Changing the culture: emerging themes in support of a personalised approach to practice in safeguarding adults

Safeguarding practice has been slow to adopt a personalised approach, despite the narrative of personalisation having been centre stage for over a decade. For example, in 2005 a Green Paper (DH 2005, p.30) acknowledged that:

The person's own assessment of their needs might conflict with those of their professional assessor... The person's personal assessment must be transparent... That is what happens in the rest of our lives.

We work out what we want and then, in trying to achieve it, we may have to negotiate. (DH 2005, p.31)

In 2010 the Department of Health set out a vision, highlighting the need to empower people to understand and manage risks in their own lives:

Personalised care is for everyone, but some people will need more support than others to make choices about how they live their lives… Making risks clear and understood is crucial to empowering service users and carers, recognising people as 'experts in their own lives'. (DH 2010a, pp.25–26)

Key messages for practice

These same themes are underlined by councils across England (those that engaged in MSP programmes in 2013–15) as fundamental aspects of the MSP approach to practice:

- Engaging core principles in practice about rights and risks, choice and control

- Engaging with people (having conversations) to understand what contributes to 'wellbeing' in their lives; seeking to support wellbeing alongside safety

- Ensuring that those who lack mental capacity (as well as those who have capacity) are empowered and included within safeguarding support

- Empowering people so that they are partners in understanding and managing risk in their own lives

- An emphasis on the need for transparency and openness in managing conflicting outcomes (both of the person and between the person and professionals or organisations)

- The role of advocacy in all of the above.

The *Making Safeguarding Personal Evaluation Report* for 2014/15 offers greater detail on what supports MSP and the challenges for delivery (Pike and Walsh 2015). It underlines the necessary context and support to enable the MSP approach. In particular the role of Safeguarding Adults Boards and the culture change necessary to facilitate MSP are emphasised, alongside changes in policy and procedure. Prioritising staff development, support and opportunity for reflection, high-level organisational support and engagement across sectors and organisations are all needed (Pike and Walsh 2015, pp.13–15, 59–62).

Evidence suggesting the need for change and the necessary direction for change

The necessary shift in culture has been slow. 'There are...strong messages that people feel driven (sometimes out of control) through a process... Often they want more than one outcome, which are sometimes not easy to reconcile. People generally want to feel safe but also to maintain relationships...' (LGA 2013, p.11).

This is reflected in the experience recounted by the wife of a man who was the focus of a Serious Case Review. She reflected: 'The word "protection" suggests altruistic idealism and protection of those with care and support needs. The reality is otherwise. The word is a euphemism for bullying power and a tendency to deny the positive elements that create happiness in a person's life' (Westminster Safeguarding Adults Board 2011, p.48).

There are numerous reviews (Serious Case Reviews and Safeguarding Adults Reviews) where a lack of a personalised approach is reflected in the findings of reports. These are available on council websites and include reviews into the deaths of: Steven Hoskin (Cornwall Adult Protection Committee 2007); CC (Surrey Safeguarding Adults Board 2010); Gemma Hayter (Warwickshire Safeguarding Adults Partnership 2011); Mr BB (Westminster Safeguarding Adults Board 2011); and Mrs ZZ (Camden Safeguarding Adults Board 2015). They indicate the need for application of a range of skills and knowledge in 'making safeguarding personal', including:

- listening skills

- attention to the issue of choice and the person's ability to exercise choice

- adherence to the principles of the Mental Capacity Act 2005 (MCA); and the MCA 2005 Code of Practice (2007)

- positive and person-centred approaches to risk

- empowering and including people who use services and their families

- prevention strategies, particularly in respect of those isolated in their communities

- expertise in working with people with whom it is challenging to engage and with whom finding a balance between choice and safety is crucial

- effective interpretation and application of the law.

The following case study, from the perspective of a person who was in need of safeguarding support, gets to the heart of why change is needed and what that change should look like. It sets out the experience and views of Annie, who was offered support in the form of a Family Group Conference (FGC; see Chapter 3).

CASE STUDY

Annie had experienced abuse from her husband for over 40 years. As the abuse continued and Annie was getting older, it became increasingly difficult to withstand. Traditional approaches had had little impact. A FGC was offered and accepted by Annie. Six months later she had left her husband and Annie now coordinates FGCs herself. When asked what it was about the support of the FGC that led to successful outcomes, Annie said the following about the approach:[2]

- 'It helped me move from firefighting to long-term solutions.

- It helped find the right people to support me.

- It helped us to see the severity of the risk.

- It supported my family.

- It put me at ease to share my story.

- It built my self-confidence.

---

2   The case study is based on a conversation between the author and Annie. Annie was and is keen to share what is to be gained from FGC. She shared these insights initially for a conference and gave permission for them to be shared here.

- Help and results came quickly.

- I apply the principles on an ongoing basis in my life.

- I did it myself.'

Principles into practice

MSP is supported extensively within the *Care and Support Statutory Guidance* (DH 2016) which sets out core principles for practice.

Putting the wellbeing principle into practice: a case study from research

The *Care and Support Statutory Guidance* lists aspects of life central to a person's wellbeing and offers an essential tool for putting MSP into practice (DH 2016, para.1.5). Achieving the necessary balance between wellbeing and safety can only be realised by working alongside the person and understanding the relative importance of aspects of their life. The wellbeing principle is underlined for all organisations both in the statutory guidance and elsewhere, including in the NHS England (NHSE) *Safeguarding Accountability and Assurance Framework* (2015) and *Compassion in Practice* (NHSE 2012).

Recent research on mass marketing fraud (Olivier *et al.* 2015) illustrates how the wellbeing principle can be put into practice. This research shows that some people who engage in scams do so because it presses many of the wellbeing 'buttons' as set out in the above statutory guidance. For some the loss of money is worth it when weighed against the wellbeing gains. Intervention therefore needs to look at the whole person and their social network in considering what it would be like for the person if engagement with scams ceased and what might replace the sense of wellbeing that the engagement provided (Olivier *et al.* 2015, pp.368–369). The research carried out by Croydon social workers and Trading Standards officers indicates that what success looks like here can only truly be gauged by the person at the centre. For some, engagement with scams introduces risk in every aspect of life, so it is important to understand and work with both motivation and risk.

The recommendations from this research include:

- taking time to understand the issues affecting the person: relevant biographical information; family and social relationships; and what the impact of ending engagement with scams would be like for them. This may require long-term involvement to enable the necessary level of understanding

- consideration of what might take the place of engagement with scams in the person's life

- joint working to bring in information and expertise as well as to ensure a consistent message to the person

- providing information and support to relatives

- establishing with the person an understanding of the level and nature of risk (see Chapter 6).

The outline of aspects of wellbeing as set out in the *Care and Support Statutory Guidance* (DH 2016, para.1.5) is a helpful aide-memoire for practice.

Putting the six safeguarding principles into practice

Testing out practice against the six safeguarding principles (see Appendix) can be a highly effective tool for examining and improving safeguarding arrangements and outcomes for people. This can be reflected upon in the context of live situations in team meetings, supervision or in other reflective practice sessions. It is helpful to focus on what needs to be done or considered in practice to make each of these principles come alive for the person. A case study from Swindon in respect of Mrs T provides a helpful example of how to apply the principles in practice (Research in Practice for Adults [RiPfA] 2014b, p.17).

CASE STUDY

Mrs T had been suffering with extreme depression and was an inpatient within a local mental health unit. Extended family members had heard that she made a will and the main beneficiary was a 'lodger' who paid Mrs T a nominal, small rent. The family members were also concerned about the 'state of the house'. They raised a safeguarding alert citing financial or material abuse and neglect at the hands of the 'lodger'.

There was some discussion of these concerns with Mrs T on the ward. However, there was concern about her mental capacity to consider the issues fully in her current condition, particularly in respect of financial affairs. For example, she was not able to discuss her will. Mrs T was assessed at this stage as not having the capacity to participate in assessing the concerns raised. In any case she was too unwell to do so. It was therefore decided to go back to her when her condition had improved when she would be able to engage in responding to the concerns raised.

She did not indicate any negative feelings towards the 'lodger'. When social workers visited the house they found no indication of the concerns/neglect outlined by extended family members.

After two to three weeks Mrs T was able to discuss in detail the arrangements she had with the 'lodger' and her views about recent contact with extended family members. She talked fondly of the 'lodger'. She felt the contribution he made to the household budget was adequate, that he was good company and that he provided day-to-day practical support.

Mrs T did not want any further action taken in this regard. She was supported to speak with her family, who were informed of the outcome. They accepted this and the case was closed. (RiPfA 2014b, p.17)

Applying the six principles with Mrs T
Empowerment

- Discuss the outcomes Mrs T wants. What are her views, wishes, feelings in respect of the allegations?

- Consider whether support of an advocate is indicated.

- Find the best time to involve her in view of her ill health and capacity to make decisions.

- Support and enable her to discuss issues with her family and make them aware of her rights (human rights and MCA 2005).

Prevention

- Make Mrs T aware of her options to manage her money.

- Support Mrs T to understand potential risks.

- Discuss with family regarding Mrs T's rights.

- Develop social networks.

- Discuss with Mrs T the impact of her mental health on decision making. Help her to understand early signs of deterioration in her mental health so she can seek early help.

- Help her to understand what abuse is; give contact information and advice on seeking help.

Proportionality

- Don't rush to take action whilst Mrs T is unwell. Must decisions be made now? (See MCA 2005.) Consider timing against level of risk.

- Weigh up wishes and feelings against potential risks; consider her right to take risks.

- Keep involvement of others to a minimum (depending on who she wants to be involved).

Protection

- Consider mental capacity in respect of financial considerations. Refer to MCA (2005) and Code of Practice (2007). Will she understand more later when her health improves? Does she require an advocate?

- Have conversations with Mrs T about her wishes and preferred outcomes and explore whether these change as her awareness of the situation and everyone's roles develops.

- Consider the least restrictive option.

- Are there financial safeguards that could be put in place? Does she want any of these?

- Enable her to discuss her position and rights assertively with the family.

Partnership

- Mrs T guides who should be involved; involve those she trusts.

- Only share information as relevant and necessary; involve Mrs T in decisions about sharing information, including with her family.

- Everyone to work to the same result specified by Mrs T.

Accountability

- Explain who the practitioners are and their roles and who Mrs T can contact in which circumstances.

- Identify one lead person and be clear about who is responsible for which actions or support.

- Explain limitations of everyone's role and what can or cannot be done.

Statutory guidance; what is demanded of practice in Making Safeguarding Personal?

Table 1.1 sets out imperatives for safeguarding practice from the *Care and Support Statutory Guidance* (DH 2016). It cross-references to findings from MSP practice (Cooper *et al.* 2016; Lawson, Lewis and Williams 2014a, 2014b; Pike and Walsh 2015).

Table 1.1 Top tips for Making Safeguarding Personal

What supports MSP? (Findings from MSP practice)[1]	Care and Support Statutory Guidance (DH 2016)[2]
• Involve people in meetings • Simplify language and guides for people using services • Review outcomes • Support wider prevention and awareness in community • Involve advocates and Independent Mental Capacity Advocates (IMCAs)	• Provide information and support in accessible ways (14.11) • Raise public awareness so communities play their part (14.11; 14.136; 14.139) • Provide an independent advocate to represent and support adults (14.10; 14.48; 14.54; 14.77; 14.80)
• Sound practice in context of MCA 2005 and Deprivation of Liberty Safeguards (DoLS) • Support people in managing risks • Reduce number of formal meetings • Empower people to manage risks in their own lives	• MCA 2005 compliance (14.55–14.61; 14.97) • Supporting adults to weigh up risks and benefits of different options (14.37; 14.56; 14.91; 14.97) • Early identification and assessment of risk (14.62)
• Enhance prevention of abuse through empowerment • Build a pathway from alerts to a range of lower-level responses	• Aim of safeguarding to prevent harm (14.11) • Strong multi-agency partnerships that provide timely and effective prevention (14.12) • Six safeguarding principles (14.13) • Early intervention to prevent abuse (14.66)
• Policies and procedures need to be revised	• Procedures should assist in personalised responses and how to involve adults in decision making (14.52) • Clear methodology which involves the person at the centre and proportionate to concerns (14.92; 14.93)
• Develop core skills and tools to support practice • Support, supervision, reflective practice • Challenging practice through supervision: 'How good are you at having difficult conversations?'	• Regular face-to-face supervision to enable staff to work confidently and competently; guidance and support for staff; skilled knowledgeable supervision focused on outcomes (14.56; 14.57; 14.202)

• Achieving the necessary cultural shift • All partners take on board benefits of outcomes focus • All partners develop personalised responses and procedures • Develop commissioners in how to build MSP into their commissioning practice	• Strong multi-agency partnership; effective responses and prevention; clarity as to roles and responsibilities; positive learning environment to help break down cultures that are risk-averse (14.12) • MSP underpins all health care delivery in relation to safeguarding (14.207) • Policies and procedures across organisations should assist the development of swift and personalised safeguarding responses and involvement of adults in decision making (14.52)
• Meaningful recording and measuring of outcomes	• Safeguarding Adults Board should consider the extent to which outcomes have been realised (14.157)
• Conversations with people and a move away from process and completing prescribed forms	• Enquiries range from a conversation through to a much more formal multi-agency action plan (14.77) • Enquiries will usually start with the adult's views and wishes, which determine next steps (14.93) • Discussion with person confirms cause for concern and agrees outcomes (14.92)
• Focus on the person's outcomes and wellbeing	• Outcomes reflect the adult's wishes and/or best interests and are proportionate to concerns (14.79) • Everyone must focus on improving the person's wellbeing (14.92)

1 This column references findings from MSP national programmes 2013–16.
2 This column shows related references from Chapter 14 of the *Care and Support Statutory Guidance*.

Priority areas for enhancing practice and outcomes

Applying core principles is fundamental to ensuring personalised safeguarding practice. There are a number of aspects of practice that emerge from the above as consistent priorities for MSP. These are described briefly below whilst being explored in greater detail elsewhere in this book.

The MCA 2005 and Making Safeguarding Personal

In 2013/14 the national MSP programme underlined the need to ensure that people who lack capacity are offered equal access to person-centred safeguarding support. In 2014/15, 72 per cent of councils said that they had used aspects of MCA (2005) practice and best-interests decision making within approaches to make safeguarding personal (Pike and Walsh 2015, p.24). Considerations in respect of mental capacity are central in MSP and, indeed, MSP has made practitioners more aware of the need to focus on this aspect of practice.

In this context there is much scope for empowerment and inclusion, but we know that this potential is not being fully exploited. A House of Lords Select Committee (13 March 2014, p.6) underlined a range of practice areas in need of attention if the empowering ethos of the MCA (2005) is to be delivered. These included: the appropriate and timely assessment and recording of capacity and the quality of those assessments; attention to principles of supported decision making and best-interests decision making; support of an IMCA where appropriate; and tackling risk-averse cultures and cultures of paternalism that inhibit the right to make unwise decisions and the pursuing of least restrictive alternatives.

Integration of the five core principles of the MCA (2005) into safeguarding practice will have a significant impact in enhancing personalised practice. Delivery on the principles of the MCA (2005) emerges as an imperative in Serious Case Reviews and Safeguarding Adults Reviews cited above as well as in the case of Mrs T.

Advocacy

Alongside advocacy associated with the MCA (2005), advocacy is a broader consideration within safeguarding, as set out in the *Care and Support Statutory Guidance* (see Table 1.1):

> Independent advocacy plays a critical role in enabling the person using services to understand and take their own decisions about risk and its mitigation. Where the person may lack capacity, it assists in ensuring that such decisions are made in the person's best interests. (VoiceAbility 2012)

Pike and Walsh (2015, p.24) state that 'a third of councils (34 per cent) had been involved in developing advocacy and buddying responses… 31 per cent developed supported decision making (a principle of the MCA 2005) and this has clear links to provision of advocacy'. They reflect on the need to build capacity in the system for increased referrals to advocacy during safeguarding inquiries.

There was evidence from the 2013/14 MSP programme that practitioners must develop a greater understanding of when and how best to use advocacy in supporting safeguarding and that further work is needed to commission a range of appropriate advocacy. Research by the Older People's Advocacy Alliance (OPAAL) UK found that those supported through advocacy identified more 'expressive' goals than advocates, such as 'increasing the person's confidence'. These were as distinct from 'instrumental' goals such as 'getting a new care package in place' or 'a neighbour to be prosecuted' (OPAAL 2009, p.33). This research says that 'there is a tendency to push us towards attacking the problem, solve it, quick outcome and move on – but maybe we need to uncover more to be really effective' (OPAAL 2009, p.42). There is a need for longer-term investment in establishing relationships built on trust that are capable of empowering people to manage risk in their own lives over the long term. Models for commissioning advocacy need to take account of this.

Some councils have begun to develop alternative responses to safeguarding and are broadening approaches to ensuring that the person's involvement is at the centre of safeguarding support. Advocacy can form part of such support. Some of these responses are explored elsewhere in this book.

Working effectively with risk

> The real goal is to enable the person to be where they want and to do what they choose, so that this will enhance their quality of life, but without undue risk of harm to themselves or others and in line with the legal framework, respecting human rights. (DH 2010b, p.56)

A positive, person-centred approach to risk, which works alongside the person in balancing the benefits to them of a particular course of action against the potential harms, supports good practice within the principles set out earlier in this chapter (see Chapter 6). A case study concerning Susi, provided by Slough Borough Council (RiPfA 2014b, pp.6–7), illustrates practice in working with risk alongside the person. The approach supported understanding of the risks and negotiation of outcomes with the person. It took place before the Care Act (2014), and this is reflected in terminology (the case study reflects the definition of safeguarding set out in the *Care and Support Statutory Guidance* that is much broader than a Section 42 Care Act [2014] duty to make enquiries). It incorporates collective efforts alongside the person to both prevent and intervene in abuse, and to work with the person to establish what being safe means to them and how best to achieve this (DH 2016, para.14.8). Working effectively alongside people to support their understanding of risk is key to prevention and resilience.

CASE STUDY

Susi had a moderate learning disability. She lived in supported living. Historically there was acceptance by Susi of unwanted sexual relationships and tolerance of violence. There had been a number of safeguarding referrals alleging sexual abuse of Susi by her boyfriend. No police action had been taken and the situation remained unresolved. Susi had been assessed as having capacity to make decisions about her relationship.

Susi initially wanted to remain with her boyfriend. She wanted him to treat her differently and for professionals to help change his behaviour. Professionals at that point wanted to put in a range of protective measures to prevent the sexual relationship whilst the risk remained significant.

Rather than take control, professionals were able gradually to involve Susi in considering the potential benefits and harms of pursuing a range of outcomes. They supported her to have greater insight into the risks alongside what was to be gained from remaining in the relationship. Her preferred outcomes were represented at all safeguarding meetings and reviewed at every stage.

Through this approach Susi began to realise the extent and nature of the risk and that her initial preferred outcomes were not achievable. She realised that her boyfriend's behaviour towards her would not change. Susi adapted the outcomes she wanted as she began to understand what was necessary to enable her to feel safe. She weighed up the risks and took the decision to leave her boyfriend and set in place a long-term plan to live in a new environment away from him.

Situations where people choose to pursue high-risk choices present particular challenges. There are some key aspects of practice that require a focus in these situations where a person's support is declined. This can assist in negotiating safer outcomes:

- A risk assessment must be carried out to determine the level of seriousness and likelihood of each identified risk.

- Intervention must be person-centred, understanding the person and their context and involving them as far as possible in understanding the risk assessment and alternatives for managing risk.

- Information should be shared with other relevant professionals who may have a contribution to make in managing/monitoring the risks.

- Consideration must be given to the mental capacity of the person, whether they require support in decision making or, following an assessment that the person lacks capacity, whether a best interests decision might be appropriate (Camden Safeguarding Adults Board 2015, p.44).

Conversations with people

The ability to have open, honest and supportive conversations, valuing the person, is at the heart of practice that makes safeguarding personal.

The above themes rely upon such conversations so as to: establish trust; understand what constitutes wellbeing for the person; gain insight into whether decision making is problematic/mental capacity is an issue to be addressed; establish mutual understanding of risk and possible ways to address this; and understand what is important to the person/what they want to happen. Moreover, the very act of involving people in conversations and talking about outcomes is empowering in developing them and their understanding of their situation, the alternatives, their resilience and their confidence. It can lead to outcomes that protect key elements of their quality of life and wellbeing. The way in which we get to the information about outcomes is crucial. The case study in respect of Annie earlier in this chapter evidences the possibility of empowerment through engaging in a conversation and working together on specified outcomes ('I did it myself!').

What supports effective conversations?

There is evidence from councils that information and guides for people and their carers on safeguarding are important. A selection of tools used by councils participating in the MSP 2013/14 programme includes examples of accessible information to support effective practice (RiPfA 2014a). Councils participating in this programme valued having the support of aide-memoires and prompts in conversations and assessments alongside people, rather than rigid forms/assessment formats and a set of tick-boxes. These facilitate the person being listened to with their own words being recorded. Some examples of aide-memoires and recording tools that support effective conversations (RiPfA 2014a) rely upon the supported decision tool set out in the DH guidance on risk (DH 2007, pp.49–51). This suggested guide to a conversation, using simple language to identify pertinent issues for the person, offers questions such as:

- What is important to you in your life?

- What is working well?

- What things are difficult for you?

- Do you think there are any risks?

- Could things be done in a different way, which might reduce the risks?

- Who is important to you?

- Are there any differences of opinion between you and the people you said are important to you?

- What could we do (practitioner) to support you?

Conversations about what is important and about outcomes aspired to by the person need to start as soon as a concern is raised, forming a firm person-centred foundation for ongoing support. This indicates the importance of an MSP approach being adopted across all organisations who may deal with safeguarding concerns. Oxfordshire County Council safeguarding team is, for example, supporting staff across agencies to ask three consistent questions. These questions are about: what people want to happen; how people want that to happen; and what are the outcomes they want (Cooper *et al.* 2016). The *Care and Support Statutory Guidance* (DH 2016) indicates the importance of Section 42 inquiries (see Appendix) starting with conversations with the person. For example, the London safeguarding procedures suggest that the:

> strengths of the adult at risk should always be considered. Mapping out with the adult, and identifying their strengths and those of their personal network, may reduce risks sufficiently so that people feel safe without the need to take matters further. (ADASS 2015, p.77)

Sometimes such an approach will mean that the conversation will in itself be sufficient to resolve the concerns. The following case study, provided by Bracknell Forest Council (RiPfA 2014b, p.15), offers an example where this was the case.

CASE STUDY

Joyce had concerns about her neighbour. He had been asking to borrow money and then not repaying it. However, Joyce said she didn't want 'anything to be done' as he was 'very kind' and visited her regularly. Joyce said that she would like to speak with her neighbour on her own, but she wasn't sure how to start the conversation. The practitioner provided Joyce with some coaching about how she might start the conversation and what she wanted to get out of it. Joyce was then able to talk with her neighbour. Whilst the neighbour was initially defensive, after a day or so he reflected on what Joyce had said and he visited her again to apologise for putting Joyce in the position where she didn't feel able to reject his request.

Although Joyce reported that her relationship with her neighbour was 'a bit fragile', he is still visiting her and hasn't asked her for money. Joyce said that she felt she was listened to and that professionals wouldn't do anything without her permission.

Conclusion

Putting principles into practice, including a focus on wellbeing alongside safety, is of central importance in ensuring personalised safeguarding practice. Working effectively in the context of the MCA (2005) and in addressing risk must go hand in hand with those safeguarding principles. Having conversations with people that support meaningful engagement informs clear options and resolution. This may be through support from an advocate. Case studies provided have offered evidence that engagement with people and the nature of those conversations also support the development of self-esteem and self-confidence, leading to longer-term resilience and prevention. This chapter offers broad advice for practice in Making Safeguarding Personal. The chapters that follow offer a rich source of more detailed guidance for achieving this.

References

Association of Directors of Adult Social Services (2015) *London Multi-Agency Adult Safeguarding Policy and Procedures*. London: ADASS.

Camden Safeguarding Adults Board (2015) *Serious Case Review in Respect of ZZ* (Executive Summary). Available at www.camden.gov.uk/ccm/cms-service/stream/asset/;jsessionid=F375C19E1C993117729DCD51316806A6?asset_id=3372170&, accessed on 4 April 2017.

Cooper, A., Briggs, M., Lawson, J., Hodson, B., and Wilson, M. (2016) *Making Safeguarding Personal Temperature Check*. London: ADASS.

Cornwall Adult Protection Committee (2007) *The Murder of Steven Hoskin: A Serious Case Review* (Executive Summary). Available at www.cornwall.gov.uk/media/3633936/Steven-Hoskin-Serious-Case-Review-Exec-Summary.pdf, accessed on 4 April 2017.

Department of Health (2005) *Independence, Wellbeing and Choice: Our Vision for the Future of Social Care for Adults in England*. London: HMSO.

Department of Health (2007) *Independence, Choice and Risk: A Guide to Best Practice in Supported Decision Making*. London: DH, Annex A.

Department of Health (2010a) *Vision for Adult Social Care: Capable Communities and Active Citizens.* London: DH.

Department of Health (2010b) *Nothing Ventured, Nothing Gained: Risk Guidance for Dementia.* London: DH.

Department of Health (2016) *Care and Support Statutory Guidance.* London: DH.

House of Lords Select Committee (2014) *MCA 2005: Post-Legislative Scrutiny.* HL Paper 139. London: HMSO.

Lawson, J., Lewis, S., and Williams, C. (2014a) *Making Safeguarding Personal: Report of Findings, 2013/14.* London: LGA/ADASS.

Lawson, J., Lewis, S., and Williams, C. (2014b) *Making Safeguarding Personal: Guide 2013/2014.* London: LGA/ADASS.

MCA 2005, Code of Practice (2007) London: HMSO.

Mental Capacity Act (2005) London: HMSO.

NHS England (2012) *Compassion in Practice – Our Culture of Compassionate Care.* Available at www.england.nhs.uk/nursingvision, accessed on 4 April 2017.

NHS England (2015) *Safeguarding Vulnerable People in the NHS – Accountability and Assurance Framework.* Available at www.england.nhs.uk/wp-content/uploads/2015/07/safeguarding-accountability-assurance-framework.pdf, accessed on 4 April 2017.

Older People's Advocacy Alliance (2009) *Speaking up to Safeguard: Lessons and Findings from the Benchmarking Advocacy and Abuse Project, 2008–2009.* Stoke-on-Trent: OPAAL.

Olivier, S., Burls, T., Fenge, L., and Brown, K. (2015) '"Winning and Losing": Vulnerability to mass marketing fraud.' *Journal of Adult Protection 17*, 6, 360–370.

Pike, L., and Walsh, J. (November 2015) *Making Safeguarding Personal Evaluation Report.* London: LGA.

Research in Practice for Adults (2014a) *Making Safeguarding Personal 2013/14: Selection of Tools Used by Participating Councils.* London: LGA/ADASS.

Research in Practice for Adults (2014b) *Making Safeguarding Personal 2013/14: Case Studies.* London: LGA/ADASS.

Surrey Safeguarding Adults Board (2010) *A Serious Case Review in Respect of CC, Died 2009* (Executive Summary). Available at www.surreycc.gov.uk/__data/assets/pdf_file/0018/42633/Executive-Summary-CC.pdf, accessed on 4 April 2017.

VoiceAbility (2012) *Advocacy: Voice and the Protection from Crime and Abuse.* Memorandum to the Department of Health Review, following events at Winterbourne View Hospital. Available at www.voiceability.org/images/news/Winterbourne_View_VoiceAbility_summary_memorandum_to_the_DH_Review_2012-03-19.pdf, accessed on 4 April 2017.

Warwickshire Safeguarding Adults Partnership (2011) *Serious Case Review: The Murder of Gemma Hayter, 9th August 2010.* Available at https://apps.warwickshire.gov.uk/api/documents/WCCC-779-97, accessed on 4 April 2017.

Westminster Safeguarding Adults Board (2011) *A Serious Case Review in Respect of Mr BB, Died 2011* (Executive Summary). Available at http://transact.westminster.gov.uk/docstores/publications_store/westminsterscrexecsummaryfinalreportaugust2012.pdf, accessed on 4 April 2017.

Chapter 2

Working More Reflexively with Risk

HOLDING 'SIGNS OF SAFETY AND WELLBEING' IN MIND

Tony Stanley

Introduction

Recent legislative changes in England provide a unique opportunity to move beyond deficit and problem-focused practice in adult social care because the Care Act (2014) has introduced practice imperatives based on wellbeing, strengths, rights and resiliency (ADASS 2014; Fox 2013). With adult safeguarding now on a statutory footing, practitioners need to provide rigour in decision making while delivering humane practice. Consequently, we need to think more deeply about how risk discourses and everyday understandings of risk might be affecting our practice and influencing our decisions (Stanley 2013; Webb 2006). The challenge for practitioners is to offer person-centred and rights-based practice while working *with* the various risks people live with. The challenge for vulnerable people is to be heard and included in decision making based on risk and safety discourses (Beresford *et al.* 2016). We need to organise our work differently to address both.

Reorganising practice away from problem-saturated care management towards truly person-centred and person-led practice needs to happen if strengths-based approaches to wellbeing are to emerge (Burbage 2013; Fox 2013). Arguably, this is not straightforward. Put simply, risk is often contrasted with safety, with practitioners working to resolve it while securing safety as best they can. Practice decisions can easily follow a logic of risk avoidance or aims of risk elimination, with unintended and largely negative consequences for those with care and support needs and their families.

Many practitioners see 'risk' as a problem to resolve, even when they uphold collaborative practice ideals (Stanley 2013). So, professionals' understandings and definitions about risk and safety tend to dominate the work. This is often referred to as the 'risk paradigm' and it dominates statutory social care (especially in children's social work). Moving beyond the risk paradigm is possible, but requires moral and intellectual debates about the nature of risk and how much of it our society will tolerate. This chapter offers a practical way forward so that we can work more reflexively with risk, and consequently deliver human rights-based approaches and social justice ideals. It explores a strengths-based method to work with risk and wellbeing and argues that new forms of organising and delivering practice are needed. Practice frameworks offer an evidence-informed way to do so – they are an established vehicle within statutory children's social care and there is an emerging evidence base for their use within adult social care (Stanley 2016). The aim of a practice framework is to organise, in a mutually reinforcing way, principles and values that underpin practice, with notions of rights, legalisation and research included, while encouraging the use of practice wisdom – all drawn on to inform our everyday practice decisions (Connolly and Healy 2009; Stanley 2016). This is important if we are to work more reflexively with risk.

The chapter further describes the 'signs of safety and wellbeing' practice framework and shows how it helps to deliver on the aims of the Care Act (2014). A practice framework is a 'conceptual map' that guides social work practice. Designed as a tool for practitioners, the 'signs of safety and wellbeing' practice framework integrates a number of practice underpinnings, within a strengths-based design – one where risk, harm, needs and strengths are considered. The Care Act (2014) offers an opportunity to deliver practice this way, supported by a policy and research agenda that argues for the person to be truly at the centre. Moving from compliance and process-dominated systems is not straightforward, but practice frameworks are noted in the literature as helping (Connolly 2007; Healy 2005). The 'signs of safety and wellbeing' practice framework is an example that incorporates a wellbeing principle for every person worked with, while providing a guide to delivering safeguarding practice that is person-centred, theoretically rigorous and ethical. The framework saves time and paperwork for busy practitioners and offers a simple but effective one-page overview of the issues that need addressing. This is an easily understandable, logical and accessible practice method for everyone involved in adult social care.

The previous chapter explained Making Safeguarding Personal (MSP) and highlighted the wellbeing principle as an important focus for practice. This is a new and significant shift because local authorities in England now have statutory safeguarding duties. This chapter offers an innovative way to consider delivering adult social care through the 'signs of safety and wellbeing' practice framework. Following a brief overview of the legislative and policy changes, an introduction to strengths-based practice is offered to show how new ways of organising practice can deliver on the desired changes. Case studies from practice illustrate how things can work while highlighting some of the everyday practice challenges.

Taking a 'strengths-based' approach

Alongside the new legislative framework, the MSP initiative places human rights and social justice ideals at the forefront of practice. As we have seen in Chapter 1, this means engaging with people, and those important to them, about expected or desired outcomes, while reviewing as the work unfolds, and reflecting about practice. The person is positioned at the centre, and a respectful, engaged, collaborative approach to how we understand their wellbeing is crucial.

Wellbeing is at the heart of the Care Act (2014), and is best conceptualised through a human-rights and asset-based lens. Wellbeing is also defined in terms of people having access to material and emotional resources within their social and economic environment (Connolly and Morris 2012). Wellbeing involves meaningful and safe relationships, a sense of belonging, purpose, acts of participating, and sense of making a contribution. In other words, our social world is shaped and organised by interpersonal relationships. This needs a sophisticated practice approach to support, with reinforcements to promote this approach. In summary, a shift from care management to a more humane person-centred approach is needed.

Practitioners need to understand these ideas so they can work practically with strengths-based methods. The positive aspects of families, and the actual needs and experiences of adults with care and support needs, should be included as important parts of the work, so analysis and decisions are collaborative, participatory and respectful. The strengths-based methods offer an important balance to the deficit 'risk paradigm'. In a practical sense we still work with the risks but widen the 'risk lens' to include risks in everyday life, risk-taking and risk comfort levels. The work becomes less focused on risk elimination and turns towards understanding 'risk' in terms of what might be manageable or possibly a resource in someone's life. The challenge then is to locate risk issues within a strengths-based practice paradigm. This can be difficult when organisations encourage risk assessments that focus on deficits and problems.

Traditional models of assessments tend to focus on deficit and problem-resolution approaches, whereas the strengths perspective offers a less oppressive way forward. The strengths perspective emerged in the 1980s, first as a set of practice principles in response to the pathology-laden treatments available for people living with mental illness (Weick *et al.* 1989). According to Saleeby (2010), operating from a strengths-based perspective means that 'everything you do as a helper will be based on facilitating the discovery and embellishment, exploration, and use of clients' strengths and resources in the service of helping them achieve their dreams and goals' (p.1). This social work perspective orientates the practitioner to accommodate a wider lens for thinking critically about the person and their situation. Practitioners are encouraged to see the person's situation as more than a set of problems, and it asks for a profound belief that people are worth doing business with – they want to have different lives. The job of the practitioner is to help facilitate this.

Accordingly, fresh designs for practice are needed to build systems that encourage holistic and person-centred assessments that inform rigorous and ethical support planning. A move is needed from service-driven to needs-led models (Slasberg 2013). However, service-led practice has dominated adult social care organisations for over a decade. Slasberg and Beresford argue that the government's intent of the Care Act (2014) is laudable but they are critical about power in decision making ultimately resting with local authorities (2014, p.2). This is because the support needs of the person are potentially subject to the resource limits of local councils. This is a significant challenge because shrinking resources are challenged by the rising demand for services. New approaches to practice are required if we are to deliver the aims of the Care Act (2014) in these challenging times.

Different practice frameworks

Practice frameworks are noted in the literature as providing schematic templates for improving practice analysis and helping practice reform (Connolly 2007; Healy 2005; Stanley 2016; Stanley and Mills 2014). Practice frameworks are a schematic template not based on or informed by organisational imperatives but designed through and informed by a core set of professional practice values. A practice framework offers a mapping out of what we do and why, offering a rationale for practice actions and decisions, while promoting a range of practice tools in the carrying out of assessments and interventions. Connolly and Healy (2009) explain that a practice framework 'integrates empirical research, practice theories, ethical principles and experiential knowledge in a compact and convenient format that helps practitioners to use the knowledge and principles to inform their everyday work' (p.32).

A practice framework provides a logical and reinforcing way in which the service designs and then supports rigorous practice because it highlights the core practice purpose in terms of values and ethics, rather than encouraging managerial or bureaucratic imperatives. Connolly (2007) argues that practice frameworks, first, provide a guide to undertaking person- and family-centred assessment work, and second, offer practitioners an intervention logic that is theoretically and ethically grounded and supported by a set of practice questions. The goal is a depth of understanding about the situation, and solutions can be developed through the working relationship.

Learning from other areas offers some useful lessons. Strengths-based approaches are now increasingly found in children's social services, to varying degrees, with a goal of offering a more humane response to child welfare. The 'signs of safety' approach is one example of this.

The 'signs of safety' approach

The 'signs of safety' approach was developed in Western Australia in collaboration with child protection workers. The impetus to create this approach arose from dissatisfaction with existing models for working with Aboriginal families in child protection settings. The approach seeks to build partnerships with parents, families and children in situations of suspected or substantiated child abuse. It is a strengths-based, safety-oriented approach to child protection work, expanding the investigation of risk to encompass strengths and 'signs of safety' that can be built upon to stabilise and strengthen the child's and family's situation (de Haan and Marian 2011; Turnell and Edwards 1999). A format for undertaking comprehensive risk assessment – assessing for danger, strengths and safety – is incorporated within the 'signs of safety' method. The approach is designed to be used from beginning to end and to assist professionals at all stages of the child protection process, whatever the setting. This is a participatory approach that welcomes the person's experience and wisdom. Bunn (2013) noted variable reliability and rigour in use, depending on the skills of the practitioner utilising the model, but this is a problem for any framework used.

At the heart of this practice framework is working with families in an open, clear and respectful way, and by using appreciative inquiry questioning, while working collaboratively, a co-construction approach to understanding of risk, harm, need and safety is encouraged (Munro, Turnell and Murphy 2016). The appreciative inquiry process results in a series of statements that describes where the person wants to be, based on their lived experience or desired outcomes. These statements are grounded in real or lived experience; and this is important because people can then see how to repeat previous successes (Hammond 1996; Vogt, Brown and Isaacs 2003).

Sample appreciative inquiry questions:

- Describe a time when you felt you could achieve the things you wanted.

- What sort of influence do you have now to help sort things out?

- What challenges might emerge along the way, and how can we work with them?

- What could make the most difference to the future you want to have (or sorting out your situation)?

The 'signs of safety' approach supports an exploration of family and community resources and strengths. The practitioner explores the protective factors that might offer balance to the reported danger and harm, and an analysis is then made about danger, harm, safety and strengths. It avoids pathological or deficit-based analyses of problems and it utilises social constructionist thinking, showing how particular discourses are drawn on to construct 'need', 'harm', 'risk' and 'safety'. Therefore, a more reflexive engagement with risk is encouraged, and risk elimination or risk avoidance guarded against. One of the most striking things about this approach is how it renders risk clear for families, and this helps them to work collaboratively even in the most difficult of circumstances. The rights of families to understand and be clear on what practitioners are doing are upheld.

In summary, risk assessments are understood as the analysed space between the worst and best of possibilities. Plans to guide more safety and improve wellbeing are built on informal resources. The decisions reached are co-constructed. In 'signs of safety', risk is not contrasted with danger; rather, risk is seen as the space between these positions. To understand what might be too risky, the practitioner needs to understand how the person themselves understands what might be dangerous or harmful, what represents safety and strengths, and what possible resources might be needed. An understanding about wellbeing is produced collaboratively, including the views and ideas of family and friends, through the conversations that take place.

Lessons from children's social care

Several lessons from children's social care are helpful (Munro *et al.* 2016). First, the 'signs of safety' approach feels different for families and practitioners because goal-setting and being attentive to what the person wants and needs is a shift away from offering professional solutions or suggestions. A significant benefit is a sharper focus for safety planning, and less reliance on identifying perpetrators or assigning culpability. The basic template is easy to follow, with some of the tools adjusted depending on the client group. For early help and adult social care, wellbeing is an important addition to any focus on safety. Respectfully enquiring into what the person might want or desire helps elucidate personal and social assets and motivations already present. These are called 'appreciative inquiry questions' (see above) and they help to facilitate a respectful engagement, while orienting the conversation around defining self-determined goals (Hammond 1996). Change and progress is planned for and is realistic and goal-centred. As a key toolkit within the framework, the appreciative inquiry questioning technique helps to reinforce strengths-based practice. This technique helps practitioners demonstrate interest, empathy and respect which prompts people to talk and share their ideas.

The practice framework is a simple three-column design with a wellbeing continuum exercise along the bottom of the page (see below). It is easily drawn up on a blank piece of paper, so practitioners can create a one-page outline, and then apply the appreciative inquiry approach to solicit ideas and examples of assets, and explore people's dreams and wants while noting down who and what is around to help achieve the goals. A visual representation of the person's situation is created, and case planning emerges based on and informed by the conversations that have taken place. All the practitioner needs is a pad and pencil, and a creative approach to practice. This is a very different approach from traditional care management. An outline of how practitioners at Tower Hamlets experienced this way of working is given later in this chapter.

In an everyday sense, practitioners start with a brief discussion about the presenting issues or needs. This is called the 'headline news' and can be written down in bullet points. A genogram and an eco-map are drawn to highlight who and what is around the person already. This helps to orientate appreciative inquiry questions about supports already in place, or the desire for more. People that are important are listed, while gaps in the family can be explored. This might expose difficult or fraught family relationships that the practitioner may be able to help repair. Practitioners then move down the centre column, asking questions about what is already working well, and exploring the person's goals. Appreciative inquiry questioning helps to bring forward ideas, based in an everyday lived reality, and these can be framed as goals to achieve. The plans created are therefore goal-focused, realistic and a combination of everyday resources within the person's own family or social network alongside practical options from health and social care. The framework is shown in Figure 2.1, with two illustrations of the practice framework in action.

Signs of Safety and Wellbeing Practice Framework		Eco-map (who/what is around the person)
Headlines (why we are involved)		
Issues that need to be addressed	Who and what is helping	What needs to happen next
What is not going well:	Strengths/resources (what's working well):	Overall goal of the plan:
Complicating factors (things we can't change):	Contribution to safety and wellbeing:	Next steps:
Statement of overall concern/need:		Plan:
Current wellbeing score 0–10 ◄————————————————————————►		
(This is the wellbeing score of the person, the practitioner's score, and others involved, e.g. family and those in the eco-map.)		

Figure 2.1 The 'signs of safety and wellbeing' practice framework.

CASE STUDIES

George is a frail older person sent home from a local hospital, late one afternoon. He told nursing staff that his brother was taking his pension and was 'a bit of a bully'. The nurse called social services asking for home help of some sort to go in to check. The social worker initially agreed for a home visiting service to go in each evening. After completing the practice framework with

George and his brother, the social worker located more relatives that could be part of safety planning. A home visiting service was not needed or wanted by George, because family members identified that George was at risk from his brother, and the family stepped in to help.

Helen is in her mid-50s, is street homeless, drug dependent and lonely. She has major epileptic episodes, sometimes requiring hospitalisation. A nurse called social services insisting that Helen's needs were primarily a social care responsibility. The practice framework guided the practitioner to work through the needs, risks and dangers with Helen, with homelessness and misuse of prescribed drugs the initial focus. The social worker helped Helen to identify that her situation was indeed risky, and for her wellbeing to improve she needed a safe place and more social contact. The primary need was identified as an enduring health condition, and she was accepted under health provision for inpatient care and supported lodgings.

The practical steps for using the practice framework
Step one: The person has already started
The first step is to hold in mind that the person will have ideas about their own assessment needs – they will have ideas about problems to resolve in order to improve their wellbeing (Social Care Institute for Excellence [SCIE] 2011). A self-assessment is the thinking *behind* what they are asking for. This is an initial assessment, and it is the opportunity for the person's thinking to drive the decisions that underpin a support plan. This is called person-led practice.

Step two: Finding out who and what is helpful to the person, and what is working well
Next, the practitioner works through the sections of the framework with a focus on the presenting issues (why we are involved), and this is followed by developing an eco-map that shows who and what is around and potentially helpful and supportive. Thinking of the framework in this way, it becomes a conceptual and practical map, all of which helps to co-construct understandings about needs, safety, wellbeing

and risks. Isolation is a major issue for many older people, and the eco-map helps us do two things: first, identify the people already providing help informally; and second, highlight to the person how these people, and possibly others who are not currently contributing, could play more helpful roles. George's worker held respectful conversations around who and what is helpful; this included family, friends, informal networks, library and the doctor. These conversations brought into focus the meaningful and helpful things important to George.

Step three: What is in the way for improved wellbeing? What is not going so well?

This step starts with a full appreciation of the person's physical, social and emotional situation, and any impairment(s) or illness(es). George and Helen were invited to share what they thought about their wellbeing and how this might be adversely affected. The social model of disability tells us that disability arises from the combination of the person's impairment and society's attitude towards it (Beresford et al. 2016). This part of the discussion must also try and establish what *causes* these issues. There will be some things that cannot be changed. It is important to find out what this means to the person. This encourages a focus on the *impact* each issue might be having on the person's wellbeing. This is the information that is used to determine the priority of the need and any duties or powers for the council to exercise. Practitioners need to be clear whether this places the person's survival or safety at risk. Beyond that, the impact might be on matters such as dignity, self-worth, self-fulfilment or general quality of life. Being clear on the *outcomes* being sought is an important part of making safeguarding personal for both George and Helen.

Step four: Scale wellbeing and scaling any risk

Through a respectful conversational approach, and by helping people think through their particular situation, with the things that are working well and the things not working well or not working at all, and forming an overall goal with the person, the practitioner formulates their analysis. The person's judgement is sought and they are asked for what is called their 'wellbeing score'. This encourages people to take a high-level view of their wellbeing, and this might highlight other issues or problems that the person thought were not relevant, but actually are. The practice tool used here is called a 'scaling question'. This is a simple but effective tool that poses one question. Different views are not a problem in this way of working. Differences open up conversations. Subsequently questions are asked about how to improve the score. This means that plans are focused on an improvement to wellbeing and safety, and not a list of services for the person to visit or be seen by.

- *Safeguarding wellbeing scale:* On a scale of 0 to 10, if 10 is 'my safety is exactly where I want it to be' and 0 is 'I am so worried I think something dreadful might happen', what number would you give it today?

An overall statement of need or concern is then developed together with the person, and co-constructing this requires sensitivity, respect and skill. An overall goal emerges from this work, and the case planning is focused on achieving the goals. The eco-map helps to identify caring and safe people useful to be part of any safety planning work. The rights of people are also considered. Helen may have been making unwise choices sleeping rough, but she was able to make them.

Step five: Planning together to improve wellbeing or building safety

Safeguarding planning is then informed by the overall goal of the plan and the statement of need or concern. Decisions about any resources needed are added. The work is outcome-focused because the statement of overall concern and case goal orientates the practitioner towards addressing the concerns and reaching the desired goals. This is clearly understood by everyone involved. The case should proceed in a timely manner. In George's case a quick resolution happened the next day. A safety plan that the family developed was put in place and the case closed to social care. The one-page mapping of the case and the plan developed can be used as visual tools to help people who may have language or learning needs. It is important to write using language that is easy to understand without minimising the worries. Professional language can easily be a barrier to shared understandings, so choosing the words we use is important.

The case studies revisited

Family meetings and family group conferencing (see Chapter 3) are useful intervention methods that support the work of the practice framework (Local Government Association [LGA] 2015; SCIE 2012). The practice framework could be presented by George to a gathering of his family and friends with a clear message about needs, risks and possible options. Safeguarding concerns are discussed openly, and support plans are created that have family and friends involved.

For Helen the same approach was taken, and over a few weeks family members emerged and did form a support plan. Mostly this was emotional support, but that is what Helen recognised as a need. The practice framework encourages working where people are, in their homes and residences; it encourages relationship-based practice to mean *working with*. For Helen, the practice framework highlighted how dislocated she was from her family; and that isolation was an issue (Fox 2013). She told the worker she would like to see or call some of her family.

Introducing the practice framework in Tower Hamlets

The Care Act (2014) prompted a different approach to practice. A 'signs of safety' approach was adopted in Tower Hamlets in 2014, and briefing sessions on the principles behind the Care Act (2014) were organised which introduced staff to the practice research and policy debates. Many staff said that these workshops helped them to link ideas about human rights and social justice to the new legal landscape, and helped them to make logical links about strengths-based ideas to their practice. Adult social care practitioners were shown how the practice framework transformed the work in children's services, through case studies and positive family feedback, and they were asked for their ideas about how this might work in adult settings. Sensible suggestions were offered – such as the suggestion to develop a wellbeing continuum as a way to assess and understand the person's self-assessment. Occupational therapists said that this was how they always tended to work, and social workers said that this helped them to be more strengths-based. Care workers said that this way of working would help them to be less task-focused and more respectful. Legal colleagues ran workshops with case studies to illustrate practice decisions that are rigorous and able to withstand legal challenge. The most significant development was some staff feeling more confident in assessment practice and decision making. Several practitioners said that they began questioning why home-based services were routinely offered at the first visit. The practice framework showed them that this might not be wanted nor needed. Cost savings and time savings were demonstrated.

Staff were asked if they could or would rise to the new practice challenges outlined in the Care Act (2014). We were clear that this new approach required an intellectual and moral investment by them. Some staff did struggle, and some said they could not work this way. Some staff said offering a home help service was a safer option because it meant that someone was visiting the person. However, this is risk-averse practice and it needed challenging.

Introducing any new way of working is not easy and training alone is never enough (Sanderson and Stirk 2012), but Tower Hamlets found that the practice workshops helped practitioners to reflect on why they do this work. Some reignited core values about practice, and others realised this was not for them. Group supervision was introduced alongside training sessions to help embed appreciative inquiry questioning skills. The skill here is to keep questioning, and resist jumping to problem solving. This is harder than it sounds because offering professional views, suggestions and answers to problems is a customary way to work. Exploring ideas and goals through a respectful questioning and listening approach is much more difficult, but certainly worth it. These are the skills that practitioners need when they meet with adults with care needs.

Managers noticed improved rigour and confidence around decision making in safeguarding cases, and risk-taking confidence emerged. This is an important shift away from objective notions of risk and harm, as issues to resolve or avoid, towards working more constructively and respectfully with the personal meanings and understandings people have about their own wellbeing. Because of the strengths-based orientation underpinning the Mental Capacity Act (2005) and Care Act (2014), a practice framework for adult social care needs to guide practitioners and service users along a series of steps and questions that encourage respectful conversations where risk and need are understood as dynamic ideas that affect and influence personal and social wellbeing. However, a note of caution – there is a very real possibility that local authorities in England will struggle to deliver this kind of practice because they are so over-stretched (Keene 2013). Delivering on the Care Act (2014) is an ongoing challenge at a time of increased demand and tightened budgets. However, as shown in this chapter, change can be driven through frontline practice.

Conclusion – working more reflexively with risk

Adjusting practice cultures inside adult social care departments, from deficit-focused to strengths-based approaches, is challenging. It is hard work. The work is all the more difficult when professionals who have worked in particular ways are asked to think afresh in strengths-based ways. Rethinking how to do things does not come easy! But with risk work this is a vital step in a move towards strengths-based practice. Some practitioners will feel more comfortable filling in forms and tick-box approaches; but this does not deliver on the principles or aims of the Care Act (2014) or making safeguarding a personal agenda.

At a time of extraordinary resource demands, and rising numbers of people using services, practice should be effectively organised. Excellent safeguarding practice needs to be at the core of adult social care services to deliver on the promises of the Care Act (2014). Rigorous and ethical practice follows when the organisational systems of work support and encourage this. The 'signs of safety and wellbeing' practice framework offers a logical and accessible way to help staff and organisations deliver safeguarding practice that is person-led and person-centred.

The 'signs of safety and wellbeing' practice framework provides practitioners and managers, as well as people using services and their families and carers, an accessible and logical framework where practice skills, practice knowledge, theory and method, ethics and research are incorporated to inform professional judgements about wellbeing, risk and need. It encourages language that is respectful and person-centred without compromising safety. Practitioners and managers need support to help them articulate their professional judgements, and this new framework supports and guides that. Moral and intellectual debates about working more reflexively with risk can happen by using this practice framework. Staff in Tower Hamlets found that decision making and confidence in exploring personal and sensitive matters with people were enabled through the skill of appreciative inquiry questioning, and the evidence of success emerged in customer feedback and through improved care plans.

The Care Act (2014) sets out a new approach to practice, underpinned by principles of empowerment and being truly client- and person-centred. Shifting years of deficit-led, local authority-driven care management practice towards a more reflexive and respectful approach to person-centred and person-led safeguarding is possible. Family networks and local communities can and do offer resources and find strengths within to help improve the wellbeing of people. Practice frameworks such as 'signs of safety and wellbeing' can guide a strengths-based approach to working with people and those important to them. This is right and just for those who use and need our services.

References

ADASS (2014) *Making Safeguarding Personal 2013/14: Summary of Findings.* London: LGA. Available at https://www.local.gov.uk/topics/social-care-health-and-integration/adult-social-care/making-safeguarding-personal, accessed on 5 April 2017.

Beresford, P., Perring, R., Nettle, M., and Wallcroft, J. (2016) *From Mental Illness to a Social Model of Madness and Distress.* London: Shaping Our Lives.

Bunn, A. (2013) *Signs of Safety in England: An NSPCC Commissioned Report on the Signs of Safety Model in Child Protection.* London: NSPCC.

Burbage, D. (2013) 'Strengths Based Social Care.' In A. Fox (ed.) *The New Social Care: Strength-Based Approaches.* Available at www.thersa.org/globalassets/pdfs/reports/new-social-care-strength-based-approaches.pdf, accessed on 5 April 2017.

Connolly, M. (2007) 'Practice frameworks: Conceptual maps to guide interventions in child welfare.' *British Journal of Social Work 37*, 5, 825–837.

Connolly, M., and Healy, K. (2009) 'Social Work Practice Theories and Frameworks.' In M. Connolly and L. Harms (eds) *Social Work: Contexts and Practice* (Second edition). Melbourne: Oxford University Press.

Connolly, M., and Morris, K. (2012) *Understanding Child and Family Welfare.* Houndmills, UK: Palgrave Macmillan.

de Haan, I., and Marian, K. (2011) 'Building safety and deepening our practice.' *Social Work Now 47*, 35–43. Wellington: Child, Youth and Family.

Fox, A. (2013) 'A Networked Model of Care.' In A. Fox (ed.) *The New Social Care: Strength-Based Approaches.* Available at www.thersa.org/globalassets/pdfs/reports/new-social-care-strength-based-approaches.pdf, accessed on 5 April 2017.

Hammond, S. (1996) *The Thin Book of Appreciative Inquiry.* Bend, OR: Thin Book Publishing Company.

Healy, K. (2005) *Social Work Theories in Context: Creating Frameworks for Practice.* Houndmills, UK: Palgrave Macmillan.

Keene, S. (2013) 'Can Local Government Deliver the Change?' In A. Fox (ed.) *The New Social Care: Strength-Based Approaches.* Available at www.thersa.org/globalassets/pdfs/reports/new-social-care-strength-based-approaches.pdf, accessed on 5 April 2017.

Local Government Association (2015) *Making Safeguarding Personal: 2014–15 Evaluation Report*. London: LGA.

Munro, E., Turnell, A., and Murphy, T. (2016) *'You Can't Grow Roses in Concrete': Action Research Final Report*. Signs of Safety English Innovations Project. Available at http://munroturnellmurphy.com/eip-report, accessed on 5 April 2017.

Saleeby, D. (2010) *The Strengths Perspective in Social Work Practice*. Kansas: Strengths Institute, University of Kansas, School of Social Welfare.

Sanderson, H., and Stirk, S. (2012) *Creating Person-Centred Organisations*. London: Jessica Kingsley Publishers.

Slasberg, C. (2013) 'A proposed eligibility and assessment framework to support the delivery of the government's vision for a new care and support system.' *Journal of Care Services Management 7*, 1, 26–37.

Slasberg, C., and Beresford, P. (2014) 'Government guidance for the Care Act: Undermining ambitions for change?' *Disability and Society 29*, 10, 1677–1682.

Social Care Institute for Excellence (2011) *User Involvement in Adult Safeguarding*. Available at www.scie.org.uk/publications/reports/report47, accessed on 5 April 2017.

Social Care Institute for Excellence (2012) *Safeguarding Adults: Mediation and Family Group Conferences*. London: SCIE.

Stanley, T. (2013) '"Our tariff will rise": Risk probabilities and child protection.' *Health Risk and Society 15*, 1, 67–83.

Stanley, T. (2016) 'A practice framework to support the Care Act 2014.' *The Journal of Adult Protection 18*, 1, 53–64.

Stanley, T., and Mills, R. (2014) '"Signs of safety" practice at the health and children's social care interface.' *Practice 26*, 1, 23–36.

Turnell, A., and Edwards, S. (1999) *Signs of Safety: A Solution and Safety Oriented Approach to Child Protection Casework*. New York: Norton.

Vogt, E., Brown, J., and Isaacs, D. (2003) *The Art of Powerful Questions: Catalyzing Insight, Innovation, and Action*. Mill Valley, CA: Whole Systems Associates.

Webb, S. (2006) *Social Work in a Risk Society: Social and Political Perspectives*. Basingstoke: Palgrave Macmillan.

Weick, A., Rapp, C., Sullivan, W.P., and Kisthardt, W. (1989) 'A strengths perspective for social work practice.' *Social Work 34*, 350–354.

Chapter 3

Participative Practice and Family Group Conferencing

Marilyn Taylor and Linda Tapper

'But for the family conference I believe I would be dead by now! How can you tell anyone that without them thinking you are being over-dramatic? Coping is not a life and takes away your self-worth. The family conference helped me to realise that there was a future. It empowered both myself and my family to plan for a future without violence.'

This chapter explores models of empowerment that are based on the concept of enabling a family to make decisions and plan for the support of one or more of their members. It argues that this is not only a democratic principle worth supporting, but that such plans are more likely to be effective and achieve better outcomes than those made by others and imposed on an individual or family group. Such plans are likely to be more comprehensive, more successful, reduce risk, and encourage personal and family resilience. Also, they are often the more cost-effective option.

The chapter includes:

- the principles and process of family group conferences (FGC) used with adults, and how these reflect current legislation and good practice

- the importance and benefits of participative practice for the individual, community and wider society

- what empowerment really means for the individual, and how this can be achieved using FGCs

- variations on the FGC model

- research findings and evaluations of outcomes.

FGC emerged from the indigenous community of New Zealand where the Maori solved problems within their community by bringing everyone together to discuss the problem and make plans. The Maori community approached the New Zealand government in the 1980s with complaints about how their children and young people were treated by the authorities when there were issues of neglect, abuse or offending behaviour. They claimed that these children and young people were routinely being taken from their homes and placed with white families at huge distances from their communities. In addition, those exhibiting offending behaviour were disproportionately represented in the courts, and in institutions. Following these complaints, the government commissioned an inquiry, the Ministerial Advisory Committee on a Māori Perspective for the Department of Social Welfare in New Zealand (Ministerial Advisory Committee 2000), which included a consultation with the Maori community, in which these issues were highlighted.

This detailed commentary and inquiry into racism within New Zealand society, particularly within the Department of Social Welfare, was published in 1988 (Maxwell 1988). Subsequently, New Zealand mandated in law a process of involving extended family and friends in making important decisions, and called the model 'family group conferences'. This model is now being used in many places throughout the world as a means of protecting and supporting children and others who may be vulnerable within their family network and community (see below).

In England, 'Feedback from people who use, or may need to use, safeguarding adults processes is that many want to retain the support of their families, and where possible seek reconciliation with an abusive relative. By enabling a family "system" to discuss and find solutions to a difficult situation it is possible to leave the most vulnerable members of that family with a legacy of support around them. Having the opportunity to confront an abusive family member or person and hear what motivated them to abuse can help to heal the emotional damage done. It can also function to introduce a "shield" of family members around an individual to support and protect them' (Local Government Association [LGA] 2011, p.15).

What is a family group conference and how does it work?

FGCs are meetings of the extended family network and friends, together with those working professionally and directly with the family. They are essentially decision-making meetings. When used for adults, they empower and support the person to make decisions about their future, and help them to develop a plan that addresses their concerns and focuses on their desire for change. It is their meeting, and they decide who should be invited, and when and where the meeting will take place. It should be noted that the use of the term 'family', in keeping with the Maori origins of FGC, includes close and extended family members as well as friends and neighbours, and whoever the person considers to be in their 'support network'.

The FGC model is based on a set of basic principles and beliefs, including the following (Ashley *et al.* 2006):

- Family members have the intimate knowledge required, including who is safe and who is not safe or has care and support needs.

- Members of the extended family tend to have a lifelong commitment to each other.

- People are more committed to carrying out plans for their welfare and for their 'family' if they make the decisions themselves, and are not merely persuaded to carry out the decisions made by others.

- Good decisions are made based on high-quality information, and that therefore meetings need to have the benefit of openness, honesty and clarity.

- People work better together if there is a principle of mutual respect, which is an important statement of our humanity.

- If strengths of a 'family' are identified and supported, good outcomes are more likely to be achieved.

However, a FGC is more than just a meeting. It should rather be considered a process, and one of the essential ingredients in this process is the preparation time. This can take around three to six weeks, and involves the coordinator personally visiting and preparing all participants, including all family members and professionals.

This enables any concerns, difficulties, relationship issues and risk factors to be identified and addressed.

A frequent difficulty can be the complex history and long-standing grievances either within the family or between family and services. Conflict within the family can be of concern to everyone, and some family members may not have spoken to each other for some time. There may be concerns about bullying, coercion and manipulation, or even the safety of bringing together some members of the family in the same room.

The careful preparation of all potential participants is essential to ensure that any such issues are identified and addressed, and is critical for both the safety and potential success of the meeting. The experience and skill of the neutral coordinator can be key to helping individuals either resolve the issues beforehand or put them aside in the interests of a common purpose.

It is crucial that all participants fully understand the reason the FGC is being held, who will be there, what will happen at the meeting (i.e. the three stages – see below), and what their own role is within the process.

During this preparation time the person is helped to decide what sort of support they would like in order to help them participate in their meeting. This could be a trained advocate, though some people choose to have a known and trusted friend or relative for this crucial role. If this is the case, then the coordinator will need to ensure that this person is thoroughly prepared to undertake this task. Support can also be arranged for other family members, such as carers, if this is considered necessary.

The FGC meeting is comprised of three parts or stages:

- Information sharing

- Private family time

- Agreeing the plan.

The first part of the meeting, 'information sharing', involves everybody: the person for whom the meeting is being held, their family and friends, any advocate or supporter, the referrer (usually the social worker) and other professionals involved with the individual. Information about the concern is shared, and family members are encouraged to ask questions for clarification. This part of the meeting is chaired by the neutral coordinator, who facilitates the FGC process.

The second part of the meeting, which distinguishes it from any other sort of meeting, is the 'private family time'. All the professionals, including the coordinator, withdraw to another room nearby, and the person, their family and friends meet on their own to make the plan. Although this part of the meeting can be challenging for families and professionals alike, it is important to the development of self-reliance and problem-solving skills within the family, and aims to encourage negotiation and cooperation. It is during this part of the meeting that time spent on thorough preparation bears fruit.

The third part of the meeting is when the person, together with their family and friends, have come to their decisions about what they want to do. They present their 'Family Action Plan' to the referrer for discussion and, if necessary, to ask for their agreement and support. This part of the meeting is facilitated by the coordinator. Once the plan has been finalised, arrangements for monitoring progress after the meeting are agreed, with the expectation that one or more family members will take some responsibility for this. It is usual to agree a date to meet again to review the plan, and to address any outstanding issues.

The case studies below have had names and personal details changed to preserve anonymity. The cases described have been fictionalised or, as many referrals show similar circumstances, are composite studies containing elements from two or more actual cases. However, the outcomes described are true representations of actual plans and achievements. The comments at the end of each case are taken verbatim with only names changed.

The first case study illustrates how an older person with mental capacity can use a FGC to change arrangements made by members of her family with which she is not happy, whilst at the same time enhancing her relationship with her family.

CASE STUDY 1

Mrs Lomas was 80 years old and had been married for 45 years. She had a son and two step-children. Her relationship with her husband had often been difficult and for the last few years they had barely spoken to each other. Recently her health had deteriorated and she required more help with daily tasks.

Unknown to her, the family decided that she should be moved into a nursing home, taking none of her personal possessions with her, telling her that this was temporary. Once in the home, Mrs Lomas became very distressed and expressed the wish to go home. It became apparent that she had capacity to make her own decisions, but had not been consulted. While in the home Mrs Lomas was assessed as not needing nursing care, or even residential care, although she was suffering from severe depression. A safeguarding inquiry was initiated.

The family said that their decision had been made 'for her own good', but, along with Mrs Lomas, agreed to a FGC to try to resolve matters. Mrs Lomas accepted the offer of an advocate to support her at the meeting, and spent some time with her to prepare what she wanted to say. Mrs Lomas wrote her own notes about how she felt and what she wanted.

At the FGC the referring social worker presented Mrs Lomas and her family with information about mental capacity and explained several options which could be considered. Mrs Lomas, supported by her advocate, spoke very clearly about what she wanted, and how she felt about what had happened. With her advocate by her side, Mrs Lomas could express her own opinions, with a little assistance when needed. The family said they had been unaware that there were other options available.

The outcome of the FGC was that Mrs Lomas was able to be financially independent and chose not to return to live with her husband, but to try a Shared Lives placement, which by the time of the FGC Review after ten weeks everyone considered to be a great success. Mrs Lomas confirmed that she now had her jewellery and personal items and was very happy with the new arrangements. She had also maintained contact with her son, and both said that their relationship was now better than previously. The Shared Lives carers attended the review and confirmed that they all got on very well together, and the intention was that Mrs Lomas would remain with them for the foreseeable future.

Comment from the service provider who attended the FGC

'A massive change to her quality of life. Having her voice heard as an individual and not just "Stan's wife". A fantastic service. Everyone involved has been professional yet thoughtful in the process.'

It should be noted that although this chapter focuses on the use of FGC to empower and support adults to make their own choices and decisions, they are also frequently used as a 'best interests' meeting for adults who lack the relevant mental capacity. Most often this is used when there is no Power of Attorney in place, or when there is a dispute about what course of action would be in the person's best interests, or how to accomplish a specific goal. When it is established that the person lacks the capacity to make specific decisions, the FGC encourages the family, who know the person best, to consider all options, taking account of what the person themselves would have wanted, as well as the information from the professionals involved. This does not conflict with the legal responsibility of the practitioner in the role of 'decision maker'. He or she will still need to agree that the plan developed by the family is indeed in the best interest of the person.

As a best interests meeting, the FGC is particularly good at fulfilling the Mental Capacity Act (2005) requirements for full consultation, inclusion and seeking out and taking account of the person's views and wishes, especially in complex situations when there are many options to consider. It is particularly important that family carers do not feel pressured to take on more than they can cope with. Conversely, when professionals feel that the family are unable to meet the needs of the person, the FGC may help everyone come to an acceptable decision, as this next case example shows.

CASE STUDY 2

Mr Clark had been living at home, cared for by his family. He was admitted to hospital with a severe infection, and in what was described as an extremely neglected state. After several weeks in hospital Mr Clark's condition improved enough for discharge, but he was assessed as needing 24-hour care and lacking capacity to make the relevant decisions. Family members wanted to take Mr Clark home, saying they would manage all his care. A safeguarding inquiry started as there were concerns that the family would be unable to provide sufficient care for his needs. The relationship between family members and health professionals was extremely difficult, with high levels of distrust on both sides.

The family agreed to take part in a FGC, facilitated by a neutral coordinator. Extensive preparation with all participants ensured that the FGC meeting was held in a 'no blame' atmosphere, with the sole aim of agreeing a plan that would best meet Mr Clark's needs. Mr Clark did not attend due to his health, but was represented by an Independent Mental Capacity Advocate (IMCA). The family came to the meeting with a detailed plan of how they were intending to care for Mr Clark. However, they listened to reports explaining the extent of the care that Mr Clark would require and asked pertinent questions. It became clear that all the family cared deeply about Mr Clark, and wanted to do as much as they could for him.

The private family time was quite long and emotional as family members considered the options. They acknowledged that their original plan for full-time care of Mr Clark at home was not feasible; however, they wanted to be involved in his care as much as possible and, when his health improved sufficiently, to care for him at home for 1–2 days per week. They were prepared to undertake training and supervision and make all necessary adaptations to the home to enable this to happen. The family wanted to be involved in the choice of nursing home and expressed the wish to work with all the professionals to achieve this aim.

Comment from the Safeguarding practitioner

'Given the high levels of anxiety and emotion and the complexities of the case, it would have been almost impossible to broker agreement with the family through the normal methods. The FGC provided a neutral and "safe" environment for discussions and information sharing, which resulted in a positive outcome with the support of all parties.'

The FGC process can also accommodate circumstances where the person is assessed as having mental capacity to make some decisions, but not others. However, before the FGC meeting takes place, there should always be clarity about the person's capacity to make each decision relevant to the concerns, and everyone must be made aware of the capacity assessments. A frequent cause of dispute between family and professionals can be lack of understanding about mental capacity and the legal implications for decision making, as shown in the first case example.

FGC can be used preventatively in safeguarding situations: using mediation and FGCs in the early stages of disagreement or conflict can help to safeguard adults with care and support needs by empowering families to cope better before a situation gets out of hand.

The importance of participative practice

In the UK, society is based on a range of democratic principles that are reflected in concepts of basic human rights and the responsibilities of the citizen. People value the right to make decisions affecting their own lives, so long as they are within the law and do not interfere with the rights and liberties of others. This can sometimes conflict with the professionalisation of decision making, which suggests that those with specific sets of knowledge, training and qualifications have all the expertise and hence must have all the answers.

In England, the Care Act (2014) clearly states the need to transform the way we work with those requiring care and support, putting people in control of their own lives, to 'safeguard adults in a way that supports them in making choices and having control about how they want to live' (Department of Health [DH] 2016, para.14.11). This is not to say that the 'safety net' should be removed, but rather that a better balance should be achieved in taking responsibility and decision making. This requires professionals to work together with individuals, families and communities, and to develop new skills in encouraging and enabling participation in all decision making and planning for the people they work with.

Making Safeguarding Personal encourages participative approaches such as FGC as a means to 'empower the person to draw on their strengths and personal networks', supporting 'a gradual shift in culture' (LGA 2013, p.4).

Despite the new legal framework, there is still often the belief that 'increasing participation' can be achieved by inviting the person to attend any meeting held about them. Without a great deal of thought and preparation, this could be simply a 'box-ticking' exercise, as a person with care and support needs is more likely to feel nervous, confused and even intimidated, than included and part of the decision making.

Empowerment in action

Models of empowerment should involve a shift of real power from the professional to the individual and their family and/or community, but too often remain on the periphery of formal decision making. Many professionals are very enthusiastic about this way of working with people, but as noted by a number of researchers, some find this very challenging. Lupton and Nixon (1999) found that some professionals involved in a FGC found it difficult to present information in an understandable way, and to resist adding conditions to the solution, particularly when they were not trained in methods of empowerment and participation in general, and in the FGC process in particular.

Holland *et al.* (2005) found that empowering the family via a FGC can be challenging for some practitioners, who tried to influence the wording of the question, the agenda of the private meeting, and the final content of the plan.

Marmot (2015) refers to three types of empowerment: material, or being able to feed your children; psychosocial, or having control over your life; and political, or having a voice. We suggest that the FGC model discussed in this chapter promotes at least two of these.

When considering FGCs and other empowerment or participative processes, it can be helpful to consider the mandate in which they appear. Michael Doolan (2002), Chief Social Worker, who was responsible for the implementation of family group conferences throughout New Zealand, identified three types of mandate:

- Good practice mandate – when the practitioner decides to use the method.

- Procedural mandate – when institutions decide criteria for referral.

- Legal mandate – when professionals have the obligation, and users have the right, to request in certain cases, as in New Zealand and the Netherlands.

Although all can be seen to empower individuals and families, it can be argued that the strongest element of empowerment is contained in the last.

The Dutch Law of Child Welfare gave citizens the right from 2015 to develop their own action plans in cases that require intervention.

This led to an increased demand for methods that support this, including FGC, as a citizen right, rather than something that is offered or withheld by professionals. When models of empowerment are not a right of the citizen, issues of inequality of access, and limitation of the experience, can come into play.

Central to the FGC process is the empowerment of anyone who may be disadvantaged or who may feel unable to exercise their right to be heard. A crucial element of this empowerment is ensuring that the person's voice is heard and that they are enabled to participate fully in the process, and for adults to exercise their right to control over their own lives.

Models of empowerment, and in particular FGCs, are not a silver bullet for success, but because they involve those most affected by the situation, and with the most personal experience, they are more likely to be effective and successful in reaching desired outcomes. They not only fit with healthy principles of democracy, but also are more likely to achieve positive results.

The case study below describes a FGC for a young woman with learning difficulties whose relationship with her father, and her contact with other family members, had broken down because of her need for independence.

CASE STUDY 3

Nicola was 21 years old. She has learning difficulties and health problems and had been living with her grandparents and two younger siblings since her mother's death ten years ago. She had chosen, against her grandparents' wishes, to move out and live with friends. Concerns had been raised previously about the relationship between Nicola and her grandfather which had become increasingly antagonistic, but after Nicola left communication broke down entirely. Nicola was distressed at the situation, and particularly at losing contact with her siblings; however, she was adamant that she did not want to return. Her grandfather insisted that she could not see them again unless she returned home.

Nicola had capacity to decide where she wanted to live, but she was considered to have care and support needs and she agreed that she did need support. Nicola agreed to have a

FGC to try to resolve the situation, and accepted the offer of an advocate because she thought she was likely to become upset at the meeting and would then be unable to say what she really wanted.

Nicola's grandfather decided at the last moment not to attend the FGC, but her grandmother did agree to attend, along with other members of the extended family, and a long-term friend of the family. Other family members who could not be there sent letters of support and offers of help. With everyone's support Nicola made a plan which would help her work towards her goal of achieving independence. In addition, her grandmother agreed that Nicola would be able to see her siblings outside the home, as they had also expressed the wish to stay in contact with her.

At a review meeting eight weeks later, Nicola reported that she had met up with her siblings, spent time with other family members, and had all the support she felt she needed to begin her new life. Although no progress had been made in repairing the relationship with her grandfather, Nicola hoped this might happen over time. Nicola's relationship with her grandmother was, however, slowly improving, and they had met in a local café for coffee and cakes.

Comment from family member who attended the FGC

'The process was very empowering [for Nicola]. [She] now realises there is support for her and she can control her own destiny.'

Variations on the FGC model

The FGC model favoured by Daybreak, and most other UK-based programmes, follows closely the model introduced in New Zealand. However, others have diverged from this traditional model and introduced variations. A Norwegian literature review (Havnen, Karen and Christiansen 2014) refers to the Family Unity Meeting, which was developed in the USA. Differences from the traditional FGC model include: the facilitator is present all the time so there is no private time; parents can veto the selection of any family member; and the meeting begins with a discussion about what resources there are in the group, and to say something positive about the family.

Other variations of the FGC models have involved the role of the coordinator/facilitator being separated, or the FGC coordinator being an employee of the referring agency, so not completely 'independent'. Information usually shared with the group in stage one of the FGC can be distributed as written reports beforehand.

'Family meetings' and 'Network meetings' are terms which can have various interpretations, and it is important that they are not considered as alternative names for FGCs. Whereas there is undoubtedly a use for any meeting which involves the person's family and social network, it is important that they are not confused with a FGC. Often these meetings are used in 'less critical' situations, and the rigorous preparation work which characterises a FGC may be reduced or omitted. The coordinator is usually not independent and may even be the case-holding practitioner. Private family time may be considered optional or even omitted entirely.

Research findings and evaluations of outcomes

There is some research about FGCs that addresses both the process and their outcomes. Historically, family group conferences tended to focus on work with children, rather than adults, so most of the research focuses on children's FGCs. However, as many findings are also likely to be relevant to adult FGCs, they are still worth considering.

The literature review undertaken by Havnen *et al.* (2014) found that most participants have a positive experience of FGCs and stressed the importance of preparing participants well, and ensuring that the critical role of the coordinator is protected and maintained by good training and support. Reviewing some small-scale studies about participants' experiences of FGCs, they highlighted two key factors: all participants should be prepared for the special characteristics of FGCs; and coordinators must maintain their central role in a qualitatively good way (ibid.). They identified that the challenge was often to reduce the number and complexity of problems to one or very few questions, in language that is precise and understandable; and the more open-ended a question, the more opportunity for the family to find a solution. Further findings were that: families were overwhelmingly positive about the model and considered it very successful in achieving good outcomes for the individual who was the centre of the discussion; empowerment was a frequent experience, often generated by support from family and friendship networks; and some research found that satisfaction waned over time, but noted that this was the same as in public services plans (ibid.).

Further Norwegian research on the effects of FGCs on social support and mental health for adults found 'significant positive effects of the FGC process on life satisfaction and mental health – while mental distress and the measure for anxiety and depression decreased significantly. In addition, positive trends were found for emotional social support and social resources' (Malmberg-Heimonen 2011, p.964).

Research from Canada into the use of FGCs to address situations of domestic abuse reported very good outcomes for the reduction of incidents of domestic abuse, and found that the most common resources provided by family members comprised relief measures, practical help, support and counselling (Pennell and Burford 2000). However, this is a high-risk area of work, and a FGC should not be attempted without specialist coordinator training (whether or not consideration is being given to any perpetrator involvement in the process).

Australian research found that respect was best expressed in straightforward and direct communication without judgemental attitudes, rather than language characterised by professional jargon. Children and young people were mainly satisfied by the process, seeing their family there to support them, rather than the plan itself. This demonstration of support by family members can often also be experienced positively by adults who are the focus of FGC meetings (Darlington and Yellowlees 2012).

Hyrve (2006) ascertained that formulating good and manageable questions for a conference was an area for improvement. The same issue is highlighted in a Danish study (Rasmussen, Hansen and Haldbo 2002), which identified that social workers reduced the number and complexity of problems by working with the family to formulate questions in a language that was precise and understandable, without making them sound like instructions. Løfsnes (2002) describes experiences from a development project where the group tried to make questions as tangible as possible and concluded that questions should not be too detailed: the more open-ended, the more opportunity to find a solution.

Dutch research found that, with the use of FGCs, involuntary admission to hospital had been avoided when working with people experiencing mental illness. Through offering an alternative environment to think about problems, spirals of marginalisation and social isolation were countered (De Jong and Schout 2013; De Jong, Schout and Abma 2014).

In the UK, reports found that 'those using it felt that family group conferencing identified the person's networks, and the personal resources that they have to manage their situation. It helped them and their family learn how to resolve complex problems within the family by drawing on their personal resources and networks' (LGA 2013, p.17).

In the UK there are currently an increasing number of FGC programmes for adults, including:

- Essex – focusing on adults with mental health problems.

- Kent – pilot programme in 2006–07 with older people, adults with learning disabilities and young adults with physical disabilities.

- Hampshire – the Daybreak FGC programme, funded by Comic Relief, to address issues of elder abuse 2007–10, then Hampshire Adult Services, funded for all adults at risk.

- Camden – expanded its children's programme to include adults.

- Midlothian – pilot programme for adults with early stage dementia.

Most FGC programmes monitor outcomes and evaluate the success and cost efficiency of their work. However, the criteria for 'success' can be hard to define:

There can be no single criterion for a 'successful outcome', although improved safety is always a priority. However, safeguarding cannot be considered in isolation from the wishes and wellbeing of the individual, and in the eyes of the service user, it may not be the most important issue. If the service user has capacity to make their own decision, he or she may choose to leave themselves at risk; however, an outcome could still be considered beneficial if the FGC process results in greater awareness and understanding of risks and options, increased support being offered and accepted, and improved communication and relationships… Financial benefits for the local authority may also be a desired outcome, but again this cannot be a realistic aim in every case, and the needs of the service user may require, for example, that a residential placement be provided if support in the home is unable to meet those needs, or if the service user prefers it. An evaluation of cost benefits of the first 3 years of this project showed clear overall cost savings. A frequent outcome was shown to be much reduced social worker time after the FGC process, often allowing cases to be closed either completely or to safeguarding. (Daybreak 2014, p.15)

The initial Daybreak pilot programme estimated £77,360 savings from avoidable residential care costs and reductions in care packages and practitioner time. The analysis of 49 referrals (Daybreak 2014, p.25) showed that, following the FGC:

- 29 cases were closed to safeguarding

- 8 cases showed reduced risk

- 17 cases required no further action by adult social care services

- 10 cases showed increased family and community support

- 8 cases resolved housing or accommodation issues

Professor Peter Marsh evaluated the Kent FGC pilot and estimated cost savings for the local authority of around £85,000 over two years. He identified four key benefits in policy terms: cost effective professional partnerships; better integrated commissioning and planning for clients; positive engagement for their families; and more positive day-to-day experience for clients (Marsh 2007).

In conclusion, FGC is a developing area in working with adults in safeguarding situations and is becoming recognised as an important tool in safeguarding work.

'What a difference three hours can make! With the help of my family and the guidance of the family group conference coordinator, the future I never thought I would have, or was worthy of, was possible and planned for.'

References

Ashley, C. (2006) *The Family Group Conference Toolkit.* London: Family Rights Group.

Daybreak (2014) *Daybreak FGC Programme for Adults Evaluation Report, April 2013–March 2014.* Available at www.daybreakfgc.org.uk, accessed on 6 April 2017.

De Jong, G., and Schout, G. (2013) 'Breaking through marginalisation in public mental health care with family group conferencing: Shame as risk and protective factor.' *British Journal of Social Work 43,* 1439–1454.

De Jong, G., Schout, G., and Abma, T. (2014) 'Prevention of involuntary admission through family group conferencing: A qualitative case study in community mental health nursing.' *Journal of Advanced Nursing 70,* 11, 2651–2662.

Department of Health (2016) *Care and Support Statutory Guidance.* London: DH.

Doolan, M. (2002) 'Establishing an effective mandate for family group conference.' *Family Group Conference Newsletter.* London: Family Rights Group.

Havnen, S., Karen, J., and Christiansen, O. (2014) *Knowledge Review of Family Group Conferencing: Experiences and Outcomes.* Regional Centre for Child and Mental Health and Child Welfare (RKBU West), Uni Research Health, Norway.

Holland, S., Scourfield, J., O'Neill, S., and Pithouse, A. (2005) 'Democratising the family and the state? The case of family group conferences in child welfare.' *Journal of Social Policy 34,* 59–77.

Hyrve, G. (2006) Familieråd sett ut i fra saksbehandlers ståsted. In S. Falck (ed.) *Hva er det med familieråd? General report from the project: Nasjonal satsing for utprøving og evaluering av familieråd i Norge.* Oslo: NOVA-rapport 18/06.

Local Government Association (2011) *Making Safeguarding Personal: Toolkit for Responses.* London: LGA.

Local Government Association (2013) *Making Safeguarding Personal – Final Report.* London: ADASS/LGA.

Løfsnæs, B. (2002). *Bestemme selv?: familieråd som metode i praktisk arbeid.* Oslo: Gyldendal Academic Press

Lupton, C., and Nixon, P. (1999) *Empowering Practice? A Critical Appraisal of the Family Group Conference Approach.* Bristol, UK: Policy Press.

Malmberg-Heimonen, I. (2011) 'The effects of family group conferences on social support and mental health for longer-term social assistance recipients in Norway.' *British Journal of Social Work 41,* 5, 949–967.

Marmot, M. (2015) *The Health Gap: The Challenge of an Unequal World.* London: Bloomsbury.

Marsh, P. (2007) *Kent Adult FGC Development Research Final Report.* Available at https://shareweb.kent.gov.uk/Documents/childrens-social-services/carers-and-family-support/family-group-conference/Adults%20research%20findings.pdf, accessed on 6 April 2017.

Maxwell, G. (1988) 'Youth offenders – Treatment of young offenders, 1840 to 1980s.' *Te Ara – the Encyclopedia of New Zealand.* Available at www.TeAra.govt.nz/en/video/26599/puao-te-ata-tu-report, accessed on 6 April 2017.

Ministerial Advisory Committee (2000) Ministerial Advisory Committee on a Māori Perspective for the Department of Social Welfare in New Zealand, 'Puat-te-ata-tu', Wellington, NZ.

Pennell, J., and Burford, G. (2000) 'Family group decision making: Protecting children and women.' *Child Welfare: Journal of Policy, Practice, and Program 79,* 2, 131–158.

Rasmussen, M., Hansen, B., and Haldbo, T. (2002) *En beslutningsmodel med meget mere: en undersøgelse af «Det danske forsøg med Familierådslagning».* Aabenraa: UDC Børn og Familier.

Chapter 4

Working towards Recovery and Resolution, including Mediation and Restorative Justice

John Gunner

Introduction

This chapter reviews a range of approaches to recovery of relationships and the resolution of conflict or harm using methods tried and tested in other areas but currently under-used for safeguarding adults. It provides summaries of different approaches that can be adopted, together with examples to illustrate good practice.

The chapter looks at the application of restorative justice and practices as alternatives in the criminal and wider systems developed alongside their sister civil court equivalents. Restorative justice (RJ) gives victims the chance to meet or communicate with offenders, facilitated by a specialist RJ Facilitator. Its function includes helping the parties to explain and seek restitution for the real impact of a crime or harm and/or a healing transformation and understanding of each other's views and needs. Everything is confidential in order to encourage participation and prevent use of information gained from meetings being used in any further formal procedures should the restorative justice process not succeed. It is also voluntary, meaning that it only takes place if all the participants agree to it. These principles can be applied in certain circumstances to adult safeguarding. Like safeguarding principles, restorative justice and mediation are also aimed at the individual rather than the state. They are termed alternative dispute resolution (ADR), principally including mediation. Mediation is a similar approach to RJ, which is perhaps more familiar; it also involves a neutral third party, an impartial mediator, who assists those involved in conflict or disputes to reach their own decisions leading to resolution. This is used a lot in family, workplace and commercial situations. There is evidence from research on the effectiveness of these approaches that indicates potential applicability and learning for inclusion in adult safeguarding practice.

So important are RJ and mediation now that they even form a parallel part of the rules of court, making litigation a last, not first, resort in the civil arena.

Until the advent of RJ there had been no modern equivalent in the area of crime and anti-social behaviour. It is now routinely used in community, family, workplace, health, school and other areas, hence the interest in its application to safeguarding.

Principles and context of the new approach – care and the restitution of harm

The Care Act (2014) put safeguarding on a new legal footing from April 2015, enshrining six key principles of adult safeguarding in the *Care and Support Statutory Guidance* (Department of Health [DH] 2016): the first two particularly apply to mediation and restorative practices (RP) or restorative approaches (RA). RP and RA are the wider, more inclusive terms for the use of techniques, principles and processes better known in the criminal context as restorative justice. These first two principles are:

1. Empowerment – the presumption of person-led decisions and informed consent.

2. Prevention – it is better to take action before harm occurs.

In addition, a third principle of Proportionality is also relevant here (the remaining ones, Protection, Partnership and Accountability, are also improved through the application of the processes of RP and mediation). It is notable that in legal circles Proportionality is thought of in a similar way to the Care Act (2014), referring to a preference for the use of less formal, costly, delaying and damaging methods to resolve problems; this is similar to least-intrusive responses appropriate to the risk in safeguarding. This proportionality principle is entirely in keeping with both the RP and mediation approaches. Mediation should be considered and attempted before other formal and often highly intensive adversarial processes and procedures. This is also more compatible with the safeguarding principles, including Protection, in that mediation and RP provide good vehicles for improving support and representation.

The key thrust of this book is about *working with* people. This contrasts radically with a formal, forensic approach trying to find and impose what is 'right' or 'correct'. Such judgement is often irrelevant to what people want or need and does further harm to ongoing relationships. Addressing needs and relationships can only be done by working with people. The benefits of facilitative processes are that they are person-centred and include achieving better mutual understanding and the addressing of needs, more creative solutions, speed, cost, informality and control of both the process and outcome by the parties. Crucially, this provides a powerful opportunity to explore, understand and even challenge the personal values of individual participants which may be at the core of, or even the cause of, problems between the parties. Yet in order to resolve conflicts stemming from human needs, parties need to eschew traditional negotiation models. Human needs theorists point out that if agreements focus solely on material interests (as in legal distributive processes dealing only with money, property, possessions, etc.) and ignore the underlying needs of parties, they are unlikely to be stable in the long term (Mitchell and Banks 1996).

Key questions for considering a restorative justice approach
Question 1
Is this really a legal or technical matter the parties are unable or unwilling to resolve directly between themselves and so only resolvable by the imposition of a judgemental decision by an outsider? Or is it more about helping and empowering the people involved to understand and resolve their own needs and wishes between them?

Question 2
Is there an important ongoing relationship between the parties (intimate, social, family, neighbour, workplace, client/professional or other) that would benefit from repair or a 'restorative' process (or avoidance of further damage done by adversarial procedures)? Or perhaps the relationship or parties' perceptions need to change for the better ('transformative' process)?

Question 3
Have the parties been advised about the possibility of using an independent specialist in RP or mediation?

The concept of prevention and restitution of harm through restorative justice

On 16 November 2015 the transposition of the EU Victims' Directive into English law came into force.

The Directive dealt with the restitution of harm, which is the central tenet of restorative justice. In the context of the Victims Code under the Domestic Violence, Crime and Victims Act (2004), harm has a wide definition but involves 'victims' who have suffered any harm arising from criminal activity including physical, mental, emotional or economic forms. It does not, however, require prosecution first. In fact, the crime does not even have to have been reported. It does, though, usually involve an assumption that there is a 'harmed person' (and therefore a 'harmer'), but it is still possible to use RJ or RP in cases of 'unacknowledged harm' where no responsibility has been accepted, or even where not all parties agree to any facilitated process. This means that it is well placed for use in adult safeguarding practice.

RJ is described as a process actively involving those affected by wrongdoing in the process of repairing the harm and by fostering the closure and emotional healing that is largely denied in our current systems (Watchel, O'Connell and Watchel 2010). Those systems are focused on formal procedures and imposing outcomes based on them rather than addressing the underlying needs, which are more the concern of people subjected to them: 'Victims don't care how much you know until they know how much you care' (Newlove 2015, p.16).

Definitions of RJ are problematic due to a growth in approaches within the fields of community justice, transformative justice, peace-making criminology and relational justice (Bazemore 1999). This chapter follows Marshall's (1996) definition which appears to encompass the main principles: 'Restorative justice is a process whereby all the parties with a stake in a particular offence come together to resolve collectively how to deal with the aftermath of the offence and its implications for the future' (Braithwaite 1999, p.5). For 'crime' and 'offence' here, this chapter substitutes 'harm or risk of harm to be considered in order to safeguard adults at risk of them'.

The prevention of harm presents a perfect opportunity for sharing perspectives, developments and skills between professions involved in and around these and other safeguarding issues. Restorative practice is increasingly being used in schools, colleges and universities, workplaces, hospitals and communities as well as the criminal justice system. Victims Commissioners, a new part of the Offices of Police and Crime Commissioners, are a good point of contact for local social work professionals and other stakeholders (see, for example, Kuppuswamy *et al.* 2015) because they can signpost to these as part of their RJ strategy on victim support services.

An important feature of RJ is the inclusion of all those harmed by events. This means not only the inclusion of all individuals, family members, groups or entire communities, but also careful attention to the concept of secondary or tertiary harm. That is, addressing the possibility of further harm being suffered, whether emotional or physical, now or in the future, by victims again or in addition by their supporters, family or others. This stands in stark contrast to formal (especially legal) processes where the focus is on the offender and the act and an argument about which standard punishment to apply. This radical difference will be fully appreciated by professionals working within or alongside care.

There is a really interesting, equally important, point arising from restorative approaches in the environments mentioned above relevant to safeguarding. That is the well-developed services in the area of forensic mental health in First Nation communities in countries such as Canada, New Zealand and Australia. According to commentators such as Drennan, Cook and Kiernan (Gavrielides 2014), this is a link obvious to psychology practitioners as a psychotherapeutic tool yet conspicuously missing in the criminal justice setting. Family, residential community, treatment and offender circles are well known and used in the former, and so often a transformative experience for participants in terms of addressing, understanding, challenging and even changing values. In this regard, RP 'circles' may be thought of as an alternative 'talking therapy', though there is little if any recognition of this as yet.

Tools to address the new focus on 'needs' and 'wellbeing'

The concept of 'meeting needs' and the principle of individual wellbeing has, of course, always been a given in the practical professional approach to safeguarding by practitioners. The Care Act (2014), though, moves this beyond good practice to become a core legal duty.

The difficulties of third party notions about the subjective nature of needs and establishing wellbeing are well illustrated by leading legal cases on the issue and also demonstrate the reasons for the involvement of the parties themselves. In the case of *A Local Authority v DL*, Judge Sir Nicholas Wall commented on an apparent contradiction between the European Convention on Human Rights (1998) and the Care Act (2014). He highlighted 'the local authority's awareness of the conflict between its duties under ECHR (1998) Article 8 and its duty to protect Mr and Mrs L from harm'. Then, in *CC v KK*, Judge Baker referred to this again, warning of the 'risk that all professionals involved with treating and helping that person – including, of course, a judge in the Court of Protection – may feel drawn towards an outcome that is more protective of the adult and thus, in certain circumstances, fail to carry out an assessment of capacity that is detached and objective'.

He ruled that 'different individuals may give different weight to different factors', in this case, as Mrs KK attached greater importance to familiar surroundings and 'emotional security' than physical security and that Mrs KK had the mental capacity to decide to return to live in her own home.

All this judicial debate is summed up in Jackson J's statement in *Re M* [2013]:

> 'In the end, if M remains confined in a home she is entitled to ask "What for?" The only answer that could be provided at the moment is "To keep you alive as long as possible." In my view that is not a sufficient answer. The right to life and the state's obligation to protect it is not absolute and the court must surely have regard to the person's own assessment of her quality of life. In M's case there is little to be said for a solution that attempts, without any guarantee of success, to preserve for her a daily life without meaning or happiness and which she, with some justification, regards as insupportable.'

This attempt at achieving some semblance of objectivity in establishing needs is not made easier by the multi-agency working required under the Care Act (2014). Even where, for example, a practitioner can appreciate the need and perceptions of some or all of the parties, they will often fail to be seen as independent. Furthermore, this personal and individual approach does also contain a potential tension between the person with care and support needs and/ or their advocate, and the multi-agency involvement necessary. Partnership is at the heart of the safeguarding principles set out in the Care Act (2014), yet it is one of the hardest elements to get right, and an area where safeguarding practice often fails. The differing approaches, perceptions, processes, professional standards and priorities will seldom be the same amongst key partners, including: local authorities; police and victim support; health services; fire and rescue services; prison and probation services; housing organisations; voluntary, charity and independent sector and faith organisations; advocacy and support services; Coroners; Crown Prosecution Service; Disclosure and Barring Service; Healthwatch; and Office of the Public Guardian. In complex partnership arrangements an independent and neutral third party can be especially useful.

Using restorative practices in safeguarding

Restorative justice is a simple approach which enables victims of crime (including family, friends, community and anyone affected) to talk about what happened with the offender – the person responsible for the act which caused the harm. It is about finding a way to move on with everyone having understood what happened and the effects it had. Like mediation, restorative practices are voluntary. No one can be forced to take part. In sensitive cases especially, it will only happen if a specially trained RJ Facilitator confirms it is safe for everyone to do so. At the very least there needs to be a consensus on the point amongst the professionals involved in safeguarding. This is true even where 'instant', informal, on-the-spot methods are used by appropriate facilitators with at least basic informal RJ training.

CASE STUDY

Eileen (mother of Emma, her 34-year-old daughter with learning difficulties) describes her experience, starting with the hurt caused:

'The trouble started about three years ago, when some of the local kids started to torment Emma. It wasn't all of them – some of them were lovely with her – but there were a couple in the group who were causing problems. It started with name-calling and Emma would come in crying.

'At first, both myself and some of the staff who supported Emma encouraged her not to go and talk to these people. But about two years ago, it started escalating. The kids started to get into the office block behind Emma's house, and they threw snowballs at her windows, and then stones and water bombs.

'Emma's mad about music – she loves it – and she'd play her music and dance around the bedroom. But then she started saying, "Mum, those kids are copying me," and they were over in the office block mimicking her. They were also pulling their pants down and showing their bums, and sticking two fingers up and it was really upsetting her. Emma would shout and cry, but that only encouraged them, because they thought it was funny.

'The local bobby came round and tried talking to some of the parents, but they became defensive about their kids, so it didn't really help.

'Last year, two young girls and a young man, all in their mid-teens, knocked on Emma's door. Up until that point, I didn't really know what was going on. The staff who were looking after Emma would file a report each time there was an incident, but I wasn't shown any of them. When she opened the door, they screamed at her, swearing and using really nasty words, and then ran off.

'Emma was really upset, and went chasing after them. The carer who was with Emma brought her inside and calmed her down, but then the same kids started knocking on the window, and shouting horrible things. At one point, they screamed, "Go and die, you f***ing spastic!" Emma was angry and distraught.

'Emma's helpers went out and told the group that they would call the police if they didn't stop. By now, the kids were kicking a football at Emma's front door, and it was crashing into the glass. Emma was so upset that she went upstairs and broke some of her CDs in half. Then she started to cut her arms.

'For the first time, I was sent a copy of the report which was filed by Emma's carers. I was in tears – Emma had self-harmed in the past, but I had no idea that she was doing it again because of what this one group of kids were doing to her. I'd already suggested to Emma that we could sit down with the people who'd been upsetting her and tell them exactly how bad they'd made her feel. Emma didn't feel that she had the courage to do that, although I tried to reassure her. Then social services stepped in and said that Emma shouldn't take part in restorative justice – they used the term "safeguarding" – so that was the end of that.

'I decided that I definitely wanted to go ahead with the meeting, even without Emma. I knew that the young man wouldn't be there, as he was in care and had recently been moved out of the area, but the two girls would. I wanted to let these young people know how upset they had made Emma, and me.'

Eileen describes the meeting

'One of the girls was living with her grandmother, and the other was with a foster mother. I knew they were only 15-year-old girls, but I was still nervous about meeting them. When I walked in the room I got a huge surprise – the foster mother had done respite care for Emma years before. She was very supportive of her foster daughter, but also very understanding about the harm they had caused Emma.

'The grandmother of the other girl actually left the room during the meeting. She told me later that she felt her granddaughter needed to face up to what she'd done by herself. Both girls were very polite – there was no anger, or shouting – and they seemed genuinely sorry for what they'd done. They both wrote a letter of apology to Emma.

'It took me a day to get over my nerves after the meeting, but I was pleased I'd done it. It made me feel better, and I felt I'd got through to those girls. Until you meet people, you have images of them in your head. When you come face to face with them, you see them in a different light. I was able to reassure Emma that they weren't horrible people, and I think it helped her too.

'Emma's doing well now, and there hasn't been any trouble since. The police have worked hard with the local kids, and a new skate park has been opened to give them something to do. I still think Emma would have benefited from going through restorative justice herself. She was nervous, which isn't surprising – even now she feels scared when she sees a group of kids. But I feel she would have been able to do it with the right support. It would certainly have been nice to explore the option a bit more.

'I think restorative justice is a great idea, and everyone should have the chance to go through it if they need to. It gives you closure. People are never the way you imagine them to be, and it really is worthwhile looking them in the eye and telling them the hurt and the upset they've caused you.

'I always say to Emma, "Talk – tell me about how you're feeling." People with learning difficulties can benefit from restorative justice. They need proper support and to know exactly what to expect, and it might take them longer to understand and accept what's said, but I feel it can help.'

Many group meetings and conferences are facilitated after much preparation, risk assessment, arrangements and management by a qualified RJ Facilitator. The process does, however, also lend itself very effectively to use in impromptu meetings. These may be in a workplace, corridor, home, hospital, health care practice or even street where people involved in a difficult situation find themselves together with a neutral third party with an understanding of the fundamental skills and processes required. A simplified set of key questions is put to the parties in order, as outlined below.

A small impromptu restorative meeting – basic script

Ask the prime active parties involved:

- What happened?
- What were your thoughts at the time?
- What have your thoughts been since?
- Who has been affected by your actions?
- In what way have they been affected?

Ask those affected:

- What happened?
- What were your thoughts at the time?
- What have your thoughts been since?
- How has this affected you and others?
- What has been the hardest thing for you?

Next steps:

- Ask the active parties if there is anything more they want to say.
- Ask those affected what they think needs to happen next.
- Ask other parties what they think needs to happen next.

At this point the parties will start generating ideas about moving on and forming the foundation for any agreed plans or actions. If they wish, these can be put in writing to sign.

The forms and standards of restorative practice

The facilitator will guide the parties on possible appropriate options for the format and conduct of any RP intervention. Where an informal small impromptu meeting is used, the person conducting it should have been trained in RP. Short courses can be as little as half a day and trainers can be found at the Restorative Justice Council (RJC) website.

For more complex or sensitive cases, such as often encountered in adult safeguarding, further training and experience is required, and the RJC is an important resource providing confidence. RJ Facilitators are not subject to mandatory professional regulation, but the voluntary accreditation provided under the RJC is widely recognised.

In the absence of any local contacts and partnerships, this could be a valuable first point of reference. In these cases, the term 'mediation' is often used; yet, somewhat confusingly, it is usually more in the form of using a script of restorative questions rather than detailed open questioning, reframing, reflecting and summary in the format of a civil mediation. RP mediation facilitation also acknowledges and addresses harm done and those responsible, whereas civil mediation is more neutral and focuses on moving on without apportioning blame. Family group conferences (FGCs; see Chapter 3) are a well-used informal form of RP 'mediation' appropriate for domestic and family groups and are transformative in the nature of relationships addressed and restored.

Advising, preparing and risk assessment

An important consideration to be assessed by the facilitator right from the outset, and directly with the parties, is how to ensure everyone is safe and comfortable and free from any risk of further harm, whether physical, emotional, psychological or other. Where there is any doubt, separate rooms and shuttle mediation is an option so that parties either do not meet directly or only do so when they are ready and agreeable. Further indirect options include video conferencing, Skype or even written letters.

There is an enhanced entitlement under the Victims Code (2014) in cases of an intimidated or vulnerable victim, which may be of relevance in a domestic situation. This includes a right to receive information about restorative justice and how to take part, as well as how to make a complaint if you do not receive the information and services you are entitled to.

In preparing and advising parties from the outset, practitioners are in a unique position to assist with the risk assessment required by a restorative facilitator to establish whether and which forms of intervention may be appropriate for parties to consider. They will often use an outline pro-forma such as that shown below. This then can also be used in advance by the practitioner as a guide, preparation for them and their clients and as initial briefing for the facilitator.

Key entitlements for victims

People are entitled to receive services under the Victims Code (2014) if they have made an allegation to the police about having suffered harm (including physical, mental, emotional, or property or economic loss) caused by a criminal offence. This does not have to wait for conviction or even reporting. It may even follow reporting by a third party or representative or even through contact as a victim in the course of investigation. Witnesses not directly subject to harm can access services under the Witness Charter (2013), rather than the Victims Code (2014).

Risk assessment checklist

How to establish risk and suitability for parties:

- Firstly, have they all agreed to take part?

- Aims of restorative process (as agreed)

- Explore nature of complaints from Party 1 and acknowledged harm/responsibility of Party 2

  - Restorative/transformative aims (i.e. restitution of harm and/ or a change in relationships).

Information authorised to be passed:

- Non-disclosure, confidentiality items, issues, agreement

- Permission for evaluation (data and contacts)

- Introduction

- Explain RJ and Victim role not as formal or silent witness.

Listening and communication needs:

- What the participants need to say

- What they want

- Needs from the process

- What they want to hear or need from the offender.

Effects of harm:

- Emotional

- Physical

- Medical treatment or condition

- Financial

- Work

- Secondary victims

- Relationships.

Attitude:

- To the offender

- Other agencies – Social Services, GP, health visitors, Housing, Occupational Therapy, others.

Risk:

- Fears and concerns

- Vulnerability

- Re-victimisation – direct, third parties

- Potential harm in participation

- Anger levels

- Intimidation and community safety.

Information sharing:

- Make sure that confidentiality is respected, so is the agreement to remain confidential between the parties?

- Can it be revealed to third parties or outside agencies in detail, or just the fact that they have settled and agreed?

- Are there any reporting protocols?

Facilitating restorative practices

An accredited independent facilitator (or suitably trained and experienced facilitator in the case of informal small impromptu meetings) is fully responsible for arranging and managing any intervention agreed. There are a few particular points relevant to the use of RP in the social care context that the practitioner can consider in regard to arrangements and preparation.

One important consideration is advocacy. Mediation and RP interventions present a superb way for a local authority or other body applying their duty to involve people in decisions made about their safeguarding planning (DH 2016, para.14.106). In the safe and non-judgemental setting, practitioners can help to encourage people to express their wishes and feelings, support them in weighing up their options, and assist them in making their own decisions. The advocacy option arises at all points from initial contact to subsequent stages of the assessment, planning, care review, safeguarding inquiry or Safeguarding Adults Review. The duty is established where a person has substantial difficulty in being involved and if there is no one appropriate to support them (DH 2016, paras.14.54, 14.80).

Other key considerations when deciding whether RP or mediation is suitable include the capacity of the person to make decisions concerning their safety, the ability to communicate their needs and any issues of power imbalance or domestic violence. Participation must be as meaningful as possible. If there is reason to believe that a person lacks capacity to agree to engage in RP or mediation, the neutral facilitator or coordinator will make a decision to proceed under the Mental Capacity Act (2005) and related Code of Practice. This must always be in the best interests of the person with care needs and the least restrictive in terms of the person's rights and freedoms.

Participation in all these processes is voluntary, with meetings held in an environment where everyone feels comfortable and safe and is offered an independent advocate if they feel they need it. In practice, people often choose a support worker, relative or friend for support, but an independent advocate should still be considered where the criteria apply.

Monitoring restorative outcomes and follow-up

In both RP interventions and mediation it is important to seize the moment to record any progress and agreement (however apparently modest), preferably in writing, checked and double-checked. This ensures that there is no confusion or misunderstanding about what everyone expects and helps the implementation of their wishes if agreements are drafted in sufficient detail.

Parties should be reminded that anything and everything they both agree can be included, as this is totally different from any formally imposed decisions or judgements, and can be as creative as they wish. This can include, for example, physical and financial care for a parent shared between warring but caring children, a variation of grant of probate and will amongst beneficiaries to allow a relative to stay in their home on the death of the legal owner in the family, or a health care plan for a sick person's much-loved elderly pets.

It is remarkable how many disputes originate and are fuelled by the need for information and explanations, and none more so than in the health care arena. For example, a multi-million-pound claim for medical negligence was dropped through mediation where the Trust agreed to provide a full explanation and apology (without admission of legal liability) together with the inclusion of the family's input and suggestions for improvements in procedures. The family had been asking for answers for ten years, and even 'winning' the legal claim would not have provided this outcome.

Summary

Key steps in following an RJ approach are set out below:

1. Try to talk to everyone directly first. (Direct negotiation)

2. Then talk through a third party if necessary. (Third party/ indirect negotiation)

3. RP to coordinate and involve a person's family and social circles and networks where there are specific issues and possibly a formal care plan is needed. (RP)

4. Mediation where any advocate is not appropriate to be present at private family-only time, there are issues of capacity or attendees other than just family are wanted, or there are issues with a care service professional or agency or a legally binding agreement needs to be drafted. (Mediation)

5. Court or formal procedures where all these fail or an agreement needs ratifying or a yes/no judgement is necessary on all or just remaining issues. (Formal route)

Mediation and facilitation or FGCs are not mutually exclusive. Rather, it is a matter of choosing the most suitable approach, bearing in mind the dynamics, people, circumstances and preferred outcomes to achieve. Think of the whole resolution effort as a continuum. Experience of using these approaches has proved to be effective in the criminal justice arenas and is worthwhile of consideration in adult safeguarding practice.

References

Bazemore, G. (ed.) (1999) 'After Shaming Whither Reintegration: Restorative Justice and Relational Rehabititation.' In G. Bazonore and L. Walgrave (eds) *Restorative Juvenile Justice: An Exploration of the Restorative Justice Paradigm for Reforming Juvenile Justice.* Monsey, NY: Willow Tree Press.

Braithwaite, J. (1999) *Restorative Justice: Assessing Optimistic and Pessimistic Accounts.* Chicago: The University of Chicago Press.

Code of Conduct for the Victims of Crime (2015) Presented to Parliament pursuant to section 33 page i of the Domestic Violence, Crime and Victims Act 2004.

Department of Health (2016) *Care and Support Statutory Guidance*. London: DH.

Directive 2012/029/EU; Code of Practice for Victims of Crime, s.33 Domestic Violence, Crime and Victims Act 2004, Ministry of Justice 2015.

Gavrielides, T. (2014) *A Victim-Led Criminal Justice System: Addressing the Paradox*. London: Independent Academic Research Studies.

Kuppuswamy, C., McGetrick, K., Sabbagh, M., Gunner, J., Harbinja, E., and Wild, C. (2015) *Restorative Justice Strategy for Hertfordshire 2015–2018*. Hertford: University of Hertfordshire School of Law.

Marshall, T.E. (1996) *Restorative Justice: An Overview. A Report by the Home Office Research Development and Statistics Directorate*. London: Home Office.

Ministry of Justice (2013) *The Witness Charter: Standards of Care for Witnesses in the Criminal Justice System*. London: Ministry of Justice.

Mitchell, C., and Banks, M. (1996) *Handbook of Conflict Resolution: The Analytical Problem-Solving Approach*. New York: Pinter.

Newlove, Baroness (2015) *Victims Commissioner, Commissioner for Victims and Witnesses: Annual Report for 2014–15*. London: OVC.

Watchel, T., O'Connell, T., and Watchel, B. (2010) *Restorative Justice Conferencing – Real Justice and the Conferencing Handbook*. Edinboro, PA: Piper Press.

Chapter 5

Promoting Safeguarding
SELF-DETERMINATION, INVOLVEMENT AND
ENGAGEMENT IN ADULT SAFEGUARDING

Trish Hafford-Letchfield and Sarah Carr

Introduction

This chapter considers the involvement and engagement of people in adult safeguarding and how to promote it. The Care Act (2014) has sought to make adult safeguarding more outcome-focused and person-centred alongside other key policy developments and practice initiatives (Local Government Association [LGA] 2013). Making Safeguarding Personal (see Chapter 1) established that an asset-based approach, which identifies a person's strengths and networks, helps them and their family to make difficult decisions. In complex scenarios this approach reinforces empowerment and control as important aspects of adult safeguarding (LGA 2013). The policy guidance *No Secrets* (Department of Health [DH] 2000) advised the inclusion of user groups and user-led organisations in adult safeguarding work to ensure that views of people using services, families and carers are taken into account (Wallcraft 2012). Later consultation (DH 2009) established that people using services 'wanted to do their own safeguarding; they wanted help with information, options, alternatives, suggestions, mediation, "talking to" and so on' (p.18). The Care Act (2014) has strengthened and facilitated the implementation of these recommendations, referring directly to the importance of the voices of people and their carers going through assessment, support planning and care review processes necessary to a safeguarding inquiry or Safeguarding Adults Review (SAR).

The chapter draws on key concepts and philosophies underpinning the involvement and engagement of people in the design, delivery and evaluation of adult social care. Adult safeguarding is possibly one of the most challenging areas for achieving this. We review some of the research and practice evidence on participation of people in the management of risk and safeguarding and map out challenges and opportunities for achieving a genuine person-centred approach. We build on contributions from earlier chapters, which considered participative practices such as family group conferencing. We use a detailed case study in three stages (Hafford-Letchfield 2015) to emphasise the role of narrative within safeguarding practice, as a practical tool for increasing involvement, and the use of advocacy by practitioners with those who struggle to be fully involved in important decisions about their lives. We conclude with tips for best practice in promoting self-determination, involvement and engagement in adult safeguarding.

Co-production

The term 'co-production' describes a shift in policy and practice towards active input by people using services (Carr 2011). Co-production emphasises that people using services have assets such as expertise and skills in their own situations. In safeguarding, these may not be easily recognised or are subverted by the interests or influence of others involved. The main vehicle for promoting co-production is through initiatives that support personalisation. The allocation of a flexible budget combined with self-directed support can be effective in facilitating greater creativity and maximising choice and control (Hafford-Letchfield 2015). However, achieving co-production involves interdependence and the reclaiming of social work skills, knowledge and resources which reassert and re-value relationship-based practice, traditionally co-located within community social work. Recognising and investing in the transformative potential of growing involvement, within a climate of reduced resources, the demands to act swiftly and conforming to local political agendas, remains challenging. This chapter makes connections between increasing involvement and engagement of people and promoting their independence and empowerment. It identifies practical tools for people negotiating their own needs for improved care and support.

Research findings on personalising risk and safeguarding

Current research on adult safeguarding mostly addresses systemic issues, service configuration and models, decision making and practitioner concepts (Graham *et al.* 2014; Norrie *et al.* 2014). Reactive and technical approaches to risk and safeguarding cause tensions in making the shift towards person-centred practice whilst still reiterating that safeguarding is 'everybody's business' (DH 2016). People using services have reported the importance of valuing approaches that 'safeguard their self-determination' (Mitchell, Baxter and Glendinning 2012, p.17) together with prevention of abuse, which they say are their main priorities (Faulkner 2012a). This challenges more traditional views held by practitioners of the perceived characteristics and perspectives of 'victims', and the identities and intentions of those who are sources of risk, which inform the way they might construct safeguarding situations. Johnson (2011) suggests that power relations obscure other ways of understanding and making sense of the person's own perspectives and voice, particularly their distress. She stresses the context for unequal power relations, both between stakeholders and between competing discourses, which determine how safeguarding issues are characterised. Her research demonstrated that professional assessments of harm or risk tend to hold greater weight overall than the person's own experiences. These inconsistencies in professionals' thresholds for constructing an action or omission as adult safeguarding are particularly evident where family members are implicated. For example, there may be potential conflict when services have made significant investments in the caring activities provided through family-based settings, without which any support may reduce or crumble (McCreadie *et al.* 2008). In these situations, different types of advocacy can help to avoid reframing intra-family violence as 'family support' issues and which can jeopardise authentic involvement (Johnson 2011, pp.214–215).

Some groups of people using services are particularly neglected in studies on risk and safeguarding, such as those from different black and minority ethnic communities found to be under-represented in safeguarding referrals. There is little research examining whether, and how far, attitudes towards risk and practices to manage risk might vary according to wider social factors such as the gender, cultural identity or socio-economic status of people using either services or professionals.

In mental health services, Faulkner's (2012b) unique user-led research work addressed the issue of absent user voices and revealed that fear and fearing loss of independence was a significant concern for those with mental health problems. This is not necessarily something considered by practitioners (see Wallcraft 2012) who, through expert interviews on involvement in adult safeguarding, highlighted that 'agencies tend to be risk-averse and service users do not often feel involved in their safeguarding processes' (p.142). Wallcraft recommended 'more involvement of service users in [adult safeguarding] research, more effective forms of involvement of groups who may be excluded [from Safeguarding Adults Boards or local forums], shared responsibility for risk, and more training in rights legislation' (p.142).

Risk-averse cultures within services may be disempowering for people, making them unable to be meaningfully involved in the processes of risk management, assessment and decision making that affect them. Faulkner's (2012b) research identified empowerment and choice as core to safeguarding policy and practice in mental health services by working to enable adults at risk to recognise and protect themselves from abuse with genuine choice both of and within services. Informants in her user-led study on risk emphasised a rights-based approach, proposing that 'user involvement in risk assessments and informed decision making about risks surely should itself be a right' (Faulkner 2012b, pp.3–4).

This theme of rights-based safeguarding has also been explored by Whitelock (2009), whose survey findings argued for 'a balance between autonomy – the right to a family and private life – and protection – the right not to be subjected to inhumane or degrading treatment' (p.40). Whitelock asserted that a rights-based approach takes user involvement as its starting point and uses existing legal frameworks to assess risk and intervene where there is serious risk of harm. Other UK studies have repeatedly drawn attention to the tensions and dilemmas experienced by professionals in balancing a positive approach to risk-taking with their professional and statutory duties to protect people with care and support needs, particularly with personalisation, in adult social care (Mitchell et al. 2012, p.3). This theme was amplified in a research and practice review (Carr 2011) on risk enablement and safety in people using self-directed support and personal budgets and concluded that person-centred working in adult safeguarding, along with the mechanism of self-directed support, planning and outcome review, can support the individual to identify the risks they want to take and those they want to avoid in order to stay safe. Carr (2011) noted that 'defensive [organisational] risk management strategies or risk-averse frontline practice may...result in individuals not being adequately supported to make choices and take control, therefore being put at risk' (p.122). Studies have shown that people subject to recovery-focused mental health care planning and coordination (Simpson *et al.* 2016), or to risk assessment under the Mental Health Act (Sheldon 2011), or using a personal budget (Stevens *et al.* 2014), reported a lack of information about the content of risk assessment or that one had taken place, even though they were concerned about it themselves or wanted to know more. Ryan (2010) noted that people using mental health services developed strategies to respond to risk, were frequently proactive and took the initiative, using the experiences they had gained from living with their illnesses. They however felt they were left to their own devices and in many situations adopted routine and common-sense strategies to respond to risk. Overall, there appears to be widespread uncertainty and a lack of evidence in how practitioners can best support people in positive risk-taking, particularly when their symptoms and abilities fluctuate. Finally, people with learning disabilities experiencing low-level abuse have reported how these experiences shaped and constrained their daily activities as they sought to avoid exposure to abuse, often by not going out, avoiding particular social situations and failing to report it (Hoong Sin *et al.* 2010).

The following case study helps to bring these issues to the surface.

CASE STUDY PART 1

George, a 90-year-old Eastern European man, is referred to the hospital social work team following admission after a fall at home and a mild stroke. He has regained some of his mobility and is ready for discharge. He lives next door to his daughter, Mary, aged 70. She maintains that she can manage, but the staff are concerned that George was admitted in a neglected condition, with an unexplained weight loss which, according to investigations, does not have any underlying medical cause. They have not discussed it with him or Mary, however, and raise a safeguarding concern.

The social worker, Yolanda, visits George on the ward and Mary is there. She notes that Mary constantly answers for George, who seems hardly engaged in what is happening. Mary says there is absolutely no need for social services. Yolanda has no opportunity to speak to George alone and decides not to insist on this on this first encounter. In discussion with her manager, Yolanda is reminded that she should expedite discharge, offer a carer's assessment and refer back to the community team.

Yolanda discovers from her information-gathering that George is seen by his GP as a bit of a 'charmer'. He had been a successful builder, a 'drinker', and the GP hints that there were 'altercations' in his marriage with Rizia (who died five years ago). The GP expresses concern about Mary's involvement and questions whether she has his best interests at heart. He said the living conditions during a recent home visit were extremely poor. The nursing staff tell Yolanda, however, that George is surly, rude and verbally aggressive to staff. He has made discriminatory remarks to them, but is well behaved with the hospital doctors.

Yolanda is concerned that the situation is more complex than she first suspected but cannot proceed with an assessment without the consent of George and Mary. She recognises the competing narratives: first of George, perceived as a difficult older man, but potentially vulnerable to abuse; and second of Mary, who is refusing help but may experience a challenging relationship with her father.

The use of narrative in safeguarding practice

To overcome some of the issues raised by research, practitioners can improve assessment by making better use of narratives with people subject to risk or safeguarding. For example, in the case study so far, storytelling can be used in the assessment to promote user involvement in safeguarding. Narrative analysis enhances listening and responses to people's stories, the ability to identify common themes from experience, and aids understanding about why some interventions are not working. Kleinman (1988) suggests that integrating an individual's biography into their care reduces the possibility of dehumanising and stripping them of personhood. For example, helping to move from the perception of George as a 'miserable' older person who needs caring for, to a person who desires a happier, more fulfilling, life given his newly acquired limitations and options for support.

The public inquiry into the failures of older people's care in Mid Staffordshire NHS Hospital (Francis 2013) highlighted the lack of dignity and compassion stemming from ageism and the dehumanisation of older people, highly dependent on both staff and their managers. Older people's own narratives and those of people directly caring for them were dominated by the priorities of senior management. Francis (2013) identified that seeking out patients' stories, using active listening and willingness to act upon what is heard should happen at all different levels in an organisation. This contributes to emotional resilience and positive emotional tones for the delivery of care. Establishing an appropriate climate is vital to enable people to feel comfortable about raising issues that concern them and staff to respond to the individual nature of their concerns. Caring and compassion are core values for adult safeguarding. For co-production to occur, new behaviours that actively promote a range of diverse interactions between the people involved in an individual's care are required.

Practitioners commissioning and overseeing care arrangements may use narratives to promote a person-centred approach by co-communicating the individual's needs, preferences, culture and sense of purpose within their care plan. Connecting people to a wider network acts as a preventative resource where there is isolation or vulnerability. The advocacy role that practitioners promote in these situations should enable people to clarify their own networks. These networks can be valued within the organisation as a meaningful barometer of the quality of support provided or performance of the service. This approach is evident in the Think Local Act Personal (TLAP) 'Making it Real' programme (TLAP n.d.) which has developed 'progress markers' for organisations – written by real people and their carers to help check progress towards transforming adult social care in a way which reflects authentic personalisation.

At an organisational level, Making it Real seeks solutions based on broader narratives of their local communities that actively plan to avoid or overcome crisis, and focuses on people within their communities, rather than inside service and organisational boundaries. This enables people to develop networks of support and to increase community connections which are vitally important to the prevention and detection of abuse. It is based on assessment processes which take time to listen, particularly to those whose views are not easily heard, to ensure that care and support is culturally sensitive and takes into account whole lives, including physical, mental, emotional and spiritual needs (TLAP n.d.).

The generation of 'I' statements expressing the adult safeguarding key principles are examples of using narrative (DH 2016, para.14.13). In the case study above, Yolanda might encourage George to engage, by asking him to articulate what outcomes he wants – for example: 'I want you to know a bit more about how changes in my life have been affecting me: I want to regain some of my independence so that I can remain self-confident and enjoy life more.'

Practitioners should be aware of their own role in constructing people's biography – how they record and document situations. For example, by moving from seeing George as 'not engaging' to a more appreciative stance such as: 'George does not have sufficient access to interpreters in his own language or enough guaranteed privacy to allow an in-depth exploration of the problems he is experiencing.' The practitioner can uncover details of the environment, conditions and circumstances shaping the individual's experiences assumed to need safeguarding interventions. According to Floersch *et al.* (2010), this process often leads to something being understood rather than solved, given that social work practice aims to identify individual, group, family or community problems, solutions, needs and strengths. Interventions can be designed based on a careful analysis of where the person 'is' and their perspectives on the abuse, and therefore the solution.

Oral narratives can communicate issues and make connections in supervision or team meetings in order to influence how people are perceived. The examples in Chapter 1 draw on a narrative approach as Making Safeguarding Personal aims to achieve a shift in culture and practice in response to what we know makes safeguarding effective from the perspective of the person being safeguarded. In turn this enhances involvement, choice and control as well as improving quality of life, wellbeing and safety. To value people as experts in their own lives and work alongside them, we need to collect information to demonstrate the extent to which this has a positive impact on their lives. As Lawson, Lewis and Williams (2014) assert, this involves a shift from a process supported by conversations to a series of conversations supported by a process. These cultural shifts illustrate that rediscovery of the emphasis on a personal story provides a more reliable means of bringing back the personal and subjective experiences of a person when using care and support services. This is essential during periods where they may feel vulnerable or at risk.

Townsend (2006) coined the term 'structured dependency' to describe how care institutions contribute to artificially structuring or deepening the dependency of people using services. Whilst referring specifically to older people, this theory of structured dependency comes from a conflict perspective, which asserts that people become forced into a dependent role and explores how the very structures that are said to support them can bring about isolation and depression, reinforced by the processes used to tackle these (such as unquestioning safeguarding referrals and practice). 'Deconstruction', a concept developed by critical theorists such as Foucault and Derrida, is an alternative means of analysing these assumptions and is often used in the social work literature on anti-discriminatory and anti-oppressive practice (Cocker and Hafford-Letchfield 2014). Deconstruction is a way of disturbing and overturning categories that we might ascribe to people using services or specific communities by being more active in helping to interpret meanings on behalf of subordinated voices and perspectives. Examples might include the 'burden' of older people on society as a result of changing demography; or thinking about how far people in poverty can really exercise 'choice' when designing support. Acknowledging the contribution that people using services can make, for example through their roles as volunteers, carers, advisors, mentors and active contributors to the community, can challenge dominant views about them being 'vulnerable' and 'victims'.

A narrative approach offers an alternative way of deconstructing some of these processes and beliefs by actively considering issues such as ageism, its policy rhetoric and promoting the move away from structuring dependency in public services. Challenging the system itself through asking curious or courageous questions in situations where there are assumptions about why someone is in a safeguarding situation, rather than focusing on the problems they face as a result, can individualise or pathologise the issues as well as the solutions. Such questions might be framed as: 'What would be George's view of our suspicions about his relationship with Mary around neglect?' or 'Have we really explored all of the problems from George's own point of view?'

Another imperative for using narrative in safeguarding practice is that it can help to find our voice during difficult times because it involves deliberate engagement. Rutten, Mottart and Soetaert (2010) suggest its use as a response to a positivistic evidence-based paradigm and a dominant management discourse in the profession which subject social workers to more bureaucratic procedures and fixed outcomes. In the case study, Yolanda potentially faces a number of restrictions in her practice which include timescales for discharge and resources available within certain eligibility criteria.

Narratives on older people

The Francis Report (2013) highlighted the absence of narratives at a strategic level in older people's services and a weak employee voice within organisational cultures, which lead to systemic abuse and failures of care. The report laid bare the consequence of toxic, disengaged work cultures where the leadership, management and those responsible for governance lost sight of their strategic priorities or underlying narrative, which was to serve older people and their carers. The Health Service Ombudsman report *Care and Compassion* (Abraham 2011) provided an account of ten investigations into complaints made in England about the standard of care provided to older people by the NHS. This highlighted that dignity, health care-associated infection, nutrition, discharge from hospital and personal care featured significantly more often in complaints about care of older people. The Ombudsman collated these investigations to convey the stark contrast between the reality of care the older people received and the principles and values of the NHS. Its mode of dissemination is a powerful example of using narratives, through which was revealed 'an attitude, both personal and institutional, which fails to recognise the humanity and individuality of the people concerned and to respond to them with sensitivity, compassion and professionalism' (p.2).

Within social care, systematic learning from failures in adults' services is emerging. Manthorpe and Martineau's (2011) analysis of 22 Serious Case Reviews on adult safeguarding identified that the recommendations presented were more often bureaucratic than narrative, and that more effort could be put into distilling the outcomes of Serious Case Reviews as tools for learning across a wider audience. Transferring these ideas into practice settings might involve questions such as:

- What are the main 'plots' in your safeguarding work? Are there different twists which may result in alternative narratives being exposed? Are we commissioning the right services and do our structures facilitate the community in telling us how to do things differently?

- What roles or characters do we play in our day-to-day work or within our relationships and expectations from others? Are we questioning our assumptions about particular groups of people over-represented in safeguarding investigations and what they can or cannot achieve? What about the day-to-day flexibility or institutionalisation of practice around certain issues? Do they make sense?

- How authentic are we in our assessments and support planning? Can we imagine different possibilities with people that we work with? What spaces can we create for them to tell us what they desire and need when in risky situations? Are we willing to take risks and experience the discomfort to work with their different stories?

- How far are we able and willing to connect with people's narratives in order to create an impetus for change? How does the rhetoric and reality cohere or conflict?

Stories may reveal personal, family or larger collectives, which express goals, ideals and cultural beliefs to help us identify the strengths in a given situation. Hall and Powell (2011) remind us that culturally relevant information is often embedded in the stories people tell, which provide a more holistic, culturally sensitive, contextualised knowledge of them, their families and their support networks. They distinguish between 'personal stories', which they say often include remembered chronologies of events and which may be mirrored by the design of our assessment tools, and 'identification stories', which may signify gender, race, class, relationship status and the cultural and political implications of people's identities based on these aspects of self (Hall and Powell 2011). Research on Lesbian, Gay, Bisexual and Transgender (LGBT) older people's poor experiences of care is a good example of how significant narrative is in challenging discrimination and oppression for a group of older people with a significant history of being marginalised and for some criminalised because of their cultural identities (Hafford-

Letchfield 2014). Older LGBT people may also have developed greater resilience in later life having managed and adapted to these issues over a lifetime including taking up an activist role (Hafford-Letchfield, 2016).

CASE STUDY PART 2

Yolanda returns to the ward to test out the information she has gathered about the home circumstances. George is uncooperative and answers in monosyllables, and tells her not to bother with him. Meeting with Mary gives rise to an aggressive response, particularly when she presses for a home visit.

She discusses this with her manager, who suggests writing a conciliatory letter acknowledging Mary's feelings of frustration and lack of support and arranging a phone call with her (particularly to reduce any risk of further abuse). Yolanda is surprised when Mary calls her and starts by apologising for what has happened. Mary seems sad and resigned. By focusing on George's life history and asking questions about his previous strengths and life events, Yolanda hears about the very acrimonious relationship between him and his immediate family over 20 years, his problematic alcohol use, the hard life that her mother experienced as a result of them being isolated, and some occasional violence by their father towards her and her siblings throughout their life. Yolanda learns that the other siblings have given up and moved away, and that, having come from Poland, there is little support in the local area. It also emerges that George had to leave Poland during the 1940s, having become homeless during the war. Mary admits that she hasn't been good to her father because of how angry she feels about his growing dependence on her. She has been tempted to get her own back. However, with the right questions, she is able to tell Yolanda that she feels empathy for her father and is still experiencing intense bereavement for her mother. Yolanda recognises their mutual insight and empathy from a number of new perspectives.

In summary, the theory of narrative postulates that individuals integrate their life experiences into an internalised, evolving story of the self, which provides a sense of unity and purpose in life. Recognising their life narrative enables people to integrate their reconstructed past, perceived present and imagined future.

Drawing on narratives in adult safeguarding will therefore lead practitioners to consider:

- The quality and effectiveness of communication with people; how to work with them and how they can participate in exploring the options and making decisions.

- The skills needed to facilitate conversations with people to find out what they want to achieve from their perspective, and how best to go about this. How to engage with best interests decision making in this context to achieve this, where a person lacks capacity in a particular time and space, using independent mental capacity advocates where necessary (see Chapter 7).

- How far the approach to helping people consider risk in their lives is both positive and person-centred.

There are of course limitations to using narrative with people: meaningful participation is affected by a range of issues, including cultural divisions, language barriers, gender, ill health, time and resources. However, making use of existing opportunities and structures is important, which is considered in the final stage of the case study.

CASE STUDY PART 3

Yolanda agrees some interim support for Mary to give her space to sort out some of her own emotional needs and to have some time with her partner, who has been supporting her in the background.

Yolanda then talks to George about his daughter being unwell and he reluctantly agrees to accept a visit to assess his home situation. Yolanda takes this opportunity to talk to George about the loss of his wife and George shares some of his regrets about their relationship and the gradual loss of his friends and networks. Yolanda secures his agreement to explore links with a local Polish association and support for maximising his income. She facilitates a family meeting with Mary and her brother and a friend who George has not seen for a while. A limited programme of support is secured from a local care agency and other ways of supporting him. This meeting had a strong focus on the loss of Rizia and what she would have said or wanted for them all. Yolanda picked up on these cues and found ways in which the different individuals connected or had a common tie. Yolanda also talked to the GP to request an assessment of George's mood and possible depression.

This case study initially presented a fairly typical referral in which there were safeguarding concerns with many references to lack of engagement, difficult personalities and the need to resolve the situation quickly. Continuity of family life, despite its difficulties and risks to individuals, was important to all the people involved. Although working under pressure in the hospital discharge situation, Yolanda was successful in picking up cues in her routine enquiries and was active in offering opportunities to talk about life history and identity. George could have been dismissed, given that he was presented as an unpleasant person. The narrative about Mary could also be taken at face value. Narrative approaches are primarily concerned with using yourself to promote interaction and relationships, not only between practitioners and people and their carers, but also between people and their formal or informal carers. It involves taking a curious stance, and Yolanda was able to prompt a shift and prevent further problems at a later date.

Advocacy in adult safeguarding

At certain times, people may struggle to be fully involved in important decisions about their lives and will need support. It is essential that they have access to independent advocates to assist in this. The Care Act (2014) places a duty on local authorities to ensure that independent advocacy is available for those who need such support and don't have anyone appropriate to provide it. The advocacy duty applies from the point of first contact with the local authority and at any subsequent stage of the assessment, planning and care review, as well as during the safeguarding inquiry or Safeguarding Adults Review (SCIE 2014) – see Appendix. Whilst advocacy promotes equality, social justice, social inclusion and human rights, the means by which it is provided should make things happen in the most direct and empowering ways possible.

Different types of advocacy may involve group, peer, citizen or professional paid advocacy. Self-advocacy, for example, provides people with encouragement and support to speak out and act on their own behalf and recognises their expertise by experience. It differs from other forms of advocacy in that the individual self-assesses a situation or problem and then speaks for his or her own needs. People should be supported to self-advocate as far as they are able to. Advocacy providers and advocates should be suitably knowledgeable and experienced in identifying safeguarding issues and focused on the person/s they are working with. People using advocacy services should have meaningful influence over the direction of that service by working co-productively to develop methods that determine outcomes and measures on the effectiveness of the advocacy relationship as well as complying with equality legislation. Co-production and involvement extends to the commissioning and provision of advocacy services by considering the types of advocacy services people want and need and how they might choose to access services in the future.

Top tips and pointers for good practice

This chapter has considered imperatives from legislation and policy underpinning people's involvement and participation in adult safeguarding, alongside research findings which highlight the barriers and limitations to achieving these. The case study illustrated how using a narrative approach combined with advocacy can support self-determination and co-produced personalised responses in partnership with people as well as their carers. Good practice pointers include the following:

- Maintain a stance of curiosity and stepping outside of institutionalised frameworks and procedures from time to time. Be able to deconstruct any stereotypes or conditions that are preventing expression and engagement with the person's own voice. Where there are tensions and conflicts, be active in bringing these to the attention of those able to challenge and reduce barriers or unhelpful culture for involvement.

- Use narrative and 'I' statements to increase communication and user-led meaning-making alongside provision of appropriate support for communication and participation. This might involve key people in the person's life; providing support to attend and participate in meetings; holding meetings in places more familiar which suit the person; providing accessible records; allocating time and establishing a climate of trust; relationship-based practice; and training everyone, including administrative staff, to support a more open climate.

- Take shared responsibility for exploring and managing risk with people and, where appropriate, appoint an advocate to help people understand their rights in the context of the harm itself, safeguarding procedures, interventions and the individual's rights in relation to these (Sherwood-Johnson 2016).

References

Abraham, A. (2011) *Care and Compassion: Report of the Health Service Ombudsman on Ten Investigations into NHS Care of Older People.* London: Parliamentary and Health Service Ombudsman.

Carr, S. (2011) 'Enabling risk and ensuring safety: Self-directed support and personal budgets.' *The Journal of Adult Protection 13,* 3, 122–136.

Cocker, C., and Hafford-Letchfield, T. (eds) (2014) *Rethinking Anti-Discriminatory Practice and Anti-Oppressive Theories for Social Work Practice.* Basingstoke: Palgrave.

Department of Health (2000) *No Secrets: Guidance on Developing and Implementing Multi-Agency Policies and Procedures to Protect Vulnerable Adults from Abuse.* London: DH.

Department of Health (2009) *No Secrets: Guidance on Protecting Vulnerable Adults in Care.* London: DH.

Department of Health (2016) *Care and Support Statutory Guidance.* London: DH.

Faulkner, A. (2012a) 'The right to take risks.' *The Journal of Adult Protection 14,* 6, 287–296.

Faulkner, A. (2012b) *The Right to Take Risks: Service Users' Views of Risk in Adult Social Care.* York: Joseph Rowntree Foundation.

Floersch, J., Longhofer, J.L., Krank, D., and Townsend, L. (2010) 'Integrating thematic, grounded theory and narrative analysis: A case study of adolescent psychotropic treatment.' *Qualitative Social Work 9,* 3, 407–425.

Francis, R. (2013) *Report of the Mid Staffordshire NHS Foundation Trust Public Inquiry.* London: The Stationery Office.

Graham, K., Norrie, C., Stevens, M., Moriarty, J., Manthorpe, J., and Hussein, S. (2014) 'Models of adult safeguarding in England: A review of the literature.' *Journal of Social Work 16,* 1, 22–46.

Hafford-Letchfield, T. (2014) *Practice Guide: Social Work with Lesbian, Gay, Bisexual and Transgendered Older People.* Community Care Inform Adults. Available at http://adults. ccinform.co.uk/practice-guidance/social-work-lesbian-gay-bisexual-transgendered-older-people, accessed on 12 April 2017.

Hafford-Letchfield, T. (2015) *Guide to Using Narratives in Assessments of Older People.* Community Care Inform Adults. Available at http://adults.ccinform.co.uk/practice-guidance/guide-using-narratives-assessments-older-people, accessed on 12 April 2017.

Hafford-Letchfield, T. (2016) *Learning in Later Life: Challenges for social work and social care.* London, Routledge.

Hall, J.M., and Powell, J. (2011) 'Understanding the person through narrative.' *Nursing Research and Practice.* Available at https://www.hindawi.com/journals/nrp/2011/293837, accessed on 12 April 2017.

Hoong Sin, C., Comber, N., Mguni, N., Hedges, A., and Cook, C. (2010) 'Targeted violence, harassment and abuse against people with learning disabilities in Great Britain.' *Tizard Learning Disability Review 15*, 1, 17–27.

Johnson, F. (2011) 'What is an "adult protection" issue? Victims, perpetrators and the professional construction of adult protection issues.' *Critical Social Policy 32*, 2, 203–222.

Kleinman, A. (1988) *The Illness Narratives: Suffering, Healing and the Human Condition.* New York: Basic Books.

Lawson, J., Lewis, S., and Williams, C. (2014) *Making Safeguarding Personal Guide.* London: ADASS/LGA.

Local Government Association (2013) *Making Safeguarding Personal: Sector-Led Improvement.* London: LGA/ADASS/SCIE.

Manthorpe, J., and Martineau, S. (2011) 'Serious Case Reviews in adult safeguarding in England: An analysis of a sample of reports.' *British Journal of Social Work 41*, 2, 224–241.

McCreadie, C., Mathew, D., Filinson, R., and Askham, J. (2008) 'Ambiguity and cooperation in the implementation of adult protection policy.' *Social Policy and Administration 42*, 3, 248–266.

Mitchell, W., Baxter, K., and Glendinning, C. (2012) *Updated Review of Risk and Adult Social Care in England.* York: Joseph Rowntree Foundation.

Norrie, C., Stevens, M., Graham, K., Hussein, S., Moriarty, J., and Manthorpe, J. (2014) 'Investigating models of adult safeguarding in England – A mixed-methods approach.' *Journal of Adult Protection 16*, 6, 377–388.

Rutten, K., Mottart, A., and Soetaert, R. (2010) 'Narrative and rhetoric in social work education.' *British Journal of Social Work 40*, 2, 480–495.

Ryan, T. (2010) 'Exploring the risk management strategies of mental health service users.' *Health, Risk & Society 2*, 3, 267–282.

SCIE (2014) Care Act 2014; commissioning independent advocacy, available at www.scie.org.uk/care-act-2014/advocacy-services/commissioning-independent-advocacy, accessed on 14 July 2017.

Sheldon, K. (2011) 'Service Users: Experiences of Risk and Risk Management.' In R. Whittington and C. Langan (eds) *Self-Harm and Violence: Towards Best Practice in Managing Risk in Mental Health Services.* Oxford: Wiley-Blackwell.

Sherwood-Johnson, F. (2016) 'Independent advocacy in adult support and protection work', *The Journal of Adult Protection*, 18, 2, 109–118.

Simpson, A., Hannigan, B., Coffey, M., Jones, A., *et al.* (2016) 'Cross-national comparative case study of recovery-focused mental health care planning and coordination.' *Health Services Delivery Research 4*, 5.

Stevens, M., Manthorpe, J., Hussein, S., Ismail, M., *et al.* (2014) *Risk, Safeguarding and Personal Budgets: Exploring Relationships and Identifying Good Practice.* London: Kings College, NIHR School for Social Care Research.

Think Local Act Personal (n.d.) *'Making it Real': Marking Progress towards Personalised Community Based Support.* Available at www.thinklocalactpersonal.org.uk/_assets/Resources/Personalisation/TLAP/MakingItReal.pdf, accessed on 12 April 2017.

Townsend, P. (2006) '25th Volume Celebration Paper. Policies for the aged in the 21st century: More "structured dependency" or the realisation of human rights?' *Ageing and Society 26*, 2, 161–179.

Wallcraft, J. (2012) 'Involvement of service users in adult safeguarding.' *The Journal of Adult Protection 14*, 3, 142–150.

Whitelock, A. (2009) 'Safeguarding in mental health: Towards a rights-based approach.' *The Journal of Adult Protection 11*, 4, 30–42.

WORKING WITH RISK AND USING THE LAW

Chapter 6

Assessing and Responding to Risk

Emily White

Introduction

The balance between autonomy and protection is an inherent tension in social work with adults. Since the implementation of the Human Rights Act (1998), the increased use of the language of restriction and human rights has caused social care to look again at its benign motivations and question the role it plays in 'protecting the vulnerable'.

> Physical health and safety can sometimes be bought at too high a price in happiness and emotional welfare. The emphasis must be on sensible risk appraisal, not striving to avoid all risk, whatever the price, but instead seeking a proper balance and being willing to tolerate manageable or acceptable risks as the price appropriately to be paid in order to achieve some other good – in particular to achieve the vital good of the elderly or vulnerable person's happiness. What good is it making someone safer if it merely makes them miserable? (Munby J, *Local Authority X v MM & Anor (No. 1)* [2007])

At the same time, large-scale failures to deliver good quality, dignified care in hospitals and care homes have become the subject of reviews, notably the Francis report into the failings of Mid Staffordshire NHS Trust, which was compiled following a public inquiry into the poor care provided by the Trust (Francis 2013). It examined why the failings were not spotted sooner, and highlighted unacceptable exposure to risk through a failure to provide appropriate care. This chapter provides an introduction to assessing and responding to risk from the perspectives of the person concerned, the practitioner and the organisation, through the lens of human rights, and offers a guide to changing how we think about risk.

A human rights perspective

> We've just pulled out of a station and at the end of the platform were about half a dozen people train-spotting. Whatever you may feel about the pursuit of train-spotting, you would notice them going about their business, possibly pass judgement but two minutes later, they will be gone from your head. But if those train-spotters had a learning disability, their activity will be pored over by a whole multi-disciplinary team of experts. Some of that team would decide its worth by totting up the measurable outcomes. A funding panel would chew it over to see if it merited paying for a support worker's time. The PBS (positive behavioural support) people would draw up a risk management plan for the day out. Circles of Support would be formed. A care planner would look into how train-spotting fares in the person-centred plan. Poof. All life gone. (Neary 2016)

Mark Neary is the father of a young man with autism who took his case to release his son from institutional care to the High Court. His blog is a collection of thoughts and experiences of the social care world and is an insight into the fact that, for many people with disabilities, or those with needs for care and support, even relatively low-key decisions about daily life are integrally linked with professionals and their assessment of the risk posed by such decisions. When concerns about physical or emotional harm, abuse, neglect or exploitation are added into the mix, the need to assess and respond to risk becomes paramount.

Within the present choice-based system of social care, people are prompted to draw on this plethora of professional knowledge to assess and manage their own risk (Dixon and Robb 2016). This in itself presents challenges. Some people may have been born with an impairment that means that they are unable to use their life experience or advice and information from others in a way that helps them assess risk in their lives. Others may have been so well protected throughout their lives that they have very little lived experience on which to base their own view of risk, making it very difficult to make decisions when it comes to issues of complexity. Still others are afforded little opportunity to take the time to consider their own experience, the views of others, and weigh up the advantages and disadvantages of any decision to deal with the risk.

Some people's experience of this weighing-up process is that they are not allowed to participate in it – often it is being done by others on their behalf...excluding people from decisions about their own risks has implications, not just for the accuracy of the assessment, but also for their dignity and human rights. (Faulkner 2012, p.22)

The 2006 United Nations Convention on the Rights of Persons with Disabilities (CRPD) is a legally binding international human rights treaty. It was adopted by the UK in 2006. The CRPD is based on the social model of disability, which identifies disability as arising from the interaction of an individual's impairment with wider social and environmental barriers. The CRPD represents a shift from a welfare- or charity-based approach to disability to a rights- and equality-based approach, where people with disabilities are active subjects, not passive recipients. A key implication of the CRPD in assessing and responding to risk is that people with disabilities should be offered the support they need to ensure that their rights, will and preferences are respected and are free from undue influence and conflicts of interest (Series 2014).

All too frequently, 'service users are taken out of the contexts of their environments and assessed in a vacuum of individual deficits and problematic behaviours. Such an approach is both informed by and satisfies populist demands for action to reduce risk' (Barry 2007, p.38). A rights-based approach to safeguarding and risk assessment moves away from the notion of protecting those with care and support needs to promoting rights, not only to freedom from degrading and inhumane treatment but also to liberty and to privacy and family life. Its very premise starts from the perspective of positively dealing with risk, rather than aiming to stop all risk, no matter the consequences.

Principles for working with risk in this way assume that people:

- understand their legal human rights

- are able to identify coercive, manipulative or exploitative behaviour in others (Dixon and Robb 2016)

- understand why professionals and others think they are at risk

- can make informed decisions about that risk based on potentially differing viewpoints

- can deal with the differing emotional perspectives and personal relationships that might be involved

- know and can then express without fear what they would like to happen to deal with the risk.

This highlights the importance of people who are at risk having regular practice in making independent decisions. Although most of the research and practice to improve decision-making skills has taken place with people with learning difficulties, the importance of having the knowledge, assertiveness and resistance to defend oneself might reasonably be considered to apply to all adults in potentially risky or abusive situations. (Faulkner 2012, p.22)

The Care Act (2014) requires local authorities to consider the person's own strengths and capabilities, and what support might be available from their wider support network or within the community. The strengths-based perspective (McNamara and Morgan 2016) assumes a focus on the person's *situation* and the factors that make them vulnerable, not the perceived deficits of the person themselves. This can be challenging when the person concerned is not practised at decision making. A focus on what it is that might lead them to be able to cope with their situation, and how these strengths can be maximised, needs to be developed with the support of a skilled practitioner. This involves focusing attention on identifying their unique personal qualities; seeking out and then supporting the use of all available resources, such as carers, most effectively; recapturing what has worked in the past; and identifying plans for the future (McNamara and Morgan 2016). In this way, the notion of the social care practitioner as 'expert' is replaced by that of the practitioner as advocate or facilitator. Of paramount importance is the practitioner's belief in the person's capacity for change, a key factor in supporting strengths-based work, and a move away from risk-aversive practice (Stanford 2011).

This perspective of practitioner as advocate or facilitator, collator of information (facts and opinion), and promoter of shared decision making and shared responsibility is equally and especially relevant when working under the framework of the Mental Capacity Act (2005). In all situations, regardless of the degree to which the person is able to participate in their assessment or make specific decisions, this approach leads the practitioner to consider wishes and feelings as paramount, and leads one to consider proportionality in assessing and responding to risk. The concept of proportionality is used as a criterion of fairness and justice in law, and should apply to any rights-based view of risk (see Chapters 7 and 8).

Developing collaborative and flexible approaches to risk assessment

There have been many attempts to develop risk assessment tools which have focussed on identifying problems and calculating the probability of repetition with the aim of avoidance…these approaches have been led by professionals, whose expertise and actions are intended to reduce risk by, for example, monitoring, observing, taking control, segregating, imposing restrictions and containment. (Boardman and Roberts 2014, p.4)

CASE STUDY

During a reflective case discussion with a manager, a practitioner was expressing her anxiety about a situation which involved an older, physically disabled woman (Margaret) who allowed her adult son with problematic substance use (Dave) to continue to live with her. He was stealing her money, subjecting her to extreme emotional stress, and allowing his associates to come into her house to deal drugs. The practitioner described a scenario over a long period of time where safeguarding concerns would be raised by neighbours, professionals and Margaret herself. The team was structured in such a way that 'cases' were opened and closed in response to contacts to the team, but in this case the same practitioner was assigned each time a new incident was reported, in recognition of the complexity of the situation and that she had built a rapport with Margaret. The practitioner would visit and discuss options, Margaret would choose a week of respite in residential care to get away from her son, would return home again and continue as before, until it became too much and made contact with social services again; this pattern continued for some months.

Any simple risk assessment tool would clearly describe the situation as high risk – significant impact; high likelihood of ongoing incidents. The practitioner, used to operating in a task-orientated team, wanted a resolution, to fix the issues and to make Margaret safe. In the absence of Dave seeking help for his problems, the ultimate safety solutions appeared to be for Margaret to move, possibly into residential care, or have support to evict Dave from her home, making him homeless. Margaret did not want either of these options, and seen through the lens of a rights-based perspective it is clear that these would have been restrictive in terms of her liberty and family life. The practitioner offered respite when requested, consistency when contacted, and advice and guidance for Dave on help for addiction and a housing application, when asked. When describing her frustration at achieving so little, and anxiety at what might happen to Margaret, the practitioner was surprised at the reflection back: in assuming the role of advocate and facilitator, she was doing exactly what Margaret needed in order to be able to cope with the risks in her life at that time.

A greater understanding of assessing and responding to risk from a rights-based perspective may have assisted this practitioner in developing her thinking and confidence about her actions in this situation, which effectively were:

- understanding that all the choices faced by Margaret may have led to some degree of harm from her perspective

- working collaboratively on understanding risk and underwriting safety, leading to a more mutually satisfying relationship based on trust (Boardman and Roberts 2014)

- exploring the protective value of increased choice and developing techniques to detect abuse or make it more difficult to occur (Stevens et al. 2014). This involved putting in place proactive strategies and contingency planning within a support plan.

High expectations are placed on practitioners and organisations through legislation, regulations and policy (Skills for Care 2011). Fook and Gardner (2007) identify a context of powerlessness linked to uncertainty, and a fear of risk and increased complexity for practitioners. Dixon and Robb (2016) make the point that the desire to make professional decision making more transparent and risk-reduction strategies more explicit has prompted the ever-increasing use of tools and procedure manuals. These are a way of managing anxiety and trying to increase predictability (Fook and Gardner 2007); if the assessment is completed, adverse events can be predicted, and a solution can be found.

It is possible that the quasi-scientific notion of risk assessment and its associated tools promotes risk-averse decision making by professionals, or at minimum the over-professionalisation of risk assessment, resulting in failure to recognise the role of ethics, morals and values in professional decision making (Stanford 2011). If the solution to risk is to prevent it or stop it, it is easy to see why practitioners may leap to risk-averse, restrictive actions – the 'place of safety'. Conversely, over-reliance on tools to predict risk may lead to a false sense of security and a failure to recognise issues, leading to superficial and simplistic application of risk management techniques, insufficient efforts to engage, and a failure to recognise and take appropriate action at all (Boardman and Roberts 2014).

The review of child protection by Eileen Munro re-emphasised the need for practitioners to see risk assessment as a tool which complements professional judgement and encourages constant and critical review and reflection, rather than an end in itself (Munro 2011). Barlow, Fisher and Jones (2012), who have carried out a systematic review of tools available for assessing harm to children, comment that:

> decisions about which tool(s) to use must take account of the need for methods of assessment that are not so highly structured that they preclude practitioner judgement, but that are also not insufficiently evidence-based or structured to facilitate accuracy and rigour in decision making. (Barlow *et al.* 2012, p.69)

A shift from an over-reliance on assessment frameworks and their associated tools as revealing 'truth', towards risk assessment as a process of ongoing hypothesis building and critical reflection (Barry 2007; Fook and Gardner 2007), is linked to the need for practitioners and organisations to be continuously learning in order to manage change, complexity and risk effectively.

While this perspective is linked to the notion of defensible, evidence-based decision making, it also promotes the active participation of the person at risk. Practitioners may be able to approach the use of risk assessment tools simply as a means of gathering information to inform decision making. The tools become a means of facilitating open discussion, understanding the risks, and understanding different perspectives – a means of supported and shared decision making for both the practitioner and the person at risk. Payne (2008) reminds the practitioner of skills that are relevant to managing complexity and risk in this way: enhancing resilience, improving the capacity of people to respond to the issues they face; being prepared to stand alongside people as they work through what is happening to them; and an objective understanding of the trajectory of the person's history as it relates to the present.

Any risk assessment should acknowledge the degree to which it is able to be focused only on the person. There are many interests in situations of high risk outside of the person – family, neighbours, numerous professionals, and the media. The practitioner needs to be able to balance the potentially competing rights associated with the risk posed and the strategy employed to respond. 'The principal objective of a Human Rights-based approach for risk assessment is to enable decisions to be collaboratively arrived upon at each stage, where the individual is as thoroughly immersed and involved in the decision tree as possible' (Mersey Care NHS Trust 2008).

> Risk assessment in any social work theme should incorporate the views of those whose needs are being addressed by such assessments. What they want, why they want it, what their abilities are and whether there are extraneous risk factors all need to be taken into account, otherwise the service user may not feel committed to or 'own' the resulting intervention. (Barry 2007, p.20)

The person at the centre of the assessment needs to be made aware as far as possible of all the competing views affecting how they respond to their situation. While this may sound uncontentious, it presents challenges for the practitioner who may find themselves at the centre of challenging family or professional dynamics. Methodologies such as family meetings, family group conferences, professionals' meetings or even mediation may need to be considered, and would form part of the ongoing assessment of risk (see Chapters 3, 4 and 5).

Undertaking risk assessment

'Faced with a decision alone, most people will be risk-averse: if something goes wrong it will be our fault and our responsibility. Sharing that decision helps us think through the options more clearly from different perspectives' (Morgan and Williamson 2014). There is a plethora of risk assessment and response models available for use within health and social care settings. (Examples can be found at www.scie.org.uk.) All of them have themes in common – gathering as much information as possible and sharing decision making, with the ultimate goal of making a 'good decision' in relation to the risk, not eliminating the risk altogether.

Barlow *et al.* (2012), having reviewed the tools available for assessing harm to children, conclude that, in order to be effective, tools must:

- provide a balance of structure between professional judgement and standardisation

- support professional competence and confidence

- ensure that complexity is not minimised

- increase the accuracy of identifying harm and whether there is a likelihood of that harm recurring

- encourage assessment and analysis of information across the 'ecology' of the individual

- be sensitive to different stages within an assessment

- provide guidance as to how the tool is to be employed in the organisational context

- be underpinned by a model of 'partnership working'

- be clearly based on best available evidence related to the risk being assessed.

This chapter does not aim to prescribe a tool for assessing risk, but suggests a framework to support the assessment of risk in safeguarding. It is built largely on the Department of Health's (2010) framework for enabling risk when supporting people with dementia, alongside the other references for this chapter.

Step 1: Understanding the person's wishes and feelings in relation to the risk

Listen to what the person is saying about their situation, gather biographical information, pay attention to past wishes, formal or otherwise, and speak to everyone who knows them and who has an interest in the situation. 'The process of listening to people's views and concerns can then begin to develop trust and an understanding of the need for a shared responsibility for safety' (Boardman and Roberts 2014). Wellbeing is promoted through attention to psychological and social as much as physical need, and listening to wishes and feelings ensures that psychological and social needs are accounted for in the initial assessment. Working with the person to put different wishes or needs in order of relative importance may help find out what is most important to them, help to understand what they see as the benefits in their situation, and help them feel listened to.

Step 2: Understanding the impact of risks on the person

Listing the risks identified through speaking to the person and others, and applying a simple test of likelihood of occurrence and severity of impact against each one, remains the most straightforward way of analysing the true extent of perceived risks. This must be undertaken in the context of the person's wishes and feelings, and used as a means of sharing information and challenging perceptions. It is not a 'professional's tool' but should be used as the basis for discussion with the person, their representatives and other professionals. Now is the time to view the issues from a strengths-based perspective – what strengths or positive factors exist that might mitigate some of the impact of the risks?

Next is to look at how far the risks might contribute to the person's quality of life (wellbeing) against the risk of harm. It is possible that the benefits the person gains from remaining in this risky situation actually do outweigh the risks, or alternatively the person may change their view of their situation when seeing the information presented in this way. This analytical process may also help to gain understanding of how far the person really does understand their situation and the level of risk they face. If limited benefits (always bearing in mind human rights) can be identified, and yet the person remains unable to see the risks posed, now is the time to begin to test their view and understanding.

This approach is also useful in informing a best interests decision (see Chapter 7) where the person lacks mental capacity to make a decision on a particular issue. Criticism of this 'balance sheet' type approach in considering best interests is that the process tries to compare the value of things that are not comparable. However, as with assessing the likelihood and impact of risks, its use as a means to aid thinking and document decision-making processes is helpful in trying to arrive at a good decision.

Step 3: Enabling and responding to risk

Before moving on to responding to the assessed risk, practitioners need the opportunity to acknowledge what they bring to the table – preconceptions based on experience, opinions about the person's ability to make decisions, anxiety about possible consequences, and the organisational culture in which they work. Fook and Gardner (2007) highlight the importance of acknowledging emotion in relation to challenging case work. Any possible action based on practitioner or organisational concerns should be explored in reflective sessions with managers and other professionals, building on the principles and guidance relating to mental capacity and human rights legislation.

Three key questions to be answered at this stage are the following:

- Can we promote the person's safety without interfering with the benefits they gain from the situation or infringing their rights?

- Are there ways in which we can help to change the situation to reduce the risk to acceptable levels whilst still respecting their choices and promoting their quality of life? (Department of Health 2010)

- Accepting that some things can go wrong – what could go wrong, and how could we respond in that case? Who can help support with the consequences and associated fear or guilt? (Morgan and Williamson 2014)

Step 4: Planning and contingency

The final step is to bring together the findings from steps 1 to 3 into a support or risk enablement plan. The plan will summarise the person's wishes and feelings, the risk assessment, enablement solutions and the agreed actions to respond to residual risk and contingency planning.

> 'Safety planning' really only has meaning for the person in the context of their personal life goals. That is what will engage the person and get them to be motivated to take part in the process...a shared responsibility for promoting safety: what the person will do, what staff will do, what others who are important to the person will do... Developing a negotiated safety plan facilitates careful experimentation and the opportunities for people to discover what works best for them. (Boardman and Roberts 2014)

Developing a culture of sensitive risk management

'A new governance...includes clear accountability frameworks, the protection of professional autonomy, learning from mistakes and strong leadership. The extent to which these aspirations can be met within a climate of risk, responsibilisation and regulation poses challenges' (Barry 2007). How can health and care organisations, especially those that are regulated, support practitioners to facilitate and advocate, to operate within a rights-based model, and meaningfully share decision making? The idea of trust and handing over of responsibility has been discussed in terms of the individual/practitioner relationship; organisationally this can and should be modelled by having in place a governance structure that trusts and supports staff and hands over responsibility. As Birkis and Aspinall (2016) point out, safety in acute health care settings concentrates on minimising the incidence and impact of adverse events by encouraging reporting of all such events and attempting to foster a culture that reduces individual blame. However, this concept is challenging to translate into many safeguarding situations as standardised approaches are unlikely to be able to reflect individual preferences. In services delivered in community settings and in a person's home, risk is often a more negotiated possibility and responsibility for adverse outcomes is less clear.

In grappling with these tensions, organisations need to consider:

- reviewing the language of blame or an over-emphasis on safety, towards a no-fault approach which encourages cooperation and learning

- accepting the goal is not safety at the expense of all else, and seeking consensus on what is 'acceptable' risk

- viewing shared decision making as a means to address risk rather than making it worse

- accepting uncertainty insofar as risk cannot be predicted or prevented and working to identify imminent risk

- clearly defining for practitioners their core duties and their margin of judgement and creativity in responding to the risk.

(Barry 2007; Fook and Gardner 2007; Neill *et al.* 2008)

The Department of Health (2010) describes moving from a narrow towards a broader view of risk and balancing the positive benefits that are likely to follow from taking risks against the negative effects of attempting to avoid risk altogether. This means moving from expert judgements and technical expertise to seeking the opinions of all involved; from individual accountability and blame to sharing learning from mistakes and near misses; from trying to control the environment to being responsive to risk.

In supporting practitioners to use tools and processes as a means to aid decision making rather than ends in themselves, organisations need to reconsider their use of process to assess and respond to risk. For example, reporting safeguarding concerns or safety incidents to the regulator or local authority is often the default response to risk. This absolves those reporting of responsibility and fails to evaluate the risk issue on its own merit. A more reflective approach, taking responsibility for the concern, and questioning the purpose of any reporting, is required. Creating opportunities for open discussion about risk issues, through critical reflection in supervision and audit, or models such as a serious incident learning process, appreciative inquiry or action learning, is crucial (Fook and Gardner 2007; Mitchell and Glendinning 2007). The Professional Standards Authority is an organisation that aims to protect the public by improving the regulation and registration of people who work in health and care. It argues in *Rethinking Regulation* (2015) that the focus of regulation on safety processes has contributed to this simplistic, process-driven response to risk, and that regulation should move away from the efficient completion of process to a focus on the prevention of specific types of harm.

Individuals, their families, practitioners, the regulator, commissioners, employers, the public and the media may take different views of any given situation in terms of assessing and responding to risk. The concept of defensible decision making in supporting organisational approaches to risk is helpful, as it focuses on the quality of the approach, rather than on the eventual outcome. The Department of Health cites Kemshall in describing defensible decision making. Organisations should be able to evidence that:

- all reasonable steps have been taken to respond

- reliable assessment methods have been used to inform decisions

- information has been collated and thoroughly evaluated

- decisions are recorded, communicated and thoroughly evaluated

- policies and procedures have been followed

- practitioners and their managers adopt a proactive, analytical approach.

(Department of Health 2010)

The above considerations should prompt organisations into thinking about moving beyond incident reporting and process to adopting an open culture, not only within but between organisations. As well as increased transparency, discussing risk issues and sharing responsibility may create a more positive view of risk within the wider system as well as risk as it relates to individuals.

The potential for different organisational approaches, different approaches between practitioners and managers and also different approaches amongst practitioners depending on the clients they work with has implications for multi-agency working and developing a shared understanding of 'risk' and accepted practices or management strategies. (Mitchell and Glendinning 2007)

As Chris Hatton reminds us in his blog:

> Social care providers have a responsibility to ensure that they are promoting good health amongst the people they are supporting, not only in aspects of people's lives such as nutrition and diet, physical activity, and substance use, but also in areas such as promoting meaningful social relationships with partners, family and friends, employment and being respected as a citizen of value. (Hatton 2014)

Quigley (2014) draws several parallels between public health and adult safeguarding, one being how to confront the problem of state intervention in people's lives for the purpose of preventing harm. At policy level both are focused on behaviour change to prevent harm. However, Quigley points out that there is a great difference between the reliance of adult safeguarding on criminal justice interventions and moral condemnation compared with public health's reliance on consensus-based methods that shape public values and culture.

This broader, public health view of risk is compatible with organisations being willing to share and discuss their assessments of risky situations in order to contribute to the intelligence within the system, but is also compatible with a rights-based approach to risk assessment. It means that organisations need to take into account the impact that any restrictive, safety-led responses might have on the emotional wellbeing of the person they care for. One of the impacts of the 2014 Supreme Court judgement on deprivation of liberty, known as 'Cheshire West' (*P v Cheshire West and Chester Council* and *P&Q v Surrey County Council*), was to bring the language of restriction, no matter how benign or well intentioned, into the everyday language of care organisations.

Leadership within organisations plays a vital role in changing the language of risk and ensuring that positive messages about risk are heard by all who work within them. The organisation ImROC (Implementing Recovery through Organisational Change) is a collaboration between the Centre for Mental Health and the NHS Confederation's Mental Health Network to promote recovery in mental health. It promotes the use of quality improvement models, processes of agreed goal-setting and review, as a means of testing how teams and organisations might start to think differently about responses to risk (see https://imroc. org). Leaders should consider how far their organisations promote the messages below in relation to risk within their settings:

- There is no such thing as a risk-free decision; the risk-averse option comes with its own risks.

- The focus of positive risk-taking is on making good decisions about risk; it is the taking of calculated and reasoned risks, not leaving things to chance (Morgan and Williamson 2014).

- Risk assessment is based on sound evidence and analysis.

- Risk-assessment tools inform discussion and shared decision making.

- Professionals involved in risk assessment use a common language for risk.

- Information-sharing for risk assessment is important and is based on agreed protocols and understanding of the use of such information.

- Risk assessment is not a discrete process but is integral to the ongoing response to and minimisation of risk (Barry 2007).

Conclusion

Stanford (2011, p.1526) identifies practitioners who can work positively with risk as being able to:

- 'contemplate personal and professional morals, ethics and values;

- reconsider the reality of risk for clients and themselves;

- believe in the possibility of change for clients; and

- reflect on theoretical and practice frameworks.'

Being able to think about risk and make good decisions in safeguarding situations may be challenging at a time when a person is most vulnerable, within a context of a life disabled by a society that may not have previously supported them to make risk-based decisions. Notions of risk are socially constructed and context-specific. However, they are often presented as a technical or scientific fact, which can be assessed by professionals through an opaque process which is invisible to critical analysis. If practitioners are able to relinquish their expert status, and view risk through the lens of human rights, they may be able to approach the use of risk assessment tools as a participative means of gathering information to inform decision making, and take the role of advocate or facilitator in supporting the person to make difficult decisions about their situation. Organisations play their part in changing the language and understanding of risk, to support their staff in making good decisions instead of eliminating the risk altogether, and in moving away from seeing risk purely from the viewpoint of organisational liability.

References

Barlow, J., Fisher, J.D., and Jones, D. (2012) *Systematic Review of Models of Analysing Significant Harm.* Berkshire: Department for Education. Available at www.gov.uk/government/uploads/system/uploads/attachment_data/file/183949/DFE-RR199.pdf, accessed on 12 April 2017.

Barry, M. (2007) *Effective Approaches to Risk Assessment in Social Work: An International Literature Review.* Edinburgh: Education Information and Analytical Services, Scottish Executive.

Birkis, Y., and Aspinall, D. (2016) *Safeguarding, Safety and Risk Scoping Review 13.* London: School for Social Care Research

Boardman, J., and Roberts, G. (2014) *Risk, Safety and Recovery.* London: Centre for Mental Health and Mental Health Network, NHS Confederation.

Department of Health (2010) *Nothing Ventured, Nothing Gained: Risk Guidance for People with Dementia.* Guidance. London: Department of Health.

Dixon, J., and Robb, M. (2016) 'Working with women with learning disability experiencing domestic abuse: How social workers can negotiate competing definitions of risk.' *The British Journal of Social Work 46,* 773–788.

Faulkner, A. (2012) *Risk, Trust and Relationships in an Ageing Society, the Right to Take Risks: Service Users' Views of Risk in Adult Social Care.* York: Joseph Rowntree Foundation.

Fook, J., and Gardner, F. (2007) *Practising Critical Reflection: A Resource Handbook.* Berkshire: Open University Press.

Francis, R. (2013) *Report of the Mid Staffordshire NHS Foundation Trust Public Inquiry.* London: The Stationery Office.

Hatton, C. (2014) *A Place of Greater Safety? Risk and People with Learning Disabilities.* Chris Hatton's Blog. Available at http://chrishatton.blogspot.co.uk/2014/03/a-place-of-greater-safety-risk-and.html, accessed on 12 April 2017.

McNamara, R., and Morgan, S. (2016) *Risk Enablement: Frontline Practice Briefing.* Dartington: Research in Practice for Adults.

Mersey Care NHS Trust (2008) *Human Rights Joint Risk Assessment and Management Plan.* Liverpool: Mersey Care NHS Trust.

Mitchell, W., and Glendinning, C. (2007) *A Review of the Research Evidence Surrounding Risk Perceptions, Risk Management Strategies and Their Consequences in Adult Social Care for Different Groups of Service Users.* York: University of York, Social Policy Research Unit.

Morgan, S., and Williamson, T. (2014) *How Can 'Positive Risk-Taking' Help Build Dementia-Friendly Communities?* York: Joseph Rowntree Foundation and Mental Health Foundation.

Munro, E. (2011) *The Munro Review of Child Protection: Final Report – A Child-Centred System.* London: Department for Education.

Neary, M. (May 2016) *The Best Interests.* Love, Belief and Balls Blog. Available at https://markneary1dotcom1.wordpress.com/2016/05/20/the-best-interests, accessed on 12 April 2017.

Neill, M., Allen, J., Woodhead, N., Reid, S., Irwin, L., and Sanderson, H. (2008) *A Positive Approach to Risk Requires Person-Centred Thinking.* London: Think Local Act Personal. Available at www.thinklocalactpersonal.org.uk/_assets/Resources/Personalisation/Personalisation_advice/A_Person_Centred_Approach_to_Risk.pdf, accessed on 12 April 2017.

Payne, M. (2008) 'Complexity and social work theory and practice.' *Social Work Now 39,* 15–20.

Professional Standards Authority for Health and Social Care (2015) *Rethinking Regulation.* London: Professional Standards Authority for Health and Social Care.

Quigley, L. (2014) 'Policy making, adult safeguarding and public health: A formula for change.' *The Journal of Adult Protection 16,* 2, 68–86.

Series, L. (2014) *On Risk and Making Hard Choices.* Small Places Blog. Available at https://thesmallplaces.wordpress.com/2014/11/14/postscript-on-risk-and-making-hard-choices, accessed on 12 April 2017.

Skills for Care (2011) *Learning to Live with Risk: An Introduction for Service Providers.* Leeds: Skills for Care.

Stanford, S. (2011) 'Constructing moral responses to risk: A framework for hopeful social work practice.' *British Journal of Social Work 41,* 1514–1531.

Stevens, M., Manthorpe, J., Hussein, S., Ismail, M., *et al.* (2014) *Risk, Safeguarding and Personal Budgets: Exploring Relationships and Identifying Good Practice.* London: Kings College, NIHR School for Social Care Research.

Chapter 7

Mental Capacity Act and Adult Safeguarding

Dan Baker

The Mental Capacity Act 2005 (hereafter referred to as the MCA 2005 or the Act) provides a legal framework to empower individuals to make their own decisions and, where this is not possible due to the person lacking mental capacity,[1] protects their best interests through enabling decisions to be made on their behalf whilst focusing on them as individuals and upholding their rights and freedoms.[2] The Act embodies the two threads of empowerment and protection within the five statutory principles set out in section(s.) 1.[3] They reflect two competing demands that must be carefully balanced: a person's right to make their own decisions and their right to be protected where this is not possible.

This dilemma goes to the very purpose of the MCA 2005, and is also intrinsic to adult safeguarding. These same threads run straight to the very heart of many, if not all, adult safeguarding situations where an individual is experiencing, or at risk of, abuse or neglect. They often result in questions, such as:

- Can and should this individual make their own decisions in their situation or be protected from harm?

- Do they understand the concerns? Do they understand the likely and foreseeable consequences?

- Who would be blamed if the individual came to harm? Whose risk is it to take?

---

1   See Appendix, s. 2 [1] of the MCA 2005.
2   See Appendix, s. 4 of the MCA 2005. The term 'best interests' is not actually defined in the Act, but s. 4 explains how to workout the best interest of a person who lacks capacity to make a specific decision at the time it needs to be made.
3   See Appendix, s.1 of the MCA 2005.

Balancing such competing demands is by no means new: before the MCA 2005, Braye and Preston-Shoot (1995) referred to 'conflicting imperatives' including 'rights versus risks, care versus control'. The MCA 2005, however, introduced a statutory pathway to guide practitioners in balancing such imperatives, but it is widely accepted that the 'prevailing cultures of paternalism and risk-aversion' have thus far limited its empowering potential (House of Lords Select Committee 2014). The desire to protect those with care and support needs at all cost, referred to as the 'protection imperative',[4] is considered to be skewing many assessments of mental capacity and best interests. The protective side of the Act is inadvertently being over-used, with insufficient focus on the empowering aspects. This is acutely relevant in adult safeguarding situations where risks, or perceived risks, to a person can often be very high, and so the desire to protect is understandably strong.

A refocusing on the spirit and intention of the Act is required: 'The Act is intended to be enabling and supportive of people who lack capacity, not restricting or controlling of their lives' (Department for Constitutional Affairs [DCA] 2007, p.19). This is central to how practitioners should apply the MCA 2005 in all adult safeguarding situations: empowerment first and foremost, protection second and when needed. This mindset demands a change in culture and practice, a repositioning of health and social care practitioners, away from protection being the primary consideration, towards 'ambassadors of human rights and creative enablers' (Baker 2017).

An adult safeguarding case study provides practical application of these issues throughout this chapter.

CASE STUDY

Margaret Jackson is 91 years old, with a diagnosis of Alzheimer's disease dementia. She lives in her own home supported by carers three times a day, assisted with her personal care and preparing meals. Margaret is in good physical health, but she is becoming increasingly confused and forgetful, often leaving her front door wide open during the day and not closing her windows at night.

---

4   *Oldham MBC v GW and PW* [2007] EWHC 136 (Fam); *PH v A Local Authority, Z Ltd and R* [2011] EWHC 1704 (Fam); *CC v KK and STCC* [2012] EWCOP 2136, [2012] EWHC 2136 (COP).

Margaret's daughter Janet lives in the same village and visits regularly. Janet has reported to Margaret's practitioner that she is concerned that local children are perhaps stealing from her mother, as money and jewellery have gone missing from the property. Janet has come to this opinion having spoken with neighbours and being told that local children were seen knocking at the front door, whilst others enter the property via the kitchen. The neighbours were not able to identify the children, and were reluctant to report their concerns formally to the police. Janet says she is beginning to feel that it may be time for her mother to move into a care home.

The first three principles protect and support individual autonomy

This chapter is primarily focused on making best interests decisions for individuals assessed as lacking mental capacity in their safeguarding situation; however, it cannot be emphasised enough that this is not the starting place. The first three principles of the Act are fundamental to how practitioners should approach any adult safeguarding situation. These principles should be considered and applied collectively because they are all part of the same empowering spirit. As a whole they represent the default position, the primary driving force of the Act, and should form the initial focus of any adult safeguarding situation. They respect individual autonomy and demand supported decision-making approaches.

The first three principles can be collectively paraphrased as:

- **Assume** capacity regardless of any particular decision(s) the individual is making, even if considered to be **unwise**, and provide the individual with **all practical support** and help to make their own decision.

It is not appropriate or legal to make best interests decisions, for any individual, without having first provided all practical assistance to help them make their own decisions and established a lack of mental capacity in the safeguarding matter.

Particularly in adult safeguarding situations, where it may be tempting to leap straight to protective considerations, these principles have the potential to be the primary defender of individual liberty and autonomy against a prevailing paternalistic and risk-adverse culture. The aim is not to take decisions away from people but to support them to make their own decisions, with whatever assistance required. Just as people with physical disabilities might require a ramp to facilitate accessing a building, supported decision making should be seen as the means to reasonably accommodate people with cognitive disabilities to exercise their legal capacity (Salzman 2010).

The 'practicable steps' available to maximise a person's mental capacity will largely depend upon the individual's needs and circumstances. Chapter 3 of the MCA 2005 Code of Practice (DCA 2007) is dedicated to this.

A good example of assisted decision making can be seen in the case of *LBX v K, L, M* [2013] where the court-appointed assessor was commended for their person-centred planning techniques.[5] There are various tools and person-centred planning techniques which can be used depending upon the individual's needs. For examples, Research in Practice for Adults (RiPfA) published a helpful handbook (Nosowska and Series 2013). Helen Sanderson Associates, a Social Enterprise seeking to promote person-centred practices, also have a range of tools accessible from their website.[6]

CASE STUDY CONTINUED

Following referral, the practitioner visited Margaret to understand the situation from her perspective, assess the risks, and support her to make any required decisions relating to the concerns. Her daughter was present to provide reassurance.

The practitioner started from the presumption of mental capacity, despite the reported confusion, and sought to provide all practical support to maximise Margaret's decision-making abilities. Furthermore, the report that Margaret would often leave her front door wide open during the day, an action others might consider as unwise, did not necessarily mean Margaret lacked mental capacity. The practitioner considered all the relevant information that Margaret would need to know and made sure it was available. She explained the details of the concerns and the options available to Margaret, which included the following:

5   *LBX v K, L, M* [2013] EWHC 3230 (Fam) and [2013] EWHC 4170 (Fam) (Theis J).
6   See www.helensandersonassociates.co.uk.

- No decisions or changes being made at all.
- Notifying the police.
- A range of options to protect Margaret and improve the security of her home:

  1. prompts that could be stuck on the back of the door, such as 'Margaret, please make sure the door is locked'
  2. the use of telecare systems to notify a central office if the door was left open
  3. additional evening care
  4. a visit from the 'Bobby Van' (a service for adults with care needs in the community to improve home security and provide advice, which might potentially include a new lock being fitted for the kitchen door).

- A placement in a local residential home, identified by her daughter as a possible option to consider.

The practitioner used person-centred planning tools to frame the discussion, which covered subjects including: What makes Margaret feel safe? Who or what is important to Margaret? What possessions are important to Margaret and how should they be kept safe?

Through this discussion it became evident that Margaret was at times confused about who visited her at home as well as the concerns about the door being left open. She knew that money and jewellery had gone missing but did not think they had been stolen by local children, referring to them as her friends.

The assessment of capacity: the bridge

The assessment of capacity can be considered as a bridge between the first three principles, which focus on upholding rights of autonomy, and the last two principles, which allow for decisions to be made on an incapacitated individual's behalf. It is intended that the supported decision-making approach should continue whilst the practitioner assesses capacity; it is not a stand-alone, out-of-context assessment.

The assessment of capacity is always time- and issue-specific – 'to make a particular decision at the time it needs to be made' (DCA 2007). It is applicable both to people with temporary or fluctuating capacity and those whose decision-making ability is permanently impaired.

This leads the practitioner on to two primary questions: when should an individual's capacity be formally assessed, and then, how is this assessment of mental capacity carried out?

The MCA 2005 Code of Practice (DCA 2007) provides helpful guidance as to when an assessment might be required, such as when a person 'repeatedly makes unwise decisions that put them at significant risk of harm or exploitation' (p.25) or 'behaviour or circumstances cause doubt' (p.52).

The test of capacity given at ss.2 and 3 of the Act[7] is further explained in Chapter 4 of the MCA 2005 Code of Practice (DCA 2007). 39 Essex Street Chambers, a long-established barristers' chambers based in London, have also produced a very helpful resource in this regard (Ruck Keene *et al.* 2016a).

CASE STUDY CONTINUED

Margaret presented with confusion during the initial discussion, and there were concerns about her ability to recognise potential risk of harm or exploitation. A recent visit to a memory clinic had confirmed a diagnosis of dementia, so it was decided that her mental capacity should be formally assessed. When the practitioner visited again she explained to Margaret, and her daughter, that she would be assessing her ability to decide upon the protective measures previously discussed.

Having defined the precise decision, the practitioner then identified the salient and relevant details required to be understood and processed as part of making the decision. This included details on the concerns, options identified, and the likely consequences of choosing one way or another for each option. During the assessment the practitioner referred back to the person-centred planning tools in an effort to promote Margaret's ability to understand all the relevant information, retain that information for long enough to weigh and use it, as

---

7   See Appendix, ss.2 and 3 of the MCA 2005.

well as communicate a decision on each protective measure. The practitioner aimed to be very clear and precise, ensuring that the actual decision was put to Margaret whilst taking account of her individual needs.

The practitioner remembered the case-law guidance which described the 'weigh or use' element of the functional test as: 'actually to engage in the decision-making process itself and to be able to see the various parts of the argument and to relate the one to another'.[8] Reflecting on this, the practitioner considered that, although Margaret could understand and retain some of the relevant information with support, she could not relate how the concerns about the door being left open, or reports of children entering via the kitchen door, might potentially relate to the money and jewellery going missing. Also Margaret could not understand that if she was talking with one child at the front door, a different child could potentially go around to the kitchen door without her knowledge, repeating, 'but I was talking with the boy at the door'.

The practitioner concluded that on the balance of probabilities, and despite starting from the position of applying the first three principles, Margaret was unable to make the required decisions using the MCA 2005 test of capacity.

This was all recorded in detail, citing the questions asked and Margaret's responses.

Making a 'best interests' decision

A best interests decision is not a particular type of outcome; rather, it is a specific process. The protection from liability[9] does not come from selecting a particular option but through following the process outlined in s.4 of the Act and subsequent case law guidance. This process is commonly referred to as the best interests 'checklist', with a mixture of considerations and requirements, as well as types and sources of information, which should be considered when making a decision.

In adult safeguarding situations it may be tempting to select an option that quickly reduces or removes presenting risks in the

---

8   *The PCT v P, AH & the Local Authority* [2009] EW Misc 10 (COP).
9   See Appendix, s.5 of the MCA 2005.

belief that it is 'in the person's best interests'. However, unless the practitioner (hereafter referred to as the decision-maker) adheres to the requirements in s.4 of the Act, this is not a MCA 2005 best interests decision. To aid this process, a best interests meeting may prove helpful, but this is not a statutory requirement. In practice there are often times when the decision-maker may understandably require time for reflection outside of the meeting environment to carefully consider all the information and circumstances. Removing the expectation of a decision being made there and then can often take the heat out of discussions, allowing for a more fruitful and open exchange.

The best interests decision-making process is summarised by the following six stages:

1. Define the decision.

2. Follow s.4 of the MCA 2005.

3. 'Balance sheet' approach.

4. Least restrictive way of achieving the desired outcome.

5. Make and record the decision.

6. Risk reduction and contingency planning.

Stage 1: Define the decision

The aim is to ensure that the decision has been defined correctly, including the options available and purpose. If the aim is not fully understood, the decision-maker may struggle to determine the least restrictive way of achieving it. The decision should be framed in a way that is objective and inclusive of all the available and realistic options. Instead of it being about consenting to one particular safeguarding option, such as consenting to respite care, the decision should be phrased much more widely, incorporating all the options – including any considered less favourable by the professionals involved.

The decision is not an abstract question, rather the actual options available to the individual at the time the decision is required.

Stage 2: Follow s.4 of the MCA 2005

S.4 of the Act is the process that, if followed correctly, enables the decision-maker to refer to their eventual decision as made in the person's best interests and protects them from liability.[10] For ease of application in practice, the 'checklist' has been separated into two broad categories: overarching requirements; and sources of information.

a. Overarching requirements

1. Avoid discrimination – do not base decisions upon assumptions about the person's age, appearance, condition or behaviour.[11]

2. Delay the decision, where possible, if there is a chance that the person may regain capacity.[12]

3. Permit and encourage the person to participate.[13]

4. The decision must not be motivated by a desire to bring about the person's death.[14]

b. Sources of information
Identify and consider all the 'relevant circumstances'
The decision-maker must consider 'all the relevant circumstances'.[15] This includes 'all relevant factors that it would be reasonable to consider, not just those that they think are important' (DCA 2007, p.68). In practice the 'relevant circumstances' are likely to be a mixture of case-specific factors as well as more universal interests or rights, and it is worth considering relevant circumstances from both these perspectives. Case-specific factors might include the person's circumstances, relationship dynamics, care and support needs and options available, whereas universal interests and rights might include elements contained in the Care Act (2014) definition of wellbeing[16] and the European Convention of Human Rights.[17]

---

10   See Appendix, s.4 of the MCA 2005.
11   Ibid. at s.4 [1].
12   Ibid. at s.4 [3].
13   Ibid. at s.4 [4].
14   Ibid. at s.4 [5].
15   Ibid. at s.4 [2].
16   The Care Act 2014, s.1 [2].
17   See www.echr.coe.int/Documents/Convention_ENG.pdf.

Case law has repeatedly emphasised that best interests decisions are akin to a holistic welfare assessment. They must incorporate such things as emotional welfare,[18] relationships and belonging,[19] and happiness.[20] Safeguarding must be more than protecting physical safety; when we safeguard a person we must also safeguard their rights, wellbeing and happiness. The relevant circumstances should reflect the person and situation as a whole.

The wishes, feelings, beliefs and values of the person

The decision-maker must 'permit and encourage' the person to participate in the decision-making process as much as possible,[21] and therefore the supported decision-making approach does not stop at the point a person is assessed as lacking mental capacity. The aim is not to take decisions away from people but to support them in directing and influencing the eventual decision as far as possible. The best interests decision-making process should be considered as shared or supported decision making, not paternalistic or purely substitute (Essex Autonomy Project 2012).

It is important to clearly record the steps taken to improve the person's understanding and ability to express their own wishes; attempting to really understand their past and present, and what is important to them in their situation. Of particular relevance are their past and present wishes, feelings, beliefs and values[22] as they 'will always be a significant factor'.[23] Nevertheless, any potential inconsistency, degree of incapacity or doubts of them being rational or safe if carried out is likely to have relevance in terms of the weight of influence attributed to them upon the eventual decision.

The Supreme Court judgement of Aintree University Hospitals NHS Foundation Trust[24] highlights the importance of considering 'matters from the patient's point of view' and making the right decision for 'an individual human being'.[25] Practitioners must see the

---

18   For example see *Re A [medical treatment: male sterilisation]* [2000] 1 FCR 193.
19   For example see *FP v GM and A Health Board* [2011] EWHC 2778 [21].
20   For examples see *Re MM (an adult)* [2007] EWHC 2003 (Fam) [120]; *PB v RB and London Borough of Haringey* [2016] EWCOP 12.
21   S.4 [4] of the MCA 2005.
22   S.4 [6] of the MCA 2005.
23   *Re M; ITW v Z* [2009] EWHC 2525 (Fam) [35].
24   *Aintree University Hospitals NHS Foundation Trust (Respondent) v James (Appellant)* [2013] UKSC 67.
25   Ibid. at para.45.

uniqueness of every person, with their own values, likes and dislikes, and consider their best interests in a person-centred way, taking account of their 'own assessment of the quality of their life'.[26]

This is of particular importance in adult safeguarding situations. There is little purpose in safeguarding an individual if the outcome does not achieve what is important to them. The decision-maker must carefully consider the outcome(s) they are trying to achieve through the best interests decision, ensuring that physical health and safety are not bought at too high a price in terms of the person's happiness and emotional welfare.[27] This demands that the safeguarding practitioner really gets to know the person as much as possible, so that they can genuinely consider the matter from their point of view.

The Essex Autonomy Project published a briefing paper in 2014 entitled *Does the MCA 2005 Respect the Will and Preferences of Disabled Persons?*, in which they concluded that the MCA 2005 was not fully compliant with article 12 (4)[28] of the United Nations Convention on the Rights of Persons with Disabilities (UNCRPD) 2006. They suggested amending the MCA 2005 best interests decision-making process with a 'rebuttable presumption that, when a decision must be made on behalf of a person lacking in mental capacity, and the wishes of that person can be reasonably ascertained, the best-interests decision-maker shall make the decision that accords with those wishes' (Essex Autonomy Project 2014).

This greater emphasis on the person's will and preferences appears to be the future direction of the MCA 2005. The Law Commission's published report (2017) on proposed changes to Mental Capacity and Deprivation of Liberty legislation includes amendments to ss.4 and 5 of the MCA 2005 in respect of ascertaining and applying the person's wishes, feelings, beliefs and values in best interests decision making. In particular, amongst other amendments, the proposals would, if enacted, place a more defined duty on decision-makers to ascertain the person's wishes, feelings, beliefs and values and then attribute 'particular weight' to them when determining the best interests decision at hand. Moreover, for certain decisions, the protection from

---

26   *Re M (Best Interests: Deprivation of Liberty)* [2013] EWHC 3456 (COP) [38].

27   *Local Authority X v MM & Anor (No. 1)* [2007]; *PB v RB and London Borough of Haringey* [2016] EWCOP 12.

28   UNCRPD art. 12 (4) requires safeguards to ensure respect for the rights, will and preference of disabled persons in matters pertaining to the exercise of legal capacity.

liability afforded to the decision-maker is proposed to be subject to a written record being in place, including, where applicable, a description of the person's wishes, feelings, beliefs and values ascertained and reasoning of why any departure from them is considered necessary. The intention, the Law Commission (2017) explains, is that 'the stronger and clearer the ascertainable wishes and feelings, the greater the weight that should be given to them' (para.14.17), and 'departing from such wishes and feelings should be permitted only where it is necessary and proportionate' (para.14.18).

Despite the Law Commission's call for 'pressing urgency', legislative change is likely to be a slow process. Nevertheless, prior to the proposed changes, legal commentators had already observed that court judgements have been moving in this direction, advising that the greater the departure from a person's expressed wishes and feelings, the greater the justification required (Ruck Keene and Auckland 2015). This would appear to be, until further development, a very prudent and pragmatic approach to take.

The views of other people

The decision-maker must take into account, if practicable and appropriate, the views of other people. This includes anyone named by the person engaged in caring for them or interested in their welfare.[29] This is a broad range of people and therefore should not be reduced to speaking with the one person who appears closest to the individual. Others may have known the person all or most of their life, often before the person lost mental capacity, and their insights are invaluable.

The decision-maker must avoid conflating the interests of others with the best interests of the person. Although there may be occasions when these are virtually inseparable, the focus should remain on the person and what is in *their* best interests. It is helpful to ask them about their family member or friend: What were/are *their* interests? What is/was important to *them*? What informed previous similar decisions *they* made? What would likely be the *person's* views, opinions or attitude on such matters? Having initially framed the discussion from this perspective, the decision-maker can move on to asking those being consulted about their personal views on the matter. This can be

---

29   S.4[7] of the MCA 2005.

an area of challenge in adult safeguarding, especially if the concern is associated with a person within the scope of those that should be consulted.[30] The dilemma should be tackled with great caution and is unavoidably case-specific; however, the status of adult safeguarding should not, in and of itself, be reason to exclude any close family member or friend. In some circumstances this may be appropriate, for example when it will place the person's welfare or wellbeing at significant risk, but in the majority of situations it should be more about the nature and degree of consultation rather than total exclusion. The decision-maker *may* also instruct an Independent Mental Capacity Advocate (IMCA) if the individual cannot consent to one or more of the proposed protection measures, and there is believed to be a benefit to the person. Furthermore, if the person has nobody to represent them or no one appropriate to consult – commonly referred to as being 'unbefriended' – an IMCA is vital.

It is very important that any Power of Attorney or Deputy[31] appointed by the court must be consulted, as they are the decision-maker for any health and welfare or property and affairs matters, depending upon the nature of the Lasting Power of Attorney (LPA) or Deputyship Order.[32]

CASE STUDY CONTINUED

The practitioner understood that a best interests decision was not simply a matter of selecting what Margaret, her family or the practitioner considered to be the best option or what would quickly remove all risks. It was understood that the focus should be on the fourth and fifth principles of the MCA (2005) and, in particular, the decision should be arrived at applying s.4 of the Act.

The practitioner explained the process to Margaret, and her daughter, emphasising that both their views and opinions would be vital in coming to the right decision, especially those

30   For examples see *Milton Keynes Council v RR and Ors* [2014] EWCOP B19; *G v E and Others* [2010] EWHC 621 (fam); and *Somerset v MK (Deprivation of Liberty: Best Interests Decisions: Conduct of a Local Authority)* [2014] EWCOP B25.

31   See Chapter 8 for more on LPA or www.gov.uk/government/organisations/office-of-the-public-guardian.

32   S.4 [7] of the MCA 2005.

of Margaret. Margaret did not appear anxious about this but reiterated her wish to remain at home. The practitioner explained that it is her role to find the right decision for Margaret as an individual, in her own unique situation.

The practitioner took the view that Margaret did not require an IMCA because her daughter was willing to be involved in the decision-making process and was appropriate to consult.

The decision was clearly defined from the outset, to choose between which, if any, protection measures identified as available should be put in place. These were the same options discussed with Margaret during the supported decision approach and capacity assessment.

Margaret seemed indifferent about suggestions such as prompts that could be stuck on the back of the door, and the telecare system, but was adamant that she did not like care homes. Regarding the option of a home assessment from the 'Bobby Van', Margaret appeared anxious about someone coming to her home.

Whilst discussing the options with Margaret the practitioner worked through the considerations listed in s.4 of the Act; holding in her mind that she must encourage Margaret's participation, the eventual decision must not be based upon discriminative assumptions, the decision should be delayed if there is a chance that Margaret might be able to make it herself at a later date, and not motivated by a desire to bring about her death.

Stage 3: 'Balance sheet' approach

The MCA 2005 Code of Practice advises that once the decision-maker has applied the above s.4 process they should 'weigh up all these factors in order to work out what is in the person's best interests' (DCA 2007, p.66). In response to this requirement the courts have continued to endorse the 'balance sheet' approach, first developed by Thorpe LJ.[33]

This approach starts with listing all options available, the same discussed with the person previously. It should include any options identified by the person themselves or others involved. If options

---

33   *Re A* [2000] 1 FLR 549.

are not available or ruled out, because of viability for example, it is vital that the rationale for this is clearly recorded. It is important to remember that making no decision at all may also be relevant.

The influencing factors, such as those identified through following s.4 of the Act, are then entered against each option, either as a benefit or disadvantage to the person, whilst considering their weight of importance each time.

In adult safeguarding situations this often means trying to identify the option that balances maximum reduction in the presenting concerns, be they aspects of neglect or abuse, with minimal negative impact upon the person and their private autonomous life. The decision-maker is aiming to identify the option with acceptable burdens or risks in order to secure some identified greater good for the individual. Options that might at first sight appear clearly unfavourable must also be considered and recorded, even if only to be later ruled out.

Munby articulated this elegantly, recommending 'sensible risk appraisal, not striving to avoid all risk, whatever the price, being willing to tolerate manageable or acceptable risks as the price appropriately to be paid [...] to achieve the vital good of the elderly or vulnerable person's happiness'.[34]

In some circumstances one or more features might have 'magnetic importance' capable of overriding all other considerations.[35] This is inevitably a professional 'value judgement',[36] but the reasoning that informed the weight of importance, for each factor, should be given. The *likelihood* of any risks or benefits occurring, as well as the relative *seriousness and/or importance* to the individual, is highly relevant in this regard (Ruck Keene *et al.* 2016b).

Stage 4: Least restrictive way of achieving the desired outcome

Regardless of any safeguarding concerns, a best interests decision is not an 'off-switch' for the rights and freedoms of the individual.[37] The decision-maker must ensure that, as far as possible, basic human

---

34   *Local Authority X v MM, KM* [2007] EWHC 2003 (Fam) [120].
35   *White v White* [1999] Fam 304; *Crossley v Crossley* [2007] EWCA Civ 1491; *Re M, ITW v Z, M and Others* [2009] EWHC 2525 (Fam)[32].
36   *Re P* [2009] EWHC 163 (Ch) (Lewison J) [39].
37   *Wye Valley NHS Trust v Mr B* [2015] EWCOP 60 [11].

rights and freedoms are upheld. This involves considering whether the purpose can be 'as effectively achieved in a way that is less restrictive of the individual's rights and freedom of action'.[38] Ultimately this includes considering whether there is genuine need to act or make a decision at all. Nevertheless, 'the final decision must always allow the original purpose of the decision or act to be achieved' (DCA 2007, p.27).

There are two further considerations that must be taken into account when a proposed option is intended to restrain[39] the person. The decision-maker must reasonably believe that the restraint is necessary to prevent harm to them, and the type of restraint used, and the amount of time, must be a proportionate response to the likelihood and seriousness of harm.[40]

Where a particular course of action or decision may engage a fundamental right or freedom, such as right to liberty (article 8, ECHR) or private and family life (article 5, ECHR), the decision-maker should seek legal advice. Depending upon the circumstances, authorisation may be required through the Court of Protection or the Deprivation of Liberty Safeguards. Either way, the decision-maker should keep a record of how they attempted to avoid this eventuality. Detailed record-keeping of the decision is particularly important where there is a dispute or the chosen option has significant disadvantages to the person. For example, distress to the person, loss of independence or difficulties in sustaining important relationships.

Stage 5: Make and record the decision

The decision-maker is required to make the decision that he or she 'reasonably believes' to be in the best interests of the person.[41] This is not about being 100 per cent sure, or that the chosen decision has absolutely no disadvantages, but the decision-maker has come to their decision on the balance of probabilities in a fair, objective and balanced way. It is good practice to set out a conclusion clearly stating why the decision was needed to be made, how the decision-maker permitted and encouraged the person to contribute, the eventual

---

38   MCA 2005 s.1.
39   MCA 2005 s.6[4] – 'uses, or threatens to use, force to secure the doing of an act which P resists, or restricts P's liberty of movement, whether or not P resists'.
40   MCA 2005 s.6[2–3].
41   MCA 2005 s.4 [9].

decision, the reasons for not selecting any lesser restrictive options, and, if applicable, any disagreements between those consulted.

The MCA 2005 Code of Practice provides guidance on resolving disputes, such as mediation, second opinions and complaints processes, but 'ultimately, if all other attempts to resolve the dispute have failed, the court might need to decide what is in the person's best interests' (DCA 2007, p.90).

Stage 6: Risk reduction and contingency planning

The reasons why any remaining risks or perceived disadvantages are thought to be outweighed by the perceived benefits must be explicitly recorded. This should lead to creating a detailed plan, with the person where possible, exploring what could be done to monitor, reduce or mitigate such risks or disadvantages further. This might include practical steps such as additional care or staff support, additional pieces of equipment, assistance to ensure that relationships can safely continue, and keeping the situation under close review. Where high risks remain, there again might be reason to seek legal advice.

CASE STUDY CONTINUED

To assist in this decision-making process, the practitioner constructed a balance sheet, entering all influencing factors against each option as either a negative or positive. The practitioner considered the weight of importance/influence for each point, recording her rationale in terms of the likelihood of the risk or benefits occurring as well as the relative seriousness and/or importance to Margaret.

The practitioner sought to take account of Margaret's own assessment of the quality of her life, her happiness and emotional welfare. Significant weight, and perhaps determinative in this case, was given to Margaret's expressed wishes to remain at home as well as her acceptance of certain protective measures aiming to make her home environment safer.

Having considered all the 'pros and cons', to avoid Margaret being admitted into a care home, the practitioner concluded that it was worth trialling the identified measures to improve Margaret's safety and security at home. Margaret even agreed for the 'Bobby Van' to visit as long as her daughter was present. Although it did not eliminate all the risks, it significantly reduced them, whilst being in line with Margaret's strong desire to remain at home. All agreed that this would be on balance the best option.

It was also agreed to be in Margaret's best interests to report the situation to the police but, because of the lack of firm evidence, they were not able to take the case further. They did, however, record the concerns for local intelligence.

The practitioner completed a safeguarding plan with Margaret, which took account of the remaining risks and how they would be monitored. Additional reviews were scheduled and the neighbours were also encouraged to report any further concerns directly to the police and the Local Authority's Adult Safeguarding Team.

Margaret and her daughter felt reassured after the telecare system was installed. Margaret was able to remain in her own home for a number of years until her health deteriorated, with no further instances of money or jewellery going missing.

References

Baker, D. (2017) *How to Achieve Best Practice in Supported Decision-Making?* Community Care, 27 February [Online]. Available at www.communitycare.co.uk/2017/02/27/achieve-best-practice-supported-decision-making, accessed on 27 February 2017.

Braye, S., and Preston-Shoot, M. (1995) *Empowering Practice in Social Care.* Buckingham: Open University Press.

Department for Constitutional Affairs (2007) *Mental Capacity Act 2005: Code of Practice.* London: DCA/The Stationery Office.

Essex Autonomy Project (2012) *Best Interests Decision-Making under the Mental Capacity Act.* Available at http://autonomy.essex.ac.uk/best-interests-decision-making-under-the-mental-capacity-act, accessed on 14 April 2017.

Essex Autonomy Project (2014) *Does the MCA 2005 Respect the Will and Preferences of Disabled Persons?* Available at http://autonomy.essex.ac.uk/is-the-MCA 2005-compliant-with-the-uncrpd-briefing-papers

House of Lords Select Committee (2014) *Mental Capacity Act 2005: Post-Legislative Scrutiny.* London: The Stationery Office. Available at www.publications.parliament.uk/pa/ld201314/ldselect/ldmentalcap/139/139.pdf, accessed on 14 April 2017.

Law Commission (2017) *Mental Capacity and Deprivation of Liberty.* London: Law Commission. Available at www.lawcom.gov.uk/project/mental-capacity-and-deprivation-of-liberty, accessed on 21 April 2017.

Nosowska, G., and Series, L. (2013) *Good Decision-Making: Practitioner's Handbook.* Dartington: Research in Practice for Adults.

Ruck Keene, A., and Auckland, C. (2015) 'More presumptions please? Wishes, feelings and best interests decision-making.' *Elder Law Journal*, 293–301.

Ruck Keene, A., Butler-Cole, V., Allen, N., Bicarregui, A. and Kohn, N. (2016a) *A Brief Guide to Carrying Out Capacity Assessments.* Thirty Nine Essex Street. Available at www.39essex.com/tag/mental-capacity-guidance-note, accessed on 14 April 2017.

Ruck Keene, A., Butler-Cole, V., Allen, N., Bicarregui, A. and Kohn, N. (2016b) *A Brief Guide to Carrying Out Best Interests Assessments.* Thirty Nine Essex Street. Available at www.39essex.com/tag/mental-capacity-guidance-notes, accessed on 14 April 2017.

Salzman, L. (2010) 'Rethinking guardianship (again): Substituted decision-making as a violation of Title II of the Americans with Disability Act.' *University of Colorado Law Review 81*, 157–245.

Chapter 8

Using the Law to Support Adult Safeguarding Interventions

Fiona Bateman

Throughout this book contributors have reinforced the importance of legal literacy for those involved in adult safeguarding. All practitioners, across all 'relevant partner' agencies, must understand the safeguarding duties that are set out in Part 1 of the Care Act (2014) (see Appendix), which is discussed later in this chapter. However, to be able to use the law effectively in interventions, practitioners must also understand the wider framework of legislative and common law[1] principles and duties, which underpin specific safeguarding duties. They must recognise which legal duties apply in different situations, including in care settings or domestic arrangements, and how these apply to private individuals, corporate bodies, employers/employees and volunteers within private, public and voluntary sector organisations.

The High Court and Court of Protection have been highly critical of practitioners, even those motivated to act because of safeguarding concerns, for failing to consider duties set out in the Mental Capacity Act (2005) [MCA], Care Act (2014) and the Human Rights Act (1998) [HRA].[2] Practitioners who understand the wider obligations within criminal, public and private law will be better able to carry out effective enquiries, correctly identify what can be done and by whom to enable people to keep themselves safe and, in line with Making Safeguarding Personal principles (see Chapter 1), successfully secure the outcomes that matter to adults who have suffered abuse and neglect.

---

1   Legal rules which have been established through judges' decisions in cases that set a precedent for future cases.
2   See, for example, District Judge Mort judgements in *Milton Keynes Council v RR, SS and TT* [2014] EWCOP B19 and [2014] EWCOP 34 or *LB Hillingdon v Neary* [2011] EWHC 1377.

Public law obligations

All practitioners carrying out public functions, including safeguarding responsibilities, must act in line with public law principles in all their activities so they can evidence, in court if necessary, that they have carried out their statutory duties properly. Schwehr (2014) summarises public law obligations as a requirement that practitioners:

- *Act lawfully.* Practitioners need to understand and apply the Care Act (2014) regarding adult safeguarding, and will also be expected to have correctly applied the obligations set out in the MCA (2005), Equality Act (2010) and HRA (1998). In addition, they must demonstrate that decision making is in line with their own professional standards, regulations, codes of practice, statutory guidance or policy which govern their practice. Non-compliance to statutory guidance may be permitted provided the practitioner can demonstrate, either on the facts of the case or by reference to a lawful policy, that there were cogent reasons for doing so.[3] Public bodies are also prohibited from applying blanket policies as practitioners must be free to exercise discretion and offer anything which is within their power, irrespective of a general policy, if the circumstances justify this.

- *Act reasonably.* Decisions which appear 'so absurd that no sensible person could ever dream that it lay within the powers of the authority'[4] are 'unreasonable' in the legal sense. This might appear a high threshold, but on a practical level public bodies often find they have crossed the line by not taking into account matters they are bound to consider or failing to ignore irrelevant matters.[5] Any dishonesty or act of bad faith will also render a decision, act or omission unreasonable. This principle requires practitioners to ask the right questions to the right people so they are able to gather sufficient information upon which to base a lawful decision, and requires that they approach their duties in a proportionate way.

---

3   *R(On the application of Munjaz) v Mersey Care National Health Service Trust* [2005] UKHL 58.

4   *Associated Provincial Picture Houses v Wednesbury Corporation* [1948] 1 KB 223, Lord Greene MR.

5   For example, in *R(SG) v Haringey London Borough Council* [2015] EWHC 2579.

- *Act fairly.* As well as ensuring that decisions are made without bias, it is also essential that individuals or groups affected by decisions are notified and given a proper opportunity to be heard as part of any decision-making process. Often there is an explicit duty within legislation that public bodies provide reasons for decisions, so it would be wise for practitioners to assume they will be required to provide an explanation and demonstrate that they have given opportunity to all relevant persons to comment before concluding their enquiries and deciding the outcome. They must also comply with any 'legitimate expectation', that is, a promise they have given someone or group of people if to do otherwise 'would be to act so unfairly as to perpetrate an abuse of power'.[6]

These fundamental principles of public law are golden threads running throughout the obligations within the Care Act (2014) and HRA (1998), including the six key principles of adult safeguarding, which champion accountability, transparency and proportionality in decision making.[7] In Cheshire West,[8] the Supreme Court unequivocally confirmed that the fundamental freedoms protected by the HRA are guaranteed to everyone. Any safeguarding inquiry could amount to an interference with these rights and can therefore only be justified if it is carried out in line with legal powers, is necessary in the circumstances, and is a proportionate response to achieve the policy objective – namely, promoting wellbeing. Local policies should provide practitioners with details of the relevant criminal, civil and statutory law relevant to adult safeguarding.

Practitioners must have the fundamental freedoms protected by the HRA (1998) at the forefront of their minds if these ideals are to positively influence practice, and because failure to comply can render decisions unlawful. People affected by failures of public bodies to meet their statutory duties are entitled to challenge this either through a complaint or Judicial Review proceedings. The courts will also impose liability on public bodies for damages suffered by individuals where they can show they have acted in breach of the HRA (1998)

---

6   *R(Bhatt Murphy) v Independent Assessor* [2008] EWCA Civ 755 Laws LJ.
7   *Care and Support Statutory Guidance*, para.14.13 (Department of Health [DH] 2016).
8   *P v Cheshire West and Chester Council* [2014] UKSC 19.

or another statutory duty of care and Parliament made provisions, explicitly or implied, for such claims.[9]

Duty of care

It isn't always easy to identify when a duty of care is owed or the extent of the duty, especially for all circumstances where safeguarding risks are identified, for example when working with adults with complex needs, fluctuating capacity or cared for by private bodies. An understanding of the underpinning legal principle and how this has been applied in legal cases will help practitioners identify when it would be 'fair, just and reasonable'[10] to impose a duty of care for the benefit of an adult at risk.

Put simply, we are all required to avoid any foreseeable harm to people we should anticipate might be affected by our actions. Courts will require anyone who has not fulfilled their duty of care to compensate those harmed by the failing. For instance, drivers owe a duty of care to all road users; negligent drivers must compensate other drivers or pedestrians harmed by their poor driving.

Generally judges will impose a duty if it is in the public interest, for example to provide for people who have been harmed by an act of bravery[11] or have care and support needs and would not otherwise have a legal remedy. However, courts consider the statutory framework which governs professional standards or responsibilities in order to determine if a duty of care is owed. Practitioners providing support care or treatment of adults must therefore understand and meet their statutory obligations to avoid a breach of the statutory or common law duty. They should also consider any separate duty of care they owe to their staff, volunteers and visitors[12] and how these duties should be managed to ensure they respond effectively to safeguarding allegations.

Practitioners who are regulated by professional bodies must comply with their respective professional conduct standards.[13] Since January 2016 the Health and Care Professionals Council have set out

9   *PI and others (minors) v Bedfordshire County Council* [1995] 2 AC 633.

10   *Caparo Industries PLC v Dickman* [1990] 2 AC 605 at 617–618.

11   *Dunnage v Randall and UK Insurance Limited* [2015] EWCA Civ 673.

12   More information is available at www.scie.org.uk/workforce/induction/standards/cis05_dutyofcare.asp.

13   More information is available at www.hcpc-uk.org/publications/standards/index.asp?id=38.

a duty for practitioners they regulate to take appropriate action to address and report concerns about the safety or wellbeing of people using services, follow up any concerns, and be open and honest if something has gone wrong. Similar duties are enshrined within the professional standards for those regulated by the General Medical Council[14] and the Nursing and Midwifery Council.[15]

Practitioners should also consider if any breach of the duty of care amounts to a crime and, if they believe it may, report this to the police for investigation. The Criminal Justice and Courts Act (2015) introduced two new offences of ill-treatment or wilful neglect committed by care workers (s.20) and care providers (s.21) providing health care to an adult or child or social care to an adult. These offences do not depend on the adult's mental health or capacity,[16] nor do they require that the ill-treatment or neglect resulted in death. S.1 of the Corporate Manslaughter and Corporate Homicide Act (2007) allows for the prosecution of senior managers of an organisation if the way in which they have managed the activities of the business amounts to a gross breach of a relevant duty of care owed by the organisation to a person and the breach is a substantial element in the cause of the person's death.

Duty to cooperate

Judges, when determining if damages could be claimed against public bodies, do not restrict themselves to the duties owed by the department in which the lead professional worked, but rather consider what duties and powers were owed by any relevant public body, given what was known or ought to have been known of the risks or needs in any particular case. It is therefore vital that practitioners inform themselves of the wider duties owed within the safeguarding context, including from other disciplines. Practitioners should never assume that another professional has a duty or power to act to prevent or stop abuse. Instead they must explore what powers might be available, whether there are any restrictions that apply in that case on using those powers, and challenge, when necessary, to secure cooperation from relevant partner agencies where there is a reasonable cause to suspect an adult is at risk.

---

14   See www.gmc-uk.org/guidance/ethical_guidance/27233.asp for more detail.

15   See www.nmc.org.uk/globalassets/sitedocuments/nmc-publications/nmc-code.pdf.

16   Criminal liability already exists for those who ill-treat and wilfully neglect a person with a mental disorder (s.127 MHA 1983) or an incapacitated person (s.44 MCA 2005).

CASE STUDY

In *X and Y v London Borough of Hounslow* [2009][17] the Court of Appeal was asked to consider whether a local authority owed a duty of care to protect X and Y from the criminal acts of others. Both adults have mild learning difficulties and were known to the local authority's Adult Social Care and Children and Family departments. When Y's allocated social worker became aware that youths had been using their flat for illicit activities, she reported to the police that they may be at risk of exploitation. She also set out her concerns to the authority's Housing and Children and Family departments, who made arrangements to carry out their relevant statutory functions. Before any action was taken, X, Y and their children were subjected to appalling sexual and physical assaults in their home by youths. Subsequently they brought a claim for negligence against the local authority, arguing that the harm was foreseeable and that the council should have taken action to protect them. X and Y conceded that Y's social worker had not been negligent, nor had there been a breach of the statutory duties owed by the council. The court, finding there was no common law duty of care in this instance, commended the social worker, despite the poor outcome of the case, as she had 'behaved impeccably throughout… She had full knowledge of the relevant facts. She appreciated and gave thought to the problems faced by the respondents at each stage and did her utmost to solve them'[18] in cooperation with her colleagues across the local authority.

This case emphasises the importance of local authorities' and their relevant partners' duties to cooperate generally (s.6 Care Act 2014) and in specific cases (s.7 Care Act 2014) when carrying out safeguarding inquiry functions and any consequent protective action. These obligations are corporate duties, meaning that, alongside responsibilities for frontline practitioners, those with managerial and governance roles within the local authority must satisfy themselves that operational systems are designed to facilitate cooperation between those carrying out duties relevant to care and support, housing, children services and

---

17   *X and Y v London Borough of Hounslow* [2009] EWCA Civ 286.
18   Ibid. at para.95.

public health functions and that staff are cooperating in fulfilling the safeguarding function. The duty to cooperate means that organisations are required to ensure they carry out their own respective functions, taking into account the duty to protect adults with needs for care and support who are experiencing, or are at risk of, abuse and neglect.[19] They may only refuse requests if they can demonstrate that it would be incompatible with its own duties or would otherwise have an adverse effect on the exercise of its functions and must give the local authority written reasons for their refusal. Simply not considering the duty or failing to make available suitable arrangements to carry out statutory functions could be a breach of statutory duty giving rise to a duty of care.

NHS bodies should, for example, set up systems to ensure that when exercising their duty of candour or investigating any serious incident[20] they also consider if there is a duty to report the incident for investigation under s.42 or s.44 of the Care Act (2014). These duties do not explicitly require a safeguarding inquiry or Safeguarding Adults Review to be undertaken in each case, nor will one be warranted in many cases; but failure to consider, as part of a complaints process or serious incident investigation, whether the facts of a particular case could require a safeguarding inquiry or review could breach the duty to cooperate under the Care Act (2014). It will inevitably impact on the Safeguarding Adults Board and local authority's ability to carry out their functions, because they cannot investigate that which they do not know about.

The Care Act (2014) statutory guidance advises the early involvement of police within any safeguarding inquiry where criminal activity is suspected and confirms that a criminal investigation by the police will take priority over all other inquiries. It also summarises the powers available to the police to gather evidence and support those victims and witnesses of crime with care and support needs.[21] Police and other criminal justice professionals (e.g. prison governors, those working with the National Probation Service or Community Rehabilitation Companies) owe offenders and the general public a duty of care. This could, in certain circumstances, include a duty to take

---

19   S.6(d) Care Act (2014).
20   See Serious Incident Framework guidance at www.england.nhs.uk/wp-content/ uploads/2015/04/serious-incidnt-framwrk-upd.pdf.
21   Care Act Guidance, at paras.14.83–14.92.

positive preventative steps to protect life (article 2, ECHR) where they have reasonable notice of risk.[22] It is therefore crucial that frontline police and offender management staff can confidently identify adults in need of care and support, recognise a risk of abuse and neglect and understand the powers they have to investigate and report concerns either through a local safeguarding process or alternative risk management processes. In addition, those in managerial or policy development roles need to design and monitor the effectiveness of processes and systems to ensure that risk is effectively identified and that responses accord to the expectations set out in Care Act (2014) guidance and local safeguarding policies.

Applying these principles and utilising the law in the safeguarding process

Practitioners responsible for determining what action to take on receipt of a report about safeguarding concerns must be motivated to act on a '*reasonable* cause to suspect'. The Care Act (2014) statutory guidance and Making Safeguarding Personal principles encourage preliminary enquiries to involve the person or their representative. Doing so will aid practitioners to explore risk within the person's context and may identify risks or concerns beyond that originally identified within the report. Practitioners reporting concerns are also expected to discuss their concerns with the person and seek their agreement to share information. They are permitted to refer concerns without consent where there is reasonable cause to suspect abuse or neglect, but it is not correct to assume it is the responsibility of the lead agency to obtain consent at a later stage.[23]

Practitioners must also actively consider if there is risk to the person by disclosing concerns to any alleged perpetrator. Public law principles require that practitioners act without bias and afford anyone affected by a decision (including one to undertake an inquiry) the opportunity to set out their case before the decision is made.[24] Failure could render the decision unlawful.[25] Where the practitioner believes contact with the person or alleged perpetrator may increase risk of

22 *Osman v United Kingdom* [1998] 29 EHRR 245.
23 For more information on information-sharing duties see www.scie.org.uk/care-act-2014/safeguarding-adults/sharing-information/what-does-the-law-say.asp.
24 See paras.14.112–14.132 of the *Care and Support Statutory Guidance* (DH 2016).
25 See *R(AB and CD) v London Borough of Haringey* [2013] EWHC 416.

harm, they must justify this on the facts of that case. They should set out why alternative actions would not enable them to alleviate risks associated with notifying the person or alleged perpetrator and ensure they have fully considered any duties they or others may owe the alleged perpetrator (e.g. under employment law). They must still take action if objectively reasonable to do so, but ensure that any intrusion on an individual's rights is proportionate.

Practitioners must take into consideration all representations made in the course of their enquiries but are entitled to use their professional judgement on the weight they place on information, provided they can demonstrate that that decision was fair and reasonable. Practitioners may encounter cases involving malicious or counter allegations and will therefore have to determine what they believed happened in order to decide any safeguarding plan. Practitioners must determine this on the balance of probability, meaning that if 'it is more likely than not that something did take place, then it is treated as having taken place'.[26] Practitioners must be careful to objectively examine evidence and look for corroborating information. It may not always be necessary to determine the truth of every allegation if there is sufficient evidence to justify lawful intervention. For example, in *London Borough of Ealing v KS & Ors* [2008],[27] the court ruled that the level of deceit and acrimony among family members was sufficient to enable the court to make a decision on whether an incapacitated adult should live with family members.

Practitioners should note that the Care Act (2014) 'eligibility criteria'[28] are not relevant in relation to safeguarding. Safeguarding inquiries should be made on the understanding of the risk of neglect or abuse, irrespective of whether the individual would meet the criteria for the provision of services.[29] Operational guidance on screening safeguarding concerns cannot advise filtering based on the setting where care is provided, the person's mental capacity or access to services, but rather requires practitioners to exercise professional judgement based on consideration of the wellbeing principle set out in s.1 fo the Care Act (2014).

---

26 *Re H (Minors)(Sexual Abuse: Standard of Proof)* [1996] AC 563.
27 *London Borough of Ealing v KS & Ors* [2008] EWHC 636.
28 Set out in s.13 of the Care Act and the Care and Support (Eligibility Criteria) Regulations 2014.
29 S.274 of the explanatory notes accompanying the Care Act and reiterated at para.14.6 of *Care and Support Statutory Guidance* (DH 2016).

Care Act (2014) statutory guidance emphasises 'making safeguarding personal' (see Chapter 1). Failure to adhere to person-centred practice without cogent reasons would leave the local authority open to criticism and court proceedings (Judicial Review) as having acted unlawfully. Similarly, not taking into account a person's mental capacity would be unreasonable in the legal sense and likely render the decision indefensible at Judicial Review. An understanding of the person's ability to make a decision or be involved in an assessment or safeguarding process is an essential component of those duties. It will determine if an advocate is required, and failure to consider that duty will undermine the legality of any subsequent decision.[30] The findings of a capacity assessment can also provide legal justification to intervene in safeguarding situations, if it is reasonable for those intervening to conclude the person lacks capacity and it is necessary to act in their best interest (see Chapter 7). But capacity is not the only factor which determines statutory bodies' duties to address persistent welfare concerns, particularly if those include a foreseeable safeguarding risk. Failure to consider other legal obligations, for example under the HRA (1998), or alternative legal remedies, for example inherent jurisdiction, could equally undermine the lawfulness of any decision.

Practitioners must consider each case on the specific facts and seek to work with people who present with persistent and/or high level of risk in respect of their wellbeing (including the risk of neglect or abuse) to explore options for intervention. This may require consulting the individual, their family, friends, carer, representative or advocate. Practitioners should only justify inaction if the evidence supports this or it is a disproportionate interference by public bodies. Even then, practitioners will need to record, with reference to the nature of the specific risks presenting, their reasons for considering they were not under a duty to act or why they have not exercised powers they (or any relevant partners) may have to safeguard the individual. This should reference relevant legislation such as s.11(2)(b) of the Care Act (2014), the Mental Health Act (1983), Children Act (1989) or Housing Act (1996) and should also address the obligations to take proactive steps to prevent discrimination or a breach of the fundamental freedoms protected by the HRA (1998) and Equality Act (2010).

This might seem like a heavy burden, but it is important to remember that, in the context of safeguarding concerns, the practitioner's role

---

30   R(SG) v Haringey London Borough Council [2015] EWHC 2579.

is to make sufficient enquiries to enable them to determine what, if anything, must be done, and by whom. The courts will expect any enquiry to be undertaken in line with Care Act (2014) guidance, and this includes ensuring relevant partners are involved.

Practitioners, including 'relevant partners', must be familiar with the different types and patterns of abuse and neglect and the circumstance in which they may take place. They should exercise inquisitive enquiry and critically review the case history so that any presenting safeguarding issue is understood in context. The Care Act (2014) guidance provides an 'illustrative guide' (DH 2016, paras.14.16–14.38) for practitioners, but as case law and learning from Safeguarding Adults Reviews develops so too will expectations for good, lawful practice. Therefore, findings from reviews and important judgements should form part of any practitioner's programme of continued professional development.

Any assessment of risk must take into account the person's capacity to protect themselves. This must focus on the specific issue and address within the assessment whether the individual 'can comprehend and weigh the salient details relevant to a decision to be made'.[31] Identifying 'salient details' in circumstances where safeguarding concerns might arise is not always straightforward.

CASE STUDY

In *London Borough of Southwark v KA & Ors* [2016][32] the Court of Protection was asked to make a declaration on whether KA, a young man with learning disabilities, had capacity to consent to sex and to marry. Proceedings were issued due to concerns that his family might arrange a marriage in order to ensure he had someone to care for him in the future if his parents couldn't. The issue to be decided was whether KA could consent to marriage and any sexual relations within the marriage. The court acknowledged that there were criminal sanctions for those who make arrangements to marry in respect of someone who lacks mental capacity to consent.[33] It accepted that state

---

31   Macur J (as she then was) in *LBL v RYJ* [2010] EWHC 2664 as quoted by Mr Justice Baker in *A Primary Care Trust v LDV and others* [2013] EWHC 272, at para.31.

32   *London Borough of Southwark v KA & Ors* [2016] EWCOP 20.

33   See www.gov.uk/guidance/forced-marriage for more information on forced marriage protection orders.

interference in such arrangements 'may be an unnecessary intrusion where capacity is not disproved' but recognised that the local authority had a legitimate interest to act to prevent a 'marriage performed with people who do lack capacity' because this 'amounts to a gross intrusion of their personal autonomy and may lead to serious sexual offences being committed'.[34] As part of the proceedings a report was commissioned from an eminent consultant psychologist and behavioural analyst who met with KA on five occasions and interviewed family members as part of her assessment. Rejecting the consultant's findings regarding KA's capacity on the basis that she had applied too high a standard, Mrs Justice Parker confirmed that capacity was a legal and not a medical judgement. She advised that it was vital for those assessing capacity to 'draw a clear distinction between: i) capacity, and ii) welfare'.[35]

Practitioners must know and apply the correct legal test that addresses the 'salient details' on the issue of capacity. As these may change with new case law, it is imperative that practitioners remain up to date with legal developments in this field. Where there is uncertainty about an adult's capacity, including where this might reduce their ability to protect themselves or leave them vulnerable to exploitation, neglect and abuse, the Court of Protection has jurisdiction to make a declaration. The court has made it clear that they expect public bodies to refer matters to court before taking action. Failure to do so may have significant consequences for the adult and their family and liability for compensation, legal costs and reputational damage for the professionals and public bodies involved. For example, in *LB Hillingdon v Steven Neary*,[36] the High Court ruled that failure by the local authority to appoint an Independent Mental Capacity Advocate, immediately refer to the court and conduct an effective review of best interests was a breach by the local authority of articles 5 and 8 of the HRA (1998).

---

34 *London Borough of Southwark v KA & Ors* [2016] EWHC 66, para.13, but see also Peter Jackson J in *Heart of England NHS Foundation Trust v JB* [2014] EWHC 342 (COP) at [7].

35 Ibid. at para.39.

36 *LB Hillingdon v Steven Neary* [2011] EWHC 1377.

If someone has been appointed as an 'agent' and has legal authority to make binding decisions on behalf of another (for example, under a Lasting Power of Attorney [LPA]), practitioners cannot ignore an agent's decision because they have a different view of the donor's best interests. Crucially, an agent, even one appointed under a welfare LPA, cannot override the capacitated decision of the person on decisions related to their welfare. Agents acting in relation to property and financial affairs could be acting under an Enduring Power of Attorney (EPA), LPA or as a Deputy (appointed by the Court of Protection). If the donor lacks mental capacity in respect of a welfare, property or financial decision, the document conferring the power must be registered with the Office of the Public Guardian (OPG). If it isn't registered it will not be valid. The document is a public record, so practitioners can verify the scope of any such power by requesting copies directly from the OPG[37] before relying on the agent's decision, particularly where there are safeguarding concerns.

Where practitioners have concerns that an agent is not acting in line with the best interests of the person, consideration should be given to whether the donor would, if aware of the concerns, have capacity to revoke the power. The decision to revoke a power can only be made by the person who granted it or, if they have lost capacity on that issue, the Court of Protection. Practitioners should also notify the OPG, who can direct a Court of Protection visitor to examine social care and health records, interview the person and report (under s.58 of the MCA 2005). Both the OPG and local authority can apply to the Court of Protection for revocation of the agent's powers. Whilst the court has powers to make interim orders and directions (under s.48 of the MCA 2005) or a declaration (s.15 MCA 2005) to authorise alternative care or treatment proposed, there is no automatic protection for liability for practitioners who act without such authorisation.

Practitioners will also need to consider whether the person's autonomy may be compromised, for example if they are subject to harassment, coercive control or acting under duress or subject to undue influence. Practitioners should know that causing (or causing someone

---

37   More information is available at www.gov.uk/government/organisations/office-of-the-public-guardian.

to fear) bodily harm,[38] acting in a way designed to intimidate or harass,[39] and repeated or continuous controlling or coercive behaviours that have a serious effect on the victim are criminal offences.[40] Statutory guidance for the police assists them to identify and investigate any allegation of this nature. Practitioners involved in adult safeguarding should be aware of patterns of behaviours that might indicate that such abuse is prevalent and be inquisitive as victims may not recognise they are subject to abuse. This is particularly relevant to domestic abuse, human trafficking, honour-based violence or financial abuse (although it could be a feature in any type of abuse).

Those who have suffered duress, undue influence or intimidation may be prevented from seeking private law remedies to protect themselves. Whilst the Court of Protection doesn't have jurisdiction to make orders in respect of capacitated adults, the High Court has an 'inherent jurisdiction' to intervene if necessary and proportionate on the facts of the case to protect the autonomy of adults at risk of abuse or neglect who, for reasons other than those covered by the MCA, are unable to protect themselves.[41]

S.79 of the Care Act (2014) permits local authorities to authorise a person to carry out certain social care functions on its behalf; however, it is important to note that s.79(2) expressly prohibits the delegation of certain functions, including the duty to cooperate and adult safeguarding functions. It also confirms that, where a function has been delegated, the local authority remains liable (and subject to Judicial Review) for anything done or omitted to be done by the person with delegated responsibility.[42] As such it should be understood that even where the local authority is not acting as lead investigator it must ensure (in line with its responsibility as the body responsible for determining if action is required[43]) that the public law principles to act lawfully, reasonably and fairly inform safeguarding practice.

---

38   The Offences Against the Person Act 1861 provides for criminal sanctions for acts causing or tending to cause danger to life or bodily harm.
39   The Protection from Harassment Act 1997 (as amended by the Protection of Freedoms Act 2012) provides for civil and criminal sanctions for behaviours such as harassment (s.2 and s.3), stalking (s.2A) and putting people in fear of violence (s.4).
40   S.76 of the Serious Crime Act 2015, statutory guidance on the offence, is available at www.gov.uk/government/uploads/system/uploads/attachment_data/file/482528/ Controlling_or_coercive_behaviour_-_statutory_guidance.pdf.
41   DL v A Local Authority [2012] EWCA Civ 253.
42   S.79(6) Care Act 2014.
43   S.42(2) Care Act 2014.

Where a safeguarding plan is required, professionals must consider whether they have legal authority to enact that plan. If the plan meets the statutory bodies' duty of care and the person has consented, this will usually be sufficient. If the person or their 'agent' is not able to provide lawful consent, or there is uncertainty regarding capacity or disagreement over what might be in the person's best interests, practitioners should refer the case to the Court of Protection. Practitioners must also obtain legal authority from the court for certain types of medical interventions.[44] It is then the responsibility of judges to determine on the evidence whether the proposed intervention can be lawfully authorised.

Practitioners should also be aware of civil law remedies which are available to adults who have suffered harm or been exploited. Adults who have been compelled by way of duress or undue influence to enter into an agreement may apply to court to request that any contract is void. Where allegations of duress are made, the person making the complaint needs to show, on the balance of probabilities, they were compelled to enter into a contract due to pressure or coercion. This will have obvious practical applications for adults who have suffered financial exploitation, but may also be applicable for adults who under duress entered into joint tenancies or loan agreements.

Practitioners should also consider civil remedies in situations where someone has influence over another and exploits their influence to direct the conduct of the other in a manner that effectively impairs their ability to express their free will. A power imbalance exists where there is 'trust and confidence, reliance, dependence or vulnerability on the one hand and ascendancy, domination or control on the other'.[45] This can include where an obligation of candour and protection has been exploited. Where such relationships exist, it is not always necessary to show there were specific, deliberate acts of persuasion. If, for example, one person places trust in another to look after his interests and the other betrays this trust to suit his own interests, the courts are likely to find undue influence and can release the exploited party from any obligations owed or set aside any transaction.

---

44   See Chapter 8 of the MCA Code of Practice and within the Reference Guide to Consent for Examination or Treatment, Department of Health, March 2001 (www. dh.gov.uk/PublicationsAndStatistics/Publications/PublicationsPolicyAndGuidance/ PublicationsPolicyAndGuidanceArticle/fs/en?CONTENT_ID=4006757&chk =snmdw8).

45   Lord Bingham of Cornhill in *Royal Bank of Scotland v Etridge* [2001] UKHL 44, para.11.

Where an adult lacks capacity to initiate proceedings, practitioners should consider whether there is a suitable person that could act as a litigation friend[46] or refer the matter to the Official Solicitor to assist them to seek redress.[47]

Conclusion

The prominence given within the Care Act (2014) to wider safeguarding duties and confirmation that these are owed by local authorities and relevant partners, as well as the civil and criminal sanctions which apply for those who fail to safeguard adults at risk, underlines the importance given to this public function. Intervening to support adults at risk requires practitioners to demonstrate adherence to the public law principles within their decision making and give careful thought to the statutory duties they and partners owe in the specific circumstance of each case. Practitioners must comply with the Care Act (2014) guidance and relevant professional conduct rules, including to continued professional development, as these reflect the wider legal principles set out within this chapter. Practitioners must also engage with the adult and their wider social network to achieve sustainable outcomes which matter to them. They must recognise when they may need to seek further guidance from their manager or legal experts, be clear about the limitations of their statutory powers and be confident to refer to the court whenever necessary.

References

Care Act 2014 and Care Act Explanatory Notes. Norwich: The Stationery Office. Subject to Crown Copyrights but available under the Open Government Licence v3.0 at www.legislation.gov.uk/ukpga/2014/23/contents, accessed on 19 April 2017.

Department of Health (2016) *Care and Support Statutory Guidance.* London: DH.

Health and Care Professions Council (2016) *Standards of Conduct, Performance and Ethics.* Publication code 20120801POLPUB/SCPE.

Schwehr, B. (2014) *Care and Health Law 'Defensible Decision-Making and Management of Legal Risk' Training Materials.* Available at www.schwehroncare.co.uk, accessed on 19 April 2017.

Transcripts of the judgements referred to within this chapter are available at www.bailii.org or www.hrcr.org.

---

46   See www.gov.uk/litigation-friend/suitability for more information.

47   For more information on the role of the Official Solicitor see www.gov.uk/government/organisations/official-solicitor-and-public-trustee/about.

Chapter 9

Managing Difficult Encounters with Family Members

Jill Manthorpe, Rebecca Johnston, Stephen Martineau, Martin Stevens and Caroline Norrie

Introduction

Family members are often the first to realise something is going wrong in the life of a relative and often the first to do something about it. Whether they are carers or 'just a relative', many feel that they are responsible for their kin. They are the source of many complaints and contacts with formal authorities. That said, there are some relatives who are very hard to engage, and this chapter considers practice and policy when this happens. Like many rare events, such situations can take up considerable professional time, and experience in managing difficult situations is often sparse.

The chapter draws on some of our current research on what helps and hinders engagement with adults at risk in the English context but is likely to have relevance to other jurisdictions too. It also draws on our ongoing analyses of Safeguarding Adults Reviews, formerly Adult Serious Case Reviews (SCRs), since these documents provide substantial detail about cases. Most of these, of course, focus on difficulties and when things went wrong, so their illustrative purpose should be seen in this context.

A brief chapter cannot convey all of the many complexities of trying to work with family members when this presents difficulties. Importantly, this chapter does not cover situations where family members find it difficult to engage with professionals when raising safeguarding concerns or when trying to resolve problems. These perspectives need to be considered.

Child protection links

For practitioners in adult services there is much to consider from child protection work about engagement with families. While social workers do have powers of access to children, they still face problems with parents who are not happy with their intervention, to put it mildly. Ferguson (2016) recently noted in his observations of child protection social worker visits to families following concerns about the child's wellbeing that 'child protection professionals experience intense emotions, from their own experience of anxiety, fear, sadness, hope, despair and the feelings of rage, hate, love, gratitude and so on that are projected into them by service users' (p.5).

There is a growing amount of valuable literature and guidance for professionals working in child protection who encounter parents that they find hostile, aggressive, threatening or intimidating (see for example Kindred 2011). These include guidance on working with uncooperative families in Scotland (NESCPC 2008) and Lincolnshire's *Working with Uncooperative and Hostile Families Practice Guidance* in the English context (Lincolnshire Safeguarding Children Board n.d.). The latter provides helpful information on the dynamics of relationships in the following areas:

- Recognition and Understanding

- Impact on Assessment

- Impact on Multi-Agency Work

- Response to Uncooperative Families

- Dealing with Hostility and Violence

- Keeping Professionals Safe

- Management Responsibility

- Supervision and Support.

While this guidance mentions the use of legal authority, its content also highlights the emotional impact of such situations and how individual professionals should be alert to them. Rather than seeing this engagement as a task for the individual practitioner to shoulder, the authors stress that practitioners need good supervision, management backing and understanding, and should be able to rely on other agencies' actions. While practitioners may fear confrontation and hostility, guidance also identifies reactions which may be harder to deal with or to see in perspective. For example, professionals may give the 'benefit of the doubt' or adopt an over-optimistic stance when they encounter reactions that might seem ambivalent. Suffolk Safeguarding Children Board (2014, p.4) states that this is encountered frequently:

> Ambivalence can be seen when people are always late for appointments, or repeatedly make excuses for missing them; when they change the conversation away from uncomfortable topics and when they use dismissive body language. Ambivalence is the most common reaction and may not amount to uncooperativeness. All service users are ambivalent at some stage in the helping process. It may reflect cultural differences, being unclear what is expected, or poor experiences of previous involvement with professionals. Ambivalence may need to be acknowledged, but it can be worked through.

In a report entitled *Ten Pitfalls and How to Avoid Them* (Broadhurst *et al.* 2010, p.28), the following self-reflective questions are posed about making a home visit if a practitioner feels concerned about their safety:

- 'Do I feel safe approaching this household?

- Do I feel safe inside this household?

- If not, why not? Exactly what in the family's behaviour and in my response made me feel unsafe?

- How do the children and young people in this household appear to cope with hostility/aggression?

- Am I able to voice my concerns and ask for support, both from colleagues and my manager?

- How do I operate when I feel challenged or threatened? What is my coping strategy? How does this affect the families I work with? Am I aggressive, collusive, accommodating, hyper alert? Do I filter out or minimise negative information?

- If I, or another professional, should go back to the household to ensure the child(ren)'s safety, what support should I ask for?

- Does my manager know I am afraid and anxious?'

To the best of our knowledge there are no similar practice guides for people working in adult safeguarding situations available from Safeguarding Adults Boards; this suggests the value of considering whether working with reluctant families is addressed sufficiently in adult social care training and in continuing professional development.

Hindering and helping

Our current research is investigating what helps and hinders when trying to access an adult about whom there are concerns that they may be at risk of abuse, most commonly as a result of an adult safeguarding concern (see the Acknowledgement at the end of this chapter). An important background to these questions is the suggestion that professionals are sometimes thwarted in gaining access to adults at possible risk of harm and in talking to them without apparent interference by other people, generally family members or carers. In England these arguments have been presented over the years in support of a power of entry to private households where permission is denied, similar to that in respect of children. Such legal authority was argued to be necessary by some of those responding to the Consultation on the review of *No Secrets* (see Norrie *et al.* 2016) and articulated by some parliamentarians in the debates on the Care Act (2014) (see Manthorpe *et al.* 2016). More recently the arguments have been revived by the campaigning organisation Action on Elder Abuse (2016) in its call for a power to access and speak to a potential victim of elder abuse in the following circumstances:

> Where there is reasonable suspicion that an older person is being subjected to elder abuse, and a Third Party denies access to see and speak to that older person, a police officer should be enabled to obtain a court order granting access. Where it is established that the Third Party was wilfully denying access they should be considered guilty of wrongful isolation. (Action on Elder Abuse 2016, p.47)

It should be noted that this proposed legislation is designed to apply in circumstances where there is no suggestion that the adult at risk is lacking decision-making capacity; powers exist in England and Wales in respect of gaining access to adults who have mental health (under the Mental Health Act 1983) or mental capacity (under the Mental Capacity Act 2005) related impairments. There are also specific powers applicable to individuals living in long-term care facilities such as care homes.

However, in England there is concern among some quarters that the state already is in possession of too many powers to invade the privacy of someone's home and acts over-zealously in executing these powers (Big Brother Watch 2015). Overall there are different views on whether an enhanced power of entry should be introduced for social workers or others, acting in conjunction with the police and as authorised by the courts, in cases where individuals seem to be hindering safeguarding inquiries in relation to community-dwelling adults at risk in England. The arguments raised in the Care Act (2014) debates about this subject prompted the government to commission a practitioner guide to the law in relation to adult safeguarding (see SCIE 2014) to clarify options available when safeguarding inquiries appear to be thwarted (see Appendix).

Experiences from Scotland

In contrast to England, Scotland has introduced powers to authorise access to those with care and support needs (with capacity) under the Adult Support and Protection (Scotland) Act 2007 (ASPA), following support being expressed in earlier consultations (Atkinson, Berzins and Garner 2002; Scottish Executive 2001). In the run-up to this legislation, references were made to key incidents or cases which had raised the public profile of adult abuse (e.g. Campbell, Hogg and Penhale 2012; Fennell 2011; Stewart 2012). In a study that incorporated face-to-face interviews with key stakeholders, Stewart (2012) detected a general consensus that such action was needed and desired to protect a group of people hitherto left unprotected. Scottish experience shows that the vexed question of how to strike the balance between 'autonomy and protection' (Preston-Shoot and Cornish 2014, p.6) still remains. On the one hand, one of the main drivers in support of change was professionals' feelings of 'helplessness and frustration' (Stewart 2012, p.37) at not being able to provide effective support or help to those with care and support needs, but on the other she observed 'an underlying perception that if existing legislation had been used appropriately then additional legislation would not have been required' (p.37). Concerns about over-intervention by the state in family life and about breaches of privacy were significantly allayed, in her opinion, by actual case examples (ibid.).

The powers of entry and intervention in the ASPA introduced a set of orders, which include orders enabling the removal of an adult at risk for the purposes of assessment and orders to ban third parties from the premises. Efforts have been made to gather data about local authorities' use of these powers; however, Ekosgen (2013) found that over half of the 32 Scottish local authorities did not provide details of the numbers of referrals, investigations, case conferences and protection orders in their areas. Consequently, national figures were unknown. Nonetheless, responding local authorities reported being granted 137 protection orders, in a context of nearly 30,000 adult protection referrals over the same period (ibid.). An earlier survey of ASPA activity during 2008–10 (de Souza 2011; Keenan 2012) found that 148 protection orders had been sought in the first two years of the Act (numbers granted are unknown). Of these 148 protection orders, 133 were banning orders. De Souza (2011) commented that these low figures were apparently expected. Figures reported by the Scottish Government (2011) for the financial year 2010/11 revealed a preponderance of banning orders (40 out of 43 orders granted).

Preston-Shoot and Cornish (2014, p.14) concluded that the small amount of protection orders applied for and granted suggested that earlier fears about overly intrusive practice as a result of the ASPA were not being realised; the low number of orders, despite fears that the Act would be used intrusively and to compel people to do what agencies saw as in their best interests (Fennell 2011), was evidence that many situations had been resolved by contact, use of relationships and voluntary measures.

Controversially, s.35 ASPA allows for protection orders to override the refusal of consent of an adult who has capacity, with the authorisation of a Sheriff (who has a similar role to a circuit judge in English law), where the adult appears to have been unduly pressurised by someone to refuse consent. This is set out in the Code of Practice, first published in 2008, and revised in 2009 and 2014 (Scottish Government 2014). These provisions throw debates about balancing autonomy, protection and pressure from others into sharp focus.

This 'natural experiment' in Scotland is interesting in respect of the preponderance of banning orders – orders that possibly refer to situations where professionals have been unable to work with relatives or other people closely involved in the lives of those with care and support needs about whom there are great concerns. In light of the small numbers it is hard to make overall judgements about whether an application for a banning order is necessary. However, Mackay *et al.* (2011) provide some examples of the casework contexts showing the chronology of problems with engagement, the presence of addictions affecting behaviour and dependencies, and, in particular, reluctance (seemingly in possible contexts of undue influence) of those with care and support needs to take action. The following example illustrates this, although does not present the long-standing concerns about the case:

> In one situation the police were contacted by the mother after her son assaulted her, and although she was initially very frightened, she quite quickly began to oppose the idea of a banning order, though when it went to court with the encouragement of her daughter and solicitor, she did agree to it. There was also evidence of undue pressure being exerted by the son. (Mackay *et al.* 2011, p.111)

In a further anonymised example, used as a vignette to stimulate discussion in research interviews, the case presented outlines the possible coercion or intimidation of those with care and support needs:

> Mr Fitzpatrick was referred to the department by his youngest son (Alex) who lives in the USA. Alex is concerned that John (another relative) is financially exploiting his father and bullying him into giving him money. When the social worker goes to the house John is reluctant to let him meet with his father; however, the social worker persists and is able to interview Mr Fitzpatrick, although John remains in the room. Mr Fitzpatrick indicates that he supports his son and his wife, paying all the bills and supplying them with a regular income as they don't work and don't feel it's appropriate to claim benefit, as it would be demeaning to them. He says he is happy to do this but appears to the social worker to be fearful of his son, often glancing in his direction whilst talking to check he is saying the right thing. (Stewart 2015, p.253)

This chapter now turns to discuss examples of cases where there is more detail of the engagement with relatives that has been difficult from the perspectives of professionals and, in hindsight, by the authors of Adult Serious Case Reviews. (Under the Care Act 2014 these are newly termed Safeguarding Adults Reviews; see Manthorpe and Martineau 2016.) It highlights what can be learned from these accounts in a threefold framework derived from a typology of different experiences of engagement problems as set out in the Lincolnshire Guidance (n.d.): ambivalence and avoidance (we have conflated these as they appear to overlap); confrontation; and violence. As will be evident, these suggest some degree of escalation which may not always occur. However, this typology seems useful in its framing of different dynamics.

Ambivalence and avoidance

Two SCRs illustrate these aspects. In the first the brother (JB) of Adult A was variously described in the SCR as capable and well presented, but his 'deceptive' behaviour contributed to Adult A becoming invisible to many professionals and the local community. It comments:

> We now know that Adult A's brother JB has been found criminally responsible for her death by gross negligence. In addition to neglecting her failing health and the condition in which she lived, he also effectively obstructed agencies, particularly North Tyneside Homes, in what may have been positive interventions that changed events and alerted services to Adult A's condition. (Wood 2011, p.22)

Interestingly the SCR does not blame adult services for any neglect or omission; Adult A was unknown to them. Her brother was deemed to have a duty of care for her; and was the person who could have helped her in her isolating life of squalor, cold and presumable pain from her pressure ulcers.

Second, in an earlier and different set of circumstances, a mother appeared to have reassured professionals that there was no real cause for concern about her son (X):

> X ceased attending one of his day care placements and reduced attendance at a second. In addition, staff were concerned at his apparent weight loss; one contacted X's mother. Three weeks after X stopped attending either placement, staff reported their concerns to the Learning Disability Team. No action was taken by the Team for a few weeks; then phone calls were made to X's mother – his main carer. She reassured the worker that X would be taking up his place again. In the event X did not. Several weeks later the same worker

visited X's home but again was unable to see X. In a further visit the worker spoke to X's mother. Subsequent efforts were made to establish X's condition and whereabouts. A few weeks later X's body was discovered in the back garden of the family home. He had been dead for some time. This followed the discovery of the body of X's mother elsewhere. (Summarised extract from Tennant 2008)

Here professionals were criticised for not following up what was happening and appearing to be reassured by X's mother, to the extent that they failed to see X and to make connections between different service contacts. X's mother appeared unchallenged with no attempt to arrange further investigation; similarly there was no exploration of her possible needs. Sadly in this case it is not clear what happened, so the potential to learn lessons, the key purpose of SCRs and their successors, is somewhat limited.

Confrontation

Laird (2014) recently researched the prevalence of aggression among parents or their partners experienced by child protection social workers. She concluded that qualifying training for social workers was not sufficient for practitioners to manage these situations. She also analysed a set of children's Serious Case Reviews in which the aggression of parents or their partners appeared to contribute to failures to protect their child from harm. While few Adult SCRs note the presence of confrontation, one provides an account of a situation where the refusal of services – at some times – by an adult with care and support needs was overshadowed by parental control of the situation:

Refusal of services and interventions was usually by the subject herself and there is widespread agreement that she had insight into her condition and also had capacity. However, on numerous other occasions it was her mother who refused the contact and this should have been challenged more assertively. Whilst the subject was in control of her condition, i.e. 'she has good insight into her difficulties'…to a considerable extent it was her mother who was in control of the interventions… Now, the very extreme circumstances and particularly the threats and intimidation made by her mother (to professional staff and to the subject herself) would be deemed a safeguarding issue and would also be addressed under domestic abuse procedures. (Tudor 2011, pp.6–7)

Here professionals are seen to be insufficiently assertive in the face of a seemingly assertive parent. This SCR appears optimistic that new safeguarding processes might limit the possibility of such a situation recurring. In contrast, the SCR (Wood 2014, p.17) following the case of Adult D (for which his son Adult E was convicted of wilful neglect) observed the potential complexities of families' recourse to legal and other proceedings:

> Whatever his motivation Adult E went to extraordinary lengths to prevent access to Adult D. In doing so Adult E mounted a classic campaign of resistance based on – delay, deny and defend. His resistance included making multiple formal complaints and eventually instigating complex and expensive litigation all of which slowed and distracted service response. The successful obstruction by Adult E did, however, present real problems for it delayed the assessment of Adult D's capacity and any potential implementation of Court of Protection proceedings under the Mental Capacity Act. In addition the disruptive presence of Adult E and an increasing number of friends/legal representation at Safeguarding Adults meetings together with the deluge of formal complaints and litigation served to slow and divert services from their prime purpose, placing them on the defensive and forcing them to give time and resource to address Adult E's incessant demands.

Newcastle Safeguarding Adults Board's (2016) statement following the publication of this SCR (White 2016) recognised that obstruction as undertaken by Adult E was rare and that the case of Adult D was 'extreme'. Questions remain about the interface in practice and working procedures of adult safeguarding and the 'grey' areas of the Mental Capacity Act 2005.

Violence

SCRs seem reticent sometimes about describing the exact nature of intimidation that professionals have encountered in addition to the type that Wood (2014) (see above) described as a 'classic campaign of resistance'. This makes it hard to conclude what type of training and support might be effective if violence is threatened or experienced. An example of the former is what is termed 'manipulation and intimidation' in the earlier SCR of another person referred to as Mr D – no doubt the professionals concerned could have given very graphic accounts of what they experienced, but SCRs are not usually so detailed:

> Manipulation and intimidation on the part of the family was not dealt with appropriately by staff who feared D would be removed from day services if they confronted the family. Despite an accumulation of concerns, and a history of deprivation and neglect, the adult protection alert was raised only months before D's death. It is expected that the implementation of the Mental Capacity Act (2005) and the role of an independent mental capacity advocate will assist in addressing such serious adult protection concerns in future. (Kent and Medway Adult Safeguarding Board 2003)

Making safeguarding relationships personal

The emphasis on Making Safeguarding Personal (MSP) as a framework for practice has been a powerful lever for change, focusing on what the adult at risk wants to happen and negotiating with them about the desired outcomes (Lawson, Lewis and Williams 2014, p.7). While there have been MSP efforts to engage with family members to improve outcomes through conflict resolution, most of these reported seem to have included family members prepared to attend mediation or family group conferences (SCIE 2012a). Care is needed about the potential for power imbalances to be under-recognised; and practice in domestic violence work suggests that a history of physical violence may render these approaches unsuitable (SCIE 2012b). For families where there are problems in engagement, early discussions are needed with a proposed facilitator or mediator about initial approaches and possible alternatives (ibid.). The SCR following the death of Adult D (Wood 2014), mentioned above, in which a campaign of non-cooperation, complaints, disruption of safeguarding meetings and legal action was carried out by his son (Adult E), observed: 'The case of Adult D demonstrates the vulnerability of Safeguarding Adults Procedures to vexatious complaint and obstruction particularly from family members of subjects (7.4.4). It is recommended that Newcastle Safeguarding Adults Board establish guidelines to cater for vexatious complaints and the role of vexatious family members within Safeguarding Adults Strategy Meetings' (Newcastle Safeguarding Adults Board 2016, p.20).

While MSP accounts helpfully provide rich pictures of current adult safeguarding practice where family members are positively engaged, we need to be alert to possible instances of wilful neglect and family abuse. In the evaluation of MSP activity in the London Borough of Enfield, for example, Brown *et al.* (2015) present four case studies of safeguarding practice where some family members were sexually abusive, removing an adult lacking decision-making capacity to another country for marriage, and exploiting and coercing a relative.

Conclusions

Wosu and Stewart (2010) cite Munro (2008) as saying that service users (families in child protection inquiries) are at risk of being seen 'as either [...] submissively docile or [...] obstreperous and refusing to engage. In the latter case these are then labelled a nuisance or resistant. They are never seen as intelligent rational people who happen to disagree with you.' In adult safeguarding there have been few opportunities to debate the relevance of children's safeguarding understandings of involuntary clients and notions of cooperation, hostility and resistance. Debate seems to have become focused on legal rather than relationship-based engagement, possibly because the rights of those with care and support needs to protection and justice are becoming more prominent, but in England there are fewer legal powers to intervene, compared with child protection. This seems to leave practitioners, particularly in England, in the position of having to work on engagement with families on a case-by-case basis, making use of skills from other aspects of their work but without a framework that acknowledges that some situations will be risky, provoke anxiety and be confrontational.

Acknowledgement and disclaimer

This chapter draws on background material for the study *Helping or Hindering in Adult Safeguarding: An Investigation of Practice* (www. kcl.ac.uk/sspp/policy-institute/scwru/res/capacity/helping-or-hindering.aspx). This study is funded by the Department of Health's

Policy Research Programme. The views expressed in the chapter are those of the authors alone and should not necessarily be interpreted as those of the Department of Health.

References

Action on Elder Abuse (2016) *Elder Abuse is a Crime – Now Let's Make it One.* London: Action on Elder Abuse.

Atkinson, J., Berzins, K., and Garner, H. (2002) *Consultation on Vulnerable Adults: Analysis of the Responses.* Edinburgh: The Scottish Office Central Research Unit.

Big Brother Watch (2015) *Entry Allowed? The Number of Local Authority Staff with the Power to Enter Your Home or Workplace. A Big Brother Watch Report.* London: Big Brother Watch. Available at www.bigbrotherwatch.org.uk/2015/01/report-entry-allowed-number-local-authority-staff-power-enter-home-workplace, accessed on 19 April 2017.

Broadhurst, K., White, S., Fish, S., Munro, E., Fletcher, K., and Lincoln, H. (2010) *Ten Pitfalls and How to Avoid Them: What Research Tells Us.* London: NSPCC. Available at www.nspcc.org.uk/globalassets/documents/research-reports/10-pitfalls-initial-assessments-report.pdf, accessed on 19 April 2017.

Brown, K., Barrett, G., Fenge, L.A., and Wincewicz, S. (2015) *Making Safeguarding Personal Evaluation: London Borough of Enfield.* Bournemouth: University of Bournemouth. Available at http://eprints.bournemouth.ac.uk/22715/1/LBE%20Evaluation%20.pdf, accessed on 19 April 2017.

Campbell, M., Hogg, J., and Penhale, B. (2012) 'Safeguarding adults at risk of harm in Scotland: Legislation, policy and practice [editorial].' *Journal of Adult Protection 14,* 4, 159–162.

de Souza, V. (2011) 'The Adult Support and Protection Act (Scotland) 2007 – Initial impact and emerging themes [part 2].' *Action Points (Action on Elder Abuse) 44 (Second Quarter),* 17–24.

Ekosgen (2013) *Adult Support and Protection in Scotland: A Detailed Review of the 2010–2012 Biennial Reports.* Glasgow: Ekosgen.

Fennell, K. (2011) 'Adult Protection: The Scottish Legislative Framework.' In T. Scragg and A. Mantell (eds) *Safeguarding Adults in Social Work* (2nd edition). Exeter: Learning Matters.

Ferguson, H. (2016) 'How children become invisible in child protection work: Findings from research into day-to-day social work practice.' *British Journal of Social Work 0,* 1–17. Available at http://bjsw.oxfordjournals.org/content/early/2016/06/29/bjsw.bcw065.abstract, accessed on 19 April 2017.

Keenan, T. (2012) *'Crossing the Acts': The Support and Protection of Adults with Mental Disorder Across the Legislative Frameworks in Scotland.* Birmingham: BASW/Venture Press.

Kent and Medway APC (2003) *Executive Summary: Serious Case Review, Case D.* Available at www.kent.gov.uk/__data/assets/pdf_file/0016/8161/Serious-case-review-D-2003.pdf, accessed on 19 April 2017.

Kindred, M. (2011) *A Practical Guide to Working with Reluctant Clients in Health and Social Care.* London: Jessica Kingsley Publishers.

Laird, S.E. (2014) 'Training social workers to effectively manage aggressive parental behaviour in child protection in Australia, the United States and the United Kingdom.' *British Journal of Social Work 44,* 7, 1967–1983.

Lawson, J., Lewis, S., and Williams, C. (2014) *Making Safeguarding Personal 2014*. London: Local Government Association. Available at https://www.local.gov.uk/topics/social-care-health-and-integration/adult-social-care/making-safeguarding-personal.

Lincolnshire Safeguarding Children Board (n.d.) *5.17 Working with Uncooperative and Hostile Families Practice Guidance*. Available at http://lincolnshirescb.proceduresonline. com/chapters/g_work_uncoop_fams.html, accessed on 19 April 2017.

Mackay, K., McLaughlan, C., Rossi, S., McNicholl, J., Notman, M., and Fraser, D. (2011) *Exploring how Practitioners Support and Protect Adults at Risk of Harm in the Light of the Adult Support and Protection (Scotland) Act 2007*. Stirling: University of Stirling. Available at www.pkc.gov.uk/media/998/ASP-Research-Report/pdf/ASP_Research_Report, accessed on 19 April 2017.

Manthorpe, J., and Martineau, S. (2016) 'Engaging with the new system of Safeguarding Adults Reviews concerning care homes for older people.' *British Journal of Social Work* bcw102.

Manthorpe, J., Martineau, S., Norrie, C., and Stevens, M. (2016) 'Parliamentary arguments on powers of access – the Care Bill debates.' *The Journal of Adult Protection 18*, 6, 318–328.

Munro, E. (2008) Keynote Speech, Signs of Safety Gathering, Gateshead (www.signsofsafety.net).

NESCPC (North East Scotland Child Protection Committee) (2008) *Inter-Agency Guidance for Working with Uncooperative Families*. Aberdeen: NESCPC.

Newcastle Safeguarding Adults Board (2016) *Statement by Newcastle Safeguarding Adults Board, 10.03.2016, Serious Case Review Concerning the Death of Edward Hedley*. Available at www.newcastle.com/sites/default/files/wwwfileroot/social-care-and-health/safeguarding-and-abuse/safeguarding-information-professionals/newcastle-safeguarding-adults-board/safeguarding-adults-reviews/serious_case_review_concerning_the_death_of_adult_d.pdf, accessed on 19 April 2017.

Norrie, C., Martineau, S., Stevens, M., and Manthorpe, J. (2016) 'Consultation on power of access.' *The Journal of Adult Protection 18*, 5, 256–265.

Preston-Shoot, M., and Cornish, S. (2014) 'Paternalism or proportionality? Experiences and outcomes of the Adult Support and Protection (Scotland) Act 2007.' *Journal of Adult Protection 16*, 1, 5–16.

SCIE (Social Care Institute for Excellence) (2012a) *Safeguarding Adults: Mediation and Family Group Conferences*. London: SCIE.

SCIE (Social Care Institute for Excellence) (2012b) *Safeguarding Adults: Mediation and Family Group Conferences. Literature Review*. London: SCIE. Available at www.scie.org. uk/publications/mediation/files/literaturereview.pdf, accessed on 19 April 2017.

SCIE (Social Care Institute for Excellence) (2014) *Gaining Access to an Adult Suspected to be at Risk of Neglect or Abuse: A Guide for Social Workers and their Managers in England*. London: SCIE.

Scottish Executive (2001) *Consultation on Vulnerable Adults*. Edinburgh: Scottish Executive.

Scottish Government (2011) *Adult Protection Committee Biennial Reports 2008–2010: Summary Report*. Edinburgh: Scottish Government.

Scottish Government (2014) *Adult Support and Protection (Scotland) Act 2007: Code of Practice*. Edinburgh: Scottish Government.

Stewart, A. (2012) *Supporting Vulnerable Adults: Citizenship, Capacity, Choice*. Edinburgh: Dunedin Academic Press.

Stewart, A.E. (2015) *The Implementation of Adult Support and Protection (Scotland) Act (2007)*. PhD thesis. Glasgow: University of Glasgow. Available at http://theses.gla. ac.uk/7083, accessed on 19 April 2017.

Suffolk Safeguarding Children Board (2014) *Working with Hard to Engage Families within the Context of Safeguarding Children Practice Guidance.* Ipswich: Suffolk Council. Available at http://suffolkscb.org.uk/assets/files/2014/2014-V3-Post-SCR-Hostile-and-Evasive-clients-draft-2014-09-.pdf, accessed on 19 April 2017.

Tennant L. (2008) Executive Summary: Summary Report into Circumstances Surrounding the Death of Adult X Aged 22 Years Worcester, Worcestershire Safeguarding Adults Committee

Tudor, P. (2011) *Serious Case Review Executive Summary, Female Subject Died Aged 40 Years.* Sandwell: Sandwell Metropolitan District Council. Available at www.sandwell.gov.uk/downloads/file/3910/scr_executive_summary_28_may_2012, accessed on 19 April 2017.

White, T. (2016) in 'Statement by Newcastle Safeguarding Adults Board, dated 10.03.2016' Newcastle, Newcastle Adult Safeguarding Board, https://www.newcastle.gov.uk/sites/default/files/wwwfileroot/social-care-and-health/safeguarding-and-abuse/safeguarding-information-professionals/newcastle-safeguarding-adults-board/safeguarding-adults-reviews/serious_case_review_concerning_the_death_of_adult_d.pdf

Wood, T. (2011) *The Death of Adult A (1951–2010) Final Report.* Gateshead: North Tyneside Safeguarding Adults Board. Available at www.northtyneside.gov.uk/pls/portal/NTC_PSCM.PSCM_Web.download?p_ID=534847, accessed on 19 April 2017.

Wood, T. (2014) *The Death of Adult D: Case Review Overview Report.* Newcastle: Newcastle Safeguarding Adults Board. Available at www.newcastle.gov.uk/sites/default/files/wwwfileroot/social-care-and-health/safeguarding-and-abuse/safeguarding-information-professionals/newcastle-safeguarding-adults-board/safeguarding-adults-reviews/newcastle_safeguarding_adults_board_-_overview_report_-_final.pdf, accessed on 19 April 2017.

Wosu, H., and Stewart, J. (2010) *Engaging with Involuntary Service Users: A Literature Review and Case Study.* Edinburgh: University of Edinburgh.

Section 3

CURRENT ISSUES FOR PRACTITIONERS

Chapter 10

Self-Neglect and Hoarding

Suzy Braye, David Orr and Michael Preston-Shoot

Introduction

This chapter explores best practice with adults who self-neglect, including those who hoard. It draws on research evidence and published Serious Case Reviews (SCRs) and Safeguarding Adults Reviews (SARs) to illustrate common pitfalls and to provide guidance for navigating dilemmas and challenges. These include tensions between autonomy and a duty of care, and between the individual's interests and those of others.

As will emerge, for effective work with self-neglect, practitioners and managers must draw on a range of literacies (Braye and Preston-Shoot 2016a; Table 10.1).

Table 10.1 Literacies for self-neglect

Legal literacy	Knowledge and skilled application of legal options or requirements
Ethical literacy	Reflective and critical consideration and application of values
Relational literacy	Engaging with people's biographies and lived experience Demonstrating concerned curiosity
Emotional literacy	Managing stress and anxiety Recognising the impact of personal orientations to practice
Knowledge literacy	Drawing on different sources of evidence
Organisational literacy	Understanding accountability and management of practice within a multi-agency context Challenging procedures, cultures and decision making where these make error more likely
Decision-making literacy	Sharing information Managing the multi-agency partnership Explicitly weighing the evidence for different options

Immediately, two myths must be dispelled. First, self-neglect is not the responsibility solely of adult safeguarding or adult social care. Second, it is not simply an older age phenomenon. SCRs commissioned in England by Local Safeguarding Children Boards (SCBs) (Derbyshire SCB 2014; Dorset SCB 2014; South Tyneside SCB 2016) have found adolescent and/or adult self-neglect alongside child neglect and other risks, such as parental mental illness, sometimes in service-resistant families. Similarly, Domestic Homicide Reviews, commissioned in England under the Domestic Violence, Crime and Victims Act 2004, have advised that self-neglect should be included in risk assessments (Gwynedd Community Safety Partnership 2014; Rochdale Safer Communities Partnership 2015).

Reviews highlight lessons for effective practice that will permeate this chapter. A multi-agency approach is required to information-sharing, communication, assessment of risk and decision making, which embraces children's services, adult services, mental health, housing and other agencies as required. Assessment should include family members' perspectives, draw on high quality history taking, and consider family dynamics, capacity and risk, and the causes and meaning of behaviour. Senior management oversight will be necessary when adults who self-neglect refuse to engage and acknowledge concerns about their self-neglect, particularly to uphold people's rights, to support the resilience of the practitioners involved, to promote relational practice, to avoid agencies closing down their involvement without thinking through the implications, and to ensure that all intervention options are evaluated.

The policy and legislative response to the challenges presented by self-neglect has varied, both within the UK and elsewhere. In England statutory guidance to the Care Act (2014) has for the first time included self-neglect as a form of abuse and neglect (Department of Health [DH] 2016). Scotland included self-neglect earlier through the Adult Support and Protection (Scotland) Act (2007), and in Wales the definition of 'adults with care and support needs' in policy guidance (Welsh Assembly Government [WAG] 2000) arguably incorporated it earlier still. Elsewhere, policy and legislative differences in whether self-neglect is included in adult safeguarding/protection services are rooted in how adults at risk, and the terms 'abuse' and 'neglect', are defined, and whether interventions are codified in civil and criminal law or in adult safeguarding/protection powers and duties (Montgomery et al. 2016).

This complex mosaic illustrates again the importance of legal literacy. It reinforces also the significance of ethical literacy, as practitioners and managers must manage the complex and contested interface between prevention, early intervention and protection, and between autonomy and intervention where justifications for both positions can be drawn from the European Convention on Human Rights (ECHR). It is this territory that the remainder of this chapter explores.

Research evidence on working with self-neglect

Statutory guidance to the Care Act (2014) notes that self-neglect covers a wide range of behaviour, including neglect of one's personal hygiene, health or surroundings and hoarding (DH 2016). This expansive definition reflects the variety of situations captured by the label of 'self-neglect' in the research literature. Living in squalor, non-maintenance of bodily hygiene, failure or refusal to observe important health behaviours, and hoarding of objects or animals have all been the focus of studies (Braye, Orr and Preston-Shoot 2011). Moreover, two or more of these sometimes present together or overlap; in other cases, only one is present.

Just as people self-neglect in varying ways, the question of why people self-neglect has many answers. Not only do different individuals self-neglect for differing reasons, but often multiple factors combine to bring about an individual's situation of self-neglect. Research identifies an extensive catalogue of factors that may or may not be implicated in any given case: physical health conditions or disabilities; impairment in aspects of cognitive functioning; emotional influences spanning from hopelessness or fear (e.g. of change or of loss of control to others), to pride or pleasure (e.g. in the possession of hoarded objects or self-perception of independent coping); mental ill-health; substance use; financial or housing challenges; loss of social networks; the influence of others on lifestyle decisions; long-standing values, self-image or personality traits; significant life events or traumas; and difficulties accessing services or individuals who might mitigate self-neglectful circumstances (Braye et al. 2011, 2014; Kyrios 2014). Furthermore, self-neglect may result from either unwillingness or inability to self-care and sometimes may involve both, with an individual's apparent choice of a particular lifestyle masking the difficulties they face in self-care or other needs that impact upon their self-care ability

(Braye et al. 2011). In such situations practitioners must avoid prematurely drawing over-neat distinctions between unwillingness and inability; it is important to explore both dimensions fully. The safeguarding literature warns against the dangers of an approach once described as 'professionals hid[ing] behind the principle of choice' (Pritchard 2001, p.239), that is to say, too readily taking a person's apparent willingness to continue self-neglecting at face value, without further exploring with them their reasons and what other options they see themselves having (Braye *et al.* 2011; Preston-Shoot 2016; Scourfield 2010).

Equally, the literature highlights the converse danger of disregarding or minimising the person's own perspectives and insights into their situation, on the implicit assumption that there could be no rational reasons to live in such self-neglect. Several studies show the importance of putting the person's perspective, not that of services, at the centre of assessment and intervention, as not doing so jeopardises relationship-building and effective planning for intervention, risks overlooking vital elements of what may be a more complex story, and creates distrust of professional involvement (Band-Winterstein, Doron and Naim 2012; Braye *et al.* 2014; Day, Leahy-Warren and McCarthy 2013; Lauder *et al.* 2005a). This calls for practitioners to work towards consensual ways forward without ignoring or downplaying the risks of the situation; they should not shy away from respectful curiosity, discussion and, when appropriate, challenge with individuals (Braye *et al.* 2014; Preston-Shoot 2016). Successfully finding the right balance can be demanding and requires practitioners to draw on ethical, relational, emotional and knowledge literacy. These enable them to weigh up decisions without losing sight of core values, to understand the person's story, to engage with them on a human level and manage tensions in the relationship, and to remain aware of the various potentially relevant causative and risk factors.

Self-neglect calls for flexibility and a person-centred approach (Braye *et al.* 2014); care and support planning should be based on the unique needs and history of the person, rather than on any formula. Any or all of medical treatment, counselling or therapy, social care, resources or benefits, or connections to organisations, activities or networks may feature, depending on the person's situation. Such approaches are more likely to lead to successful outcomes where they are informed by: a concerted attempt to 'understand the person' beyond the self-neglect; a sense of timing where professionals identify a pace that helps the individual to move forward, without 'rushing' them into unhelpful changes or rejection of the involvement; transparency and sensitivity about risks, options and legal measures; understanding of, and building on, the person's coping strategies (possibly including some self-neglectful behaviour itself); knowledge of relevant law; and coordinated multi-agency working (Braye *et al.* 2014, 2015b; Day *et al.* 2013; Lauder *et al.* 2005a, 2005b).

Negotiating agreement and coordination between the different agencies involved presents its own challenges. These can be many and varied, including not only health, social care and housing, but potentially others such as environmental protection or fire services. Effective multi-agency working brings complementary perspectives and skills to bear, while reducing the risks of practitioners working at cross-purposes. Yet research studies and SCRs/SARs alike reveal that this has frequently not been achieved in self-neglect cases. Differences in agency eligibility thresholds, priorities, value positions and resources may complicate working together (Braye *et al.* 2011, 2015b; Lauder *et al.* 2005a); additionally, lack or unawareness of mechanisms for inter-professional referrals, communication or discussion interferes with the integration of agency efforts (Braye *et al.* 2014, 2015b). However, there are also examples of creative and constructive collaboration (Braye *et al.* 2014; Lauder *et al.* 2005a). Organisational literacy should facilitate these outcomes and reinforce robust decision making; at a minimum, practitioners should familiarise themselves with the roles of others involved and work towards common understandings of any care plan.

Legal literacy for self-neglect practice

Knowledge of the powers and duties that allow intervention is a key element of effective practice. SCRs/SARs commonly criticise the degree of scrutiny given to whether available legal options can and should be used, and call for stronger legal literacy.

Legal rules, however, do not provide easy answers. They provide options, showing what *may* be done rather than what *should* be done in any individual case. Equally, legal remedies are not value-free: they reflect political priorities, which themselves derive from the broader societal and cultural context. Lauder *et al.* (2005b) argue that two cultural factors characterise the UK context – preoccupation with hygiene and sanitation, and tolerance of eccentricity, resulting in 'an ambivalent and contrary attitude to those who self-neglect' (p.47) that is embedded within social judgements and reflected in our legal systems.

Respect for autonomy is hardwired into law, with an 800-year legacy from the Magna Carta underpinning the notion of limits to state interference in citizens' lives. More recently the ECHR (integrated within UK law by the Human Rights Act 1998) has provided the right to respect for private and family life (article 8) and the right to liberty and security of the person (article 5). The Mental Capacity Act (2005) establishes the principle that making a decision others may deem unwise is not to be equated with lacking mental capacity. Professional codes of conduct (for example, Health and Care Professions Council [HCPC] 2016) emphasise respect for privacy, and support for people to make their own decisions, as does statutory guidance to the Care Act (2014) (DH 2016) with its focus on personalisation and its espousal of Making Safeguarding Personal (Local Government Association [LGA] 2015). Conversely, protection and human dignity are prominent too. The state has a duty of care towards its citizens, to protect them from foreseeable harm. The ECHR codifies a right to the protection of life (article 2) and a right to protection from inhuman and degrading treatment (article 3). The same professional code that requires practitioners to respect privacy (HCPC 2016) also expects them to respect dignity, and to take all reasonable steps to reduce risk of harm. Such values underpin coroners' comments in self-neglect cases, questioning the absence of intervention when 'surely someone, somewhere, could and should have done something'. The presence of risk to others from an individual's self-neglect is a powerful driving force for imposed measures of intervention. A proportional balance must be struck between these competing imperatives in each unique case.[1]

Knowledge of available powers and duties is a key element of effective practice, but legal literacy is not just a question of knowing the law; it is about using it in complex and uncertain situations in which deep contradictions and moral dilemmas are engaged. It is the ability to connect relevant legal rules with the professional priorities and objectives of ethical practice (Braye and Preston-Shoot 2016b). Vital components are sound understanding of legal rules, strong engagement with professional ethics, and committed promotion of

---

1   *Re Z (an adult: capacity)* [2004] EWHC 2817 (Fam).

human rights. These must be integrated and applied in the context of each set of circumstances, requiring the exercise of professional judgement, respectful dialogue with the individual about risks and their choices, wisdom in weighing options, and confidence in presenting the rationale for action.

The following case study demonstrates how practitioners might apply the legal rules.

CASE STUDY: SHEILA

Sheila, in her early sixties, lives in a ground-floor flat in a multi-occupancy building owned by a registered social landlord. She lives alone and is estranged from her only son. A diabetic, she is in very poor health. Arthritis and a heart condition mean that she has limited mobility. She rarely leaves the house, but a neighbour brings shopping and local shops make deliveries. The interior of her flat is in a poor condition according to neighbours and her GP; discarded food and packaging lie everywhere, and each room is piled high with clothes, newspapers and accumulated household debris. She has two cats who soil the floor and furniture. The level of dirt in the flat, and in the small yard outside, is extreme, and Sheila neglects her personal care too. She spends much of her time in one room, rarely washing or changing her clothes. She is a heavy drinker and chain smoker, and spends her days and often nights too in an armchair, which is surrounded by accumulated papers and debris, and is soaked with urine from her incontinence when drinking. She sometimes has falls and occasionally has been hospitalised with fractures and burns, but once discharged she refuses follow-up care. Her neighbour has become increasingly concerned that Sheila is not eating – her shopping requests are less frequent, and she appears to be losing weight; meals that the neighbour provided have been left untouched. The GP has reviewed her health needs and medication, but remains concerned about how she is living, and referred her to adult social care. A practitioner has attempted to make initial contact with Sheila, but although she is happy to talk on the doorstep she does not offer access to her flat and politely declines any help and support.

Applying legal principles to practice

- The Care Act (2014) and the statutory guidance emphasise wellbeing, noting the importance in self-neglect of working alongside the person and understanding how their past experiences influence current behaviour (DH 2016, para.1.12). Individuals are seen as best-placed to judge their own wellbeing, so regard must be paid to their views, wishes, feelings and beliefs, considerations that underpin an explicit focus on 'making safeguarding personal' (DH 2016, para.4.15).

- The Mental Capacity Act (2005) codifies five principles, including that unwise decisions do not automatically signify incapacity (see Appendix).

- The Equality Act (2010) and the Human Rights Act (1998) require protection from unlawful discrimination, promotion of equality of opportunity and human rights, and proportionality in interventions.

The response to the referral will draw upon two parallel legal duties within the Care Act (2014) (Table 10.2).

Table 10.2 Two parallel legal duties within the Care Act (2014)

Section 42 inquiries	Section 9 assessment
Self-neglect is one circumstance that constitutes 'abuse and neglect' (DH 2016). If the local authority considers that Sheila meets the criteria set out in s.42 (see Appendix) then the duty to make safeguarding inquiries is engaged. S.42 inquiries may not always be necessary; the guidance calls for careful attention to the individual's ability to take self-protective action (e.g. by accepting services).	The s.9 duty to undertake an assessment of care and support needs is engaged where an individual appears to have such needs, regardless of their level. Sheila's circumstances will satisfy this threshold. Not applicable in Sheila's case, but important where an individual who self-neglects is a carer for someone else, is the s.10 duty to assess a carer's needs for support.
An advocate must be appointed to support Sheila's participation if it appears she has difficulty understanding the process and expressing her wishes and feelings, and no other appropriate person is available (ss.67/68).	

The Care Act (2014) does not provide additional mandates for intervention specific to self-neglect and it repealed the power (s.47

National Assistance Act 1948) to remove a person living in insanitary conditions to a place of safety. Following assessment of care and support needs, further duties require the local authority to assess the eligibility of Sheila's assessed needs (s.13), to meet needs deemed eligible (s.18), to set a personal budget (s.26), to plan how care and support is provided (s.25) and to review the plan periodically (s.27).

The Mental Capacity Act (2005) provides an additional element to both s.42 inquiry and s.9 assessment, as either must identify whether Sheila has the mental capacity to understand the risks involved in her circumstances and to decide how to meet her personal and household needs. For that assessment to take place, careful negotiation and relationship-building will be needed.

Sheila will lack capacity to take a specific decision if she meets the criteria set out in ss.2–3 of the Mental Capacity Act (see Appendix). If she lacks capacity in relation to a specific decision, any decision made by others on her behalf must be in her best interests, taking account of the factors listed in s.4 of the Mental Capacity Act (see Appendix).

With certain patterns of behaviour (for example, a persistent mismatch between expressed intent and realised action), it may be important to question whether impairment of executive brain function[2] could be interfering with the individual's ability to use or weigh information in the moment when the decision needs to be made (for example, in deciding whether to eat and drink, or where and when to smoke). So, having explored Sheila's professed reasons for her choices, a multi-disciplinary approach that includes neuropsychological assessment may be appropriate.

If Sheila is deemed not to have capacity, measures to help and support her can be implemented, enabling her either to remain more safely at home or to reside elsewhere. In considering her best interests, her views, wishes, feelings and beliefs of course remain important as guides in decision making, balanced against concerns about risk. The decision in *Westminster City Council v Sykes* [2014][3] illustrates well how to manage this balance.

If the care and support arrangements amount to a deprivation of liberty (DoL) – where Sheila is under continuous supervision and control, and is not free to leave – additional legal safeguards apply. For DoL in

---

2   The literature on executive capacity is explored more fully in Braye *et al.* (2011). Naik *et al.* (2008) and Hildebrand, Taylor and Bradway (2014) provide examples of how the concept is incorporated within clinical practice.

3   *Westminster City Council v Sykes* [2014] EWHC B 9 (COP).

a care home or hospital, authorisation must be sought from the local authority, which must undertake a range of assessments. For any other setting, authorisation must be sought from the Court of Protection.

If Sheila has capacity to make relevant decisions, consideration must be given to alternative ways to mitigate risks. Here the research evidence on approaches that produce positive outcomes provides guidance (Braye *et al.* 2014): persistence in building a relationship of trust over time can facilitate gradual acceptance of support; understanding of her history and journey into self-neglect will enable a more personalised intervention; and a proportionate approach to risk containment will be more appropriate than seeking to remove all risk.

If Sheila's self-neglect is associated with mental disorder and risks are acute, intervention may prioritise attention to mental health.

- Mental Health Act (1983): Psychiatric assessment and treatment may be appropriate, and in certain circumstances compulsory admission may be necessary. Assessment by an Approved Mental Health Professional (AMHP) must identify whether the grounds for s.2 (admission for assessment) or s.3 (admission for treatment) are met.

- Guardianship (s.7) may be an alternative to hospital admission, providing a relationship of authority to determine where Sheila should live, require attendance for treatment, occupation, education or training, or facilitate access by a doctor or AMHP.

If Sheila lacks capacity to make decisions about her care and treatment, thorough consideration must be given to whether use of mental capacity or mental health legislation provides the less restrictive alternative (Braye and Preston-Shoot 2016c).

If Sheila refuses access to her flat and acute concerns persist, it may be necessary to secure entry.

- Under the Mental Health Act (1983), s.135, an AMHP may request a magistrate's warrant authorising a police constable (accompanied by an AMHP and a doctor) to enter her flat if it is believed she is mentally disordered and is being ill-treated or neglected, or lives alone and is unable to care for herself. She may be taken to a place of safety for 72 hours, in order to assess the need for hospital admission or other care arrangements.

- The Police & Criminal Evidence Act (1984) permits the police to enter premises without a warrant to save life or prevent injury, or prevent serious damage to property.

Even at the early stages of assessment, multi-agency involvement may be appropriate. The Care Act (2014) supports inter-agency practice through:

- endorsement of safeguarding partnerships as a positive means of addressing self-neglect (DH 2016, para.14.141)
- reciprocal duties of cooperation between the local authority and relevant partners (ss.6 and 7).

Thus the local authority may seek the cooperation of, for example, the fire brigade for home fire safety visits, installation of smoke detectors and/or alarms, and in some circumstances sprinklers if warranted. Whether the owner of the property is fulfilling their fire safety responsibilities should also be considered.

If Sheila is assessed as having capacity to make decisions on her care and support but continues to live as before, and assuming mental health assessment has ruled out hospital admission or guardianship under the Mental Health Act (1983), then environmental health, housing and anti-social behaviour legislation provide powers to impose measures, and the local authority may work closely with the relevant authorities.

These powers may be used to address squalor and infestation within domestic premises.

- Public Health Act (1936): If Sheila's flat is considered 'unwholesome and filthy' and 'prejudicial to health', or if vermin are present, the local authority can require it to be cleaned and disinfected (ss.83/84). It may also apply for power of entry, and can carry out the work and charge her. Sheila herself could also be 'removed and made clean' (s.85).

- The Public Health Act (1961) (s.36) provides powers to clear accumulated waste on land in the open air, and to require vacation of premises to allow fumigation.

- Under the Prevention of Damage by Pests Act (1949) the local authority can require Sheila to keep land clear of vermin by removing materials that attract them.

- The Environmental Protection Act (1990) gives the local authority power to require 'abatement of a statutory nuisance', which could constitute the state of Sheila's flat, how animals are kept, and accumulated materials outside (ss.79/80). There is power of entry, and the local authority may do the work and make a charge.

- Under the Public Health (Control of Disease) Act (1984), amended by the Health & Social Care Act 2008, the local authority may apply for a court order imposing measures applying to Sheila, her possessions or premises, to protect against infection or contamination where there is a significant risk to human health.

Powers exist to address self-neglectful behaviour that constitutes severe nuisance and annoyance to others.

- Anti-Social Behaviour, Crime and Policing Act (2014) and statutory guidance (Home Office 2014): A local authority, housing provider or the police may apply for an Injunction to Prevent Nuisance and Annoyance (IPNA), relating to 'conduct capable of causing nuisance or annoyance to any person in relation to that person's occupation of residential premises, or a housing-related nuisance or annoyance to any person'. A power of arrest for breach may be attached where risk of harm is significant. Breach of an IPNA is an absolute ground for eviction. Community Protection Notices (CPNs) are available to the local authority and the police to address unreasonable conduct that is having a 'persistent or continuing detrimental effect on quality of life' in the locality. Breach of a CPN is a criminal offence.

- The Housing Act (1985) (amended 1996) and Housing Act (1988) provide grounds for eviction of a tenant causing nuisance or annoyance to someone 'residing, visiting or otherwise engaged in lawful activity in the locality', or where a tenancy obligation has been broken.

- Acceptable Behaviour Contracts are voluntary agreements (Home Office 2007) between an individual and the police, housing department or registered social landlord. They are not legally binding, but provide an alternative, or perhaps preliminary, step to injunctions or eviction proceedings.

- Building Act (1984): The local authority may give notice of intention to remedy defective premises that are prejudicial to health or a nuisance. It may carry out the work and recover the costs. Where a building is dangerous, it may apply for a court order requiring the owner to carry out the work and, in cases of non-compliance, may do the work and recover the costs.

- The Housing Act (2004) provides duties and powers for local authorities to address hazards in buildings or land that pose risks of harm to health or safety, through use of the Housing, Health and Safety Rating System. Improvement and prohibition notices requiring remedial action by tenants and owner-occupiers may be issued. If a notice is not complied with, the local authority may organise and charge for the work.

Sheila's self-neglect may extend to neglect of her cats, and animal welfare legislation may be invoked.

- Animal Welfare Act (2006): Individuals have a duty to meet the welfare needs of their animals. Advice and education may be followed by formal warnings and prosecution. Cruelty to animals is a criminal offence.

The courts provide an avenue for resolution of uncertainty and dilemmas.

- The Court of Protection makes decisions on finance or welfare for people who lack mental capacity to decide for themselves. It can be asked to determine an individual's capacity in relation to a specific matter and/or, where capacity is lacking, to determine what is in their best interests. Its involvement is particularly important in complex, uncertain or contested cases. If the court judges an individual to have capacity in relation to a decision, it has no further jurisdiction over that matter.

- The High Court can exercise its inherent jurisdiction to set in place protective measures in relation to an individual who, while having mental capacity, cannot exercise that capacity freely because they are under constraint, subject to coercion or undue influence, or for some other reason deprived of the capacity to make the relevant decision.[4] Although more commonly used in relation to protection from a third party, it may be worthy of consideration where no statutory remedy is available and the circumstances warrant it.

Lessons from case reviews

Perhaps surprisingly, given how long self-neglect remained under the policy and legislative radar in England, it has featured explicitly or implicitly in over 60 SCRs/SARs (Preston-Shoot 2016). Their recommendations for practice (Braye *et al.* 2015a, 2015b) cover three areas (Table 10.3).

Table 10.3 Lessons from case reviews

Staff support	Training, supervision, health and safety
Procedures	Availability of guidance on referrals, assessment of need and risk, recording and (complex) case management; protocols for multi-agency working, escalation of concerns and information-sharing; awareness-raising measures
Best practice	Person-centred, relationship-based approaches, which openly explore mental capacity and reluctance to engage, involve family members, consider all available legal and service commissioning options

Further analysis has identified key components for effective practice with adults who self-neglect, including those who hoard. Person-centred approaches to intervention are strongly highlighted, which seek to understand significant historical and more contemporary events that might influence behaviour and their engagement with care and support services. Such an approach does not simply accept service refusal but expresses concerned curiosity and continues proactively to seek engagement. Knowledge is drawn from people in the person's family and social environment, family dynamics are explored where relevant, and assessment of mental capacity is thorough and reviewed routinely.

---

4   *DL v A Local Authority and Others* [2012] EWCA Civ 253.

Agencies involved must coordinate assessments, care planning and reviews, and share information. Familiarity with safeguarding procedures and available legal rules is essential. Practitioners benefit from supervision and training, reasonable workloads to enable the longer-term work that self-neglect cases frequently require, and management and specialist involvement in complex cases of high risk.

Two reviews are now considered, selected because they focus on different manifestations of self-neglect – hoarding (Cornwall and Isles of Scilly Safeguarding Adults Board 2014) and neglect of health (Gloucestershire Safeguarding Adults Board 2015). The pitfalls that they highlight and their recommendations for effective policy and practice are not atypical, and enable practitioners to audit their own practice and organisational context.

Cornwall

This case involves an older man, aged 81, who hoarded excessively and died at home, probably after a fall, with his belongings collapsed on top of him. Pivotal pitfalls in this case included incomplete risk assessments and inadequate mental capacity assessments. Presumption of capacity was too readily assumed rather than challenged, with practitioners also disempowered through believing that they could not raise questions about his refusal of help and being unclear whether or how in this context they could fulfil their duty of care. Some practitioners were unaware of available local guidance on self-neglect, did not follow pathways constructed following earlier SCRs and were confused about how to respond. Referrals lacked clear information about his hoarding and the risks his home presented; thus concerns became lost, some agencies did not engage with service provision, and decisions were made in the absence of all the available information.

Familiar messages for practice are highlighted. These include the importance of persistent efforts to engage both the individual and the agencies that might be able to offer care and support. Liaison between practitioners and agencies is crucial, especially where individuals do not fit neatly into service boundaries. Complex case panels and 'adult at risk management systems' are a valuable means of bringing practitioners and managers together when securing multi-agency engagement is proving difficult and ensuring that everyone is clear about where responsibility lies for people with interlocking needs.

Practitioners must be ready to challenge notions of 'lifestyle choice' and, rather than abandoning an individual when they refuse help, softly and skilfully negotiate an ongoing relationship and intervention. Once again this requires that organisations adapt their working culture to ensure that the infrastructure and resources support the effective management of complex cases, enabling intensive, responsive and long-term intervention.

Gloucestershire

This case concerns a man's lack of self-care and refusal of services, concluding with him surviving the potential loss of a limb due to self-neglect. The review withholds his age but reports him as having mild learning disability and controlled epilepsy. Pivotal pitfalls and familiar good practice recommendations emerge from this case (Table 10.4).

Table 10.4 Pitfalls and good practice from Gloucestershire

Pitfalls	Learning for good practice
Agencies withdrew when he was hard to engage or declined previously accepted levels of care and support; they did not explore with him concerns about hygiene and diet.	Proactive and creative approaches are required to gain someone's trust and motivation; staff must make efforts to understand the causes of behaviour, including physical and environmental deterioration.
Formal capacity assessments were not completed despite agreements that they should be done; mental capacity was assumed; staff did not check his ability to understand the consequences of decisions.	Decisions about capacity for specific decisions should be reviewed regularly; even where individuals appear to understand potential consequences of their decisions, it does not necessarily mean that they have the capacity to follow through actions or agreed behaviour changes.
Alerts and concerns were not followed up promptly or investigated thoroughly.	Levels of concern must be communicated effectively between staff and agencies; agreed actions derived from a multi-agency risk management plan must be progressed.
Commissioners did not provide care plans with required outcomes or then thoroughly evaluate the effectiveness of services being provided.	Care and support should not be reduced without a formal review.

Pitfalls	Learning for good practice
The multi-agency network missed opportunities to share concerns about risk and their collaboration was affected by differences in culture and practices.	Patterns, here of concerns followed by improvements followed by renewed concerns, should be explored.
GPs did not review medication levels.	Agencies should not close down their involvement without multi-agency discussion.
Individuals can be fearful of interventions, and reluctant to acknowledge struggles with daily living.	Time and relationship continuity help service users to know and trust staff.
Reluctance to overrule an individual.	Management challenge and support must be given to consider all available legal options.

Conclusion

The seven literacies with which this chapter began are all indispensable in self-neglect work. Understanding how self-neglect manifests and why it occurs in a particular individual is a complex task, as is weighing up the mix of ethical and pragmatic considerations that guide practice. Practitioners must be able to navigate their way through the legal framework and web of agencies that now surround self-neglect, without ever losing from sight the 'person' at the centre of their practice. This chapter has furnished a map for these tasks by briefly summarising the research literature, mapping the legal pathways of most frequent relevance, and discussing the accumulated findings of SCRs/SARs featuring self-neglect. Important steps forward have been taken in recent years, in the UK and elsewhere, to give self-neglect the attention it merits, as this evolving evidence base shows. While much focus is on challenges and failings in practice, there is also ample evidence of good practice and positive outcomes. It has been clearly demonstrated that, with commitment, knowledge, a clear value base, time and concerned curiosity, self-neglect work can improve quality of life and even save lives.

References

Band-Winterstein, T., Doron, I., and Naim, S. (2012) 'Elder self neglect: A geriatric syndrome or a life course story?' *Journal of Aging Studies 26*, 2, 109–118.

Braye, S., and Preston-Shoot, M. (2016a) *Legal Literacy in Adult Social Care.* Strategic Briefing. Dartington: Research in Practice for Adults.

Braye, S., and Preston-Shoot, M. (2016b) *Legal Literacy: Practice Tool.* Dartington: Research in Practice for Adults.

Braye, S., and Preston-Shoot, M. (2016c) *Practising Social Work Law* (4th edition). Basingstoke: Palgrave Macmillan.

Braye, S., Orr, D., and Preston-Shoot, M. (2011) *Self-Neglect and Adult Safeguarding: Findings from Research.* London: SCIE.

Braye, S., Orr, D., and Preston-Shoot, M. (2014) *Self-Neglect Policy and Practice: Building an Evidence Base for Adult Social Care.* London: SCIE.

Braye, S., Orr, D., and Preston-Shoot, M. (2015a) 'Learning lessons about self-neglect? An analysis of Serious Case Reviews.' *Journal of Adult Protection 17*, 1, 3–18.

Braye, S., Orr, D., and Preston-Shoot, M. (2015b) 'Serious case review findings on the challenges of self-neglect: Indicators for good practice.' *Journal of Adult Protection 17*, 2, 75–87.

Cornwall and Isles of Scilly Safeguarding Adults Board (2014) *Learning Together Serious Case Review: Mr L. The Reassurance of Disengagement.* Available at www.cornwall.gov. uk/media/10696931/the-reassurance-of-disengagement-2014.pdf, accessed on 20 April 2017.

Day, M.R., Leahy-Warren, P., and McCarthy, G. (2013) 'Perceptions and views of self-neglect: A client-centred perspective.' *Journal of Elder Abuse & Neglect 25*, 1, 76–94.

Department of Health (2016) *Care and Support Statutory Guidance.* London: DH.

Derbyshire Safeguarding Children Board (2014) *Overview Report: Serious Case Review in Respect of a Child. BDS 10.* Available at www.derbyshirescb.org.uk/images/serious%20 case%20review%20BDS%2010_tcm65-277904.pdf, accessed on 20 April 2017.

Dorset Safeguarding Children Board (2014) *Family S11: Serious Case Review Overview Report.* Available at www.dorsetlscb.co.uk/working-with-children/serious-case-reviews, accessed on 20 April 2017.

Gloucestershire Safeguarding Adults Board (2015) *Overview Report, 'R'.* Available at www.gloucestershire.gov.uk/media/13346/overview-report-final-draft-r-20-august-2015.pdf, accessed on 20 April 2017.

Gwynedd Community Safety Partnership (2014) *Domestic Homicide Review Executive Summary: Overview Report into the Death of Adult 1.* Available at www.gwynedd.llyw. cymru/en/Residents/Documents-Residents/Health-and-social-care-documents/ SeriousCaseReviews/Domestic-homicide-review---Executive-summary---Overview-report-into-the-death-of-Adult-1.pdf, accessed on 20 April 2017.

Health and Care Professions Council (2016) *Standards of Conduct, Performance and Ethics.* London: HCPC.

Hildebrand, C., Taylor, M., and Bradway, C. (2014) 'Elder self-neglect: The failure of coping because of cognitive and functional impairments.' *Journal of the American Association of Nurse Practitioners 26*, 452–462.

Home Office (2007) *Acceptable Behaviour Contracts and Agreements.* London: Home Office.

Home Office (2014) *Anti-Social Behaviour, Crime and Policing Act 2014: Reform of Anti-Social Behaviour Powers. Statutory Guidance for Frontline Professionals.* London: Home Office.

Kyrios, M. (2014) 'Psychological Models of Hoarding.' In R.O. Frost and G. Steketee (eds) *Oxford Handbook of Hoarding and Acquiring.* Oxford: Oxford University Press.

Lauder, W., Anderson, I., and Barclay, A. (2005a) 'Housing and self-neglect: The responses of health, social care and environmental health agencies.' *Journal of Interprofessional Care 19*, 4, 317–325.

Lauder, W., Davidson, G., Anderson, I., and Barclay, A. (2005b) 'Self-neglect: The role of judgements and applied ethics.' *Nursing Standard 19*, 18, 45–51.

Local Government Association (2015) *Making Safeguarding Personal: 2014–15 Evaluation Report.* London: LGA.

Montgomery, L., Anand, J., Mackay, K., Taylor, B., Pearson, K., and Harper, C. (2016) 'Implications of divergences in adult protection legislation.' *Journal of Adult Protection 18*, 3, 149–160.

Naik, A., Lai, J., Kunik, M., and Dyer, C. (2008) 'Assessing capacity in suspected cases of self-neglect.' *Geriatrics 63*, 2, 24–31.

Preston-Shoot, M. (2016) 'Towards explanations for the findings of Serious Case Reviews: Understanding what happens in self-neglect work.' *Journal of Adult Protection 18*, 3, 131–148.

Pritchard, J. (2001) 'Neglect: Not Grasping the Nettle and Hiding Behind Choice.' In J. Pritchard (ed.) *Good Practice with Vulnerable Adults.* London: Jessica Kingsley Publishers.

Rochdale Safer Communities Partnership (2015) *Domestic Homicide Review: Female A.* Available at www.rochdale.gov.uk/pdf/2017-01-19-Domestic-Homicide-Review-September-2015-v1.pdf, accessed on 20 April 2017.

Scourfield, P. (2010) 'Reflections on the Serious Case Review of a female adult (JK).' *Journal of Adult Protection 12*, 4, 16–30.

South Tyneside Safeguarding Children Board (2016) *Serious Case Review into the Circumstances concerning Kevin (a Pseudonym).* Available at www.southtyneside.gov.uk/article/35815/Serious-case-reviews, accessed on 20 April 2017.

Welsh Assembly Government (2000) *In Safe Hands: Implementing Adult Protection Procedures in Wales.* Cardiff: WAG.

Chapter 11

Domestic Abuse and Adult Safeguarding

Lindsey Pike and Nicki Norman

Introduction

Identifying and responding appropriately to domestic abuse is now an essential part of adult safeguarding practice. Domestic abuse can necessitate a safeguarding inquiry and is defined in the Care Act (2014) guidance (Department of Health [DH] 2016, s.14.20) using the cross-government definition:

> any incident or pattern of incidents of controlling, coercive threatening behaviour, violence or abuse between those aged 16 or over who are, or have been, intimate partners or family members regardless of gender or sexuality. The abuse can encompass, but is not limited to:
>
> - Psychological
>
> - Sexual
>
> - Financial
>
> - Emotional.

The terms 'domestic violence' and 'domestic abuse' are both in common use, so are used interchangeably here. The term 'survivor' is used to describe people who are experiencing, or have experienced, domestic abuse, and the female pronoun used to reflect that statistically women are disproportionately affected.

The central feature of domestic violence and abuse is coercive and controlling behaviour. This chapter outlines how to respond to such behaviour in a safeguarding adults context; that is, when the person who is experiencing domestic abuse has care and support needs, and due to those needs is unable to protect themselves from the abuse (see Appendix). The chapter will explore the evidence around domestic abuse of people with care and support needs; the role of gender; effective responses, including legal responses; and multi-agency working. Practice tips are provided throughout to relate the issues discussed to practice. Readers are referred to http://coercivecontrol. ripfa.org.uk for more in-depth learning materials commissioned by the Chief Social Worker and jointly produced by Women's Aid and RiPfA on this issue.

What is domestic violence and abuse?

Domestic abuse results, on average, in two women a week being killed by a current or ex-partner (Smith *et al.* 2012) and regularly requires professional support and intervention across the spectrum of statutory and voluntary sectors. It can be experienced by anyone, regardless of race, ethnic or religious group, sexuality, class, gender or disability. However, internationally, domestic abuse is recognised as a gendered issue most commonly experienced by women and perpetrated by men, and a cause and consequence of societal inequality.

Domestic abuse is not limited to or more prevalent within any particular community, class or social group. Nor can it be attributed to poverty, substance misuse or poor mental health, although these may be exacerbating factors. It can and does also take place within same-sex relationships and can be perpetrated by women towards men, although the nature, severity and impact of abuse and support required by male victims may differ to that of women (LGA and ADASS 2015). There is some evidence that trans people experience domestic abuse in at least the same prevalence as the general population, though may find it more difficult to access support (Rogers 2016).

Domestic abuse is rarely a one-off incident but most commonly a pattern of abusive and controlling behaviour by which the perpetrator asserts power and control over the victim.

Coercive, controlling behaviour is at the core of domestic abuse (Stark 2007), and this is recognised in law with the Serious Crime Act (2015), which created a new offence of controlling or coercive behaviour in intimate or familial relationships (s.76). This offence closed a gap in the law around patterns of behaviour intended to cause harm and widens the previously narrow definition of domestic abuse which focused on single incidents of physical violence. The cross-government definition of domestic abuse further defines that:

> Controlling behaviour is a range of acts designed to make a person subordinate and/or dependent by isolating them from sources of support, exploiting their resources and capacities for personal gain, depriving them of the means needed for independence, resistance and escape and regulating their everyday behaviour. (Home Office 2015, p.3)

Coercive behaviour is an act or a pattern of acts of assault, threats, humiliation and intimidation or other abuse that is used to harm, punish or frighten their victim (ibid.).

With advances in technology, the tools that abusers draw upon to monitor, control and harass have widened. For many, abuse they receive online from a partner or ex-partner is part of a pattern of abuse they also experience offline (Laxton 2014).

The Power and Control Wheel (Figure 11.1) was created by the Domestic Abuse Intervention Project (DAIP 1984) as a result of focus groups with over 200 women who shared their experiences of intimate partner gender-based violence. Perpetrators systematically use threats, intimidation and coercion to instil fear and to dominate the victim (spokes of wheel). These tactics are reinforced by his use of physical and/or sexual violence (rim of wheel), resulting in his gaining and maintaining power and control over her (centre of wheel).

The particular experiences of survivors of abuse within this context are articulated well by contributors to research about disabled women and domestic violence:

> One time, he actually took the battery out of this wheelchair... He just unplugged it so I couldn't move and if it wasn't for a mutual friend that came to the house he wouldn't have plugged it back in. And I don't know how long I'd have been staying there with a dead battery... He'd make me wait for help or he'd tut a lot or...shove me about sometimes and push me hard... (Hague *et al.* 2008)

Figure 11.1 The Power and Control Wheel (DAIP 1984).[1]

Domestic abuse and people with social care needs

Domestic abuse, as an issue for people who have care and support needs, is under-recognised and under-reported (LGA and ADASS 2015). Robbins *et al.* (2016) highlight that while social workers can be well placed to detect, investigate and support people experiencing domestic abuse, the context of social work, where domestic abuse

---

is seen as a 'children and families' issue, means this has not been a priority in adult social work to date. Most of the limited evidence available focuses on the experience of women; more research is needed about the impact of domestic abuse on men with social care needs.

The use of power and control within domestic relationships contributes to, mirrors and is supported by gender inequality, ageism and discrimination against disabled people in wider society. The impact of additional types of disadvantage are conceptualised in the idea of 'intersectionality' (Crenshaw 1993) which highlights the additional layers of oppression that an individual may face. The social model of disability describes the barriers faced by disabled people in living their lives, and looking at domestic abuse of people with social care needs through this lens can help us to understand the issues that people may face when trying to leave abusive relationships. The additional issues for people with care and support needs are twofold:

- People's condition can be used by the perpetrator as a way of gaining power over them; and they may have reduced protective factors to guard against abuse.

- There are additional barriers to accessing domestic abuse services; including disbelieving attitudes, lack of recognition of the potential for domestic abuse in this population, physical access to services, possible dependence on the perpetrator and lack of information about accessible services available.

Perpetrators of domestic abuse may use the survivor's condition to humiliate, belittle and control them (LGA and ADASS 2015). For example, DeafHope, an organisation which supports Deaf survivors of domestic abuse cite tactics used by perpetrators specific to Deaf survivors, including criticising speech, using 'hearing privilege' by excluding people from conversations, or spreading rumours in the Deaf community (DeafHope n.d.).

Disabled women

Magowan (2004) suggests that over 50 per cent of disabled women may have experienced domestic abuse. In their study for Women's Aid, Hague et al. (2008) noted that disabled women were more likely to encounter specific issues of power and control as well as isolation and dependence due to barriers they face related to their disability. Disabled women's advice to practitioners is summarised below.

Practice tips

- Be informed about disabled women's needs.

- Take advice from and consult disabled women.

- Provide accessible well-publicised domestic abuse services that disabled women know about; and tell women about them.

- Do not threaten with institutionalisation.

- Develop disability equality schemes with input from disabled women.

- Take disabled women seriously and do not patronise.

(Thiara 2015)

Practitioners need to be aware of how a person's disability might shape their experience of domestic abuse. Rich (2014) highlights the need to ask people with disabilities about love and relationships. Relating back to intersectionality, she comments that disabled women can be 'dually stigmatised' in that societal expectations around women's bodies can negatively influence their thinking, and their disability can be used as a reason to 'victim blame'. Rich found that women with physical disabilities used a range of survival strategies, including blaming the disability for the abuse, seeing the abuser as 'broken, disabled or damaged' himself, framing the abuse as accidental, or reframing the control as 'protective'. Practitioners should be aware of the impact that coercive control may have on survivors' conceptualisation of abuse.

Older people

Assumptions that domestic abuse does not affect older people may prevent practitioners from making safe enquiries about domestic abuse. This is exemplified in the Serious Case Review related to the death of Mary Russell, 81, who was killed by her husband Albert, 88, despite numerous contacts with the emergency services (Southend Safeguarding Adults Board 2011). Older women may have lived with domestic abuse over a long period of time, or may have started to experience it more recently. Longer-term abuse negatively impacts on mental health, with a range of emotions such as frustration, anger, hopelessness and low self-esteem described by older women (McGarry and Simpson 2011). It also has negative implications for physical health in later life, and relationships with family (ibid.). Where abuse is still being experienced, physical abuse can be more serious due to slower healing and greater frailty in old age, and financial abuse can limit autonomy and choice in later life. Older women face additional barriers to disclosing, which can include financial dependency on abusers, and traditional attitudes towards marriage and gender roles (ibid.). Domestic abuse services may not be seen as 'for' older women, or people with care and support needs more generally, and a lack of information for this group is also seen as a barrier to reporting of the issue.

Knight and Hester (2014) found that the onset of dementia in either the perpetrator or the survivor increases the likelihood of violence in relationships where domestic abuse has occurred in the past. This study of 22 cases found that adult safeguarding was often involved but there was no involvement from the domestic abuse sector. This highlights the importance of recognising domestic abuse in safeguarding situations, and involving the relevant specialists.

People with learning disabilities

McCarthy, Hunt and Milne-Skilman (2015) found that women with learning disabilities experienced the full range of abuse that is inflicted on other women. The researchers interviewed 15 women and recommended that all health and social care professionals:

- make safe enquiries and ask about relationships

- become alert to women with learning disabilities becoming more isolated

- be aware that physical injury may be a sign of other, multiple forms of abuse which should be enquired into

- have a greater remit to work with people who have lower levels of learning disability, who may not be eligible for any support, making them more vulnerable to abuse

- provide accessible information, and access to civil and criminal justice options where appropriate.

While some women had had positive experiences of asking for and receiving help from the police and social services, the majority had not; one said, 'When we ask for help, there's no one to help us. They seem to take your children away instead of helping you' (ibid., p.8).

Earlier research by Walter-Brice *et al.* (2012) suggested that women with learning disabilities may not know what to expect from an intimate relationship. Practitioners should be ready to discuss what a good relationship looks like, while being ready to make and respond to safe enquiries.

People who access mental health services

There is a higher prevalence of domestic abuse among people who experience poor mental health (Trevillion *et al.* 2012), and domestic abuse is likely to have a negative impact on mental health.

Perpetrators will use a person's mental ill health against them, for example by:

- using their mental ill health to discredit their version of events

- reinforcing dependency by taking an overbearing 'caring' role

- threatening that the children will be taken away

- deliberately misleading or undermining the person

- withholding medication or overmedicating.

Such behaviours are likely to worsen existing mental health conditions.

Forced marriage, female genital mutilation and so-called 'honour'-based violence

Domestic abuse takes place within intimate personal relationships. This generally means between partners, but can also include family members or carers. There are other recognised forms of domestic abuse that also take place within the context of a familial relationship, including so-called 'honour'-based violence, forced marriage and female genital mutilation. Practitioners have a crucial role in recognising and responding to these forms of abuse.

Honour-based violence

Honour-based violence is commonly defined as 'a crime or incident which has or may have been committed to protect or defend the honour of the family and/or community'.[2] Most victims of honour-based violence are women and girls who are judged to have shamed the family or community by not adhering to perceived codes of honour, normally through expressions of autonomy, but men may also be at risk.

'Honour-based crime' is an umbrella term to encompass various offences covered by existing legislation (see below under legal responses).

Forced marriage

A forced marriage takes place without the valid consent of one or both parties, where duress is a factor, and is illegal in the UK. Adults with learning or physical disabilities may be at particular risk, and in some cases may not have the mental capacity to consent to marriage. UK statistics show that, of the number of cases reported to the Forced Marriage Unit, 12 per cent (141 cases) involved people who had a physical or learning disability. Of these, 62 per cent of victims were men, in contrast to 20 per cent of the general population (Home Office and FCO 2016). HM Government (2014) published multi-agency guidance on handling cases of forced marriage, which provides useful principles for practitioners to work to.

Female genital mutilation

Female genital mutilation (FGM) is a harmful traditional practice that involves the partial or total removal of the female genitalia, or other injury to the female genital organs without a medical reason. It is an offence to either perform FGM or help anyone perform it on a UK resident either in the UK or abroad under the Female Genital Mutilation Act (2003) as amended by the Serious Crime Act (2015). Regulated health and social care professionals must report cases of FGM in under-18s that they identify in the course of their work to the police (Home Office and Department for Education 2015).

---

2   Crown Prosecution Service and Association of Chief Police Officers' common definition; see www.cps.gov.uk/legal/h_to_k/honour_based_violence_and_forced_marriage.

Adults with care or support needs identified as having had, or being at risk of, FGM should be responded to within existing safeguarding processes.

Appropriate responses and safe enquiry

At times, intentionally or unintentionally, the lives of the people being abused will interact with services; and these are key opportunities for intervention. Every point of interaction with a survivor is an opportunity for intervention and should not be missed. Agencies and the professionals working for them can help to provide opportunities for disclosure of abuse by:

- displaying information about domestic abuse and where to seek help

- creating opportunities for individuals to speak without the partner/carer present

- only using professional interpreters (when these are required)

- asking direct questions about their circumstances – for example: 'Has anyone close to you made you feel frightened?' or 'Has anyone prevented you from getting the things you need, for example food, medication, hearing aids or medical care?'

- explaining your reasons for enquiring – for example: 'We know domestic abuse affects many people; so we ask everyone about it when we observe possible indicators of abuse.'

- arranging advocates where necessary.

(LGA and ADASS 2015)

The ideal response to a disclosure is one that empowers the victim, through the provision of non-judgemental support and information, to explore the options available to them, and assists them to take appropriate action. This approach aligns well with Making Safeguarding Personal (see Chapter 1).

Practice tips for safe enquiry

- Listen and allow her time to talk; acknowledge the strength it has taken to talk about the abuse.

- Explain the limits of your confidentiality.

- Reassure her that she is not to blame – the abuser is responsible for their own behaviour – and do not ask questions that imply blame, such as 'What did you do to upset him?'

- Allow her to make her own decisions. Don't push her to leave the relationship if she is not ready to.

- Check whether she needs immediate medical attention for injuries or police protection (for example, if the abuser is waiting outside and an attack is likely). If so, offer help to contact the appropriate services.

- Check what her immediate concerns are and how you can help address these – this might relate to her health and social care needs, children or anything else.

- Help her to report the abuse to the police if she chooses to do so.

- Explore the options that are available to her and share information about organisations that can offer specialist support to people experiencing domestic abuse and their children (if relevant).

- Support her to plan safe strategies for leaving the abusive relationship.

- Allow her to create her own boundaries of what she thinks is safe and not safe; she is the expert of the risks she faces and should not be encouraged to follow strategies that she feels uncomfortable with.

- Offer a point of contact beyond your meeting or a safe way of staying in contact – perhaps agreeing a code word that will result in an agreed response, if appropriate.

- Look after yourself. Recognise your own limitations and do not put yourself into a dangerous situation; for example, by offering to talk to the abuser directly.

There will be a range of issues concerning the woman disclosing abuse, and her immediate and longer-term needs will be individual to her and her circumstances. People with social care needs, particularly if they are dependent on their abuser for care, will often face practical and logistical complications to leaving an abusive relationship. This should be acknowledged and support offered with achieving this.

Some agencies use a risk assessment checklist which comprises a list of set questions aimed at identifying the level of risk of serious injury or homicide a person is facing. A high-risk score can trigger a referral to a safeguarding meeting such as a Multi-Agency Risk Assessment Conference (MARAC), which results in the professionals present sharing information they hold about the case and developing an action plan. The limitations of the risk-based approach have, however, been highlighted within the policy arena and concerns raised that access to services is, in some cases, limited to those deemed at high risk. Furthermore, survivors can feel objectified and silenced by the MARAC process (Robbins et al. 2014). Davies (2015) outlines the pitfalls of the current UK model, including: victim blaming; disregard for consent; over-sharing of information; paternalism; referrals without purpose; and disregard for cultural safety. She advocates survivor-led, anti-oppressive multi-agency practice.

Practitioners may be anxious to meet their duties to safeguard the individual, and this can compromise an empowering response. Safety (as a basic human need) should be addressed along with other needs, but a response that focuses purely on risk is unlikely to engage the person or respond effectively to the situation. Perpetrators of abuse may also themselves have social care needs, and this can present challenging dilemmas for those supporting them. It should not automatically be assumed that the perpetrator's behaviour relates to their social care needs, nor that the abused person should be expected to accept the behaviour, even if they care for the person. Practitioners need to assess the survivor's vulnerability if they are caring or cared for by the perpetrator, and provide a response that places her safety from the perpetrator's abuse as a paramount concern.

Commissioners should refer to the National Institute for Health and Care Excellence (NICE 2014) guidelines on commissioning perpetrator programmes.

Working with parents

For the children living within families where there is domestic abuse, the effects are significant. Domestic abuse is a consistent factor in Serious Case Reviews into child deaths (Research in Practice 2016). Many children who witness it also experience other forms of abuse, and are more likely to have behavioural and emotional problems (Stanley 2011). The law is clear that domestic abuse is a child protection issue, with the Adoption and Children Act (2002) (s.120) amending the definition of 'harm' in s.31(9) of the Children Act (1989) to include 'impairment suffered from seeing or hearing the ill-treatment of another'. This makes witnessing domestic abuse a reason to take action to protect a child from harm.

The Munro (2011) report into child protection found that children's needs can be overlooked when the focus is on the needs of the parent. Equally, if professionals focus on child protection, the abused parent may be unwilling to disclose abuse for fear that their children may be removed, which in turn may mean that the impact on the abused parent is overlooked. This fear is exacerbated where the non-abusing parent has a condition that means their ability to parent is under scrutiny.

Practitioners leading on safeguarding inquiries may need to balance these competing priorities, advocating for the needs of the survivor and the child concurrently. It is important to support the non-abusing parent in a non-judgemental way to deal with the impact of abuse on themselves and their children and to parent to their fullest potential within the circumstances (Johnston 2006, p.29).

Summary of specialist services that may be available

Dedicated domestic abuse agencies (whose primary purpose is to support victims of domestic abuse) have developed a wealth of expertise in supporting survivors of abuse and offer a range of services. These include:

- refuges – safe accommodation and support for women who have no choice but to leave their home (some provide accessible accommodation, although personal care is not provided)

- outreach – support to survivors within their homes or communities

- therapy – helping survivors to overcome the psychological impact of abuse (on an individual or group basis)

- advocacy – supporting survivors to navigate the necessary criminal justice, legal, housing, financial and children-related frameworks and to access their rights

- dedicated support for children and young people affected by domestic abuse.

There are also specialist services that offer dedicated domestic abuse support for women from black and minority ethnic groups, for disabled women, for lesbian, bisexual or trans people, and for men. The range and level of services available within individual areas will vary.[3]

Programmes are also available for perpetrators of abuse to assist them in changing their behaviours, some court-mandated and others voluntary. An evaluation of perpetrator programmes found that, although improvements could still be made, for many men, women and children their lives are improved following a domestic violence perpetrator programme (Kelly and Westmarland 2015).

Strengths-based, needs-led working and safety planning

Women's Aid's 'Change that Lasts' (2015) model response to domestic abuse promotes a response within communities, specialist services and other agencies that is needs-led and strengths-based, and that has a common goal of independence for the victim of abuse. This approach strongly aligns with Making Safeguarding Personal (Lawson, Lewis and Williams 2014), which advocates that best practice ensures that the person at risk is at the centre of safeguarding inquiries.

In practice both approaches can be summarised as meaning:

---

3   Useful websites for finding out about specialist domestic abuse services are www.gov.
     uk/report-domestic-abuse and www.womensaid.org.uk.

- genuinely listening to the person

- understanding that people who have experienced abuse may have reduced self-esteem and confidence in expressing their needs and wishes

- supported decision making; informing people in language or formats that are appropriate for them about the options available to them

- asking the person what they want to happen, and accepting that their answer may not fit with your expectation of what needs to happen, but that addressing this need may break down barriers to becoming safer for them

- learning about the individual strengths and resources the person has available to them – what they can do themselves and what they might need support with

- taking progress at their pace

- keeping them informed throughout.

CASE STUDY

You visit Sukhi, a 40-year-old woman who has multiple sclerosis (MS), and her partner John at their home to discuss her social care needs. The house is immaculately clean and tidy. John talks lots about the impact of Sukhi's MS on their lives and the increasing care he has to provide. He tells you what social care support he thinks is needed. Sukhi doesn't say much, but when she does John often contradicts her, saying she is not thinking straight and that she is forgetful. Sukhi has no local family or friends, saying that they moved to the area five years ago for John's work. John gives you his mobile number as a point of further contact, stating that Sukhi struggles to use hers now.

Drawing on the guidance given within this chapter, consider how you would:

- facilitate a confidential conversation alone with Sukhi and ask direct questions to enable her to disclose any abuse she is experiencing

- respond to any disclosure of abuse non-judgementally and with sensitivity
- provide Sukhi with information and explore the options available to her in an accessible way
- ensure that Sukhi has access to ongoing support
- agree any further action to be taken and a safe way of keeping in touch that Sukhi is comfortable with.

Remember that building someone's trust can take time, so disclosure of abuse may not occur in the first meeting. In your conversations with Sukhi it would be important to look out for patterns of coercive and controlling behaviour, as well as incidents of physical or financial abuse. Ensure that you understand local safeguarding policies and procedures and are able to apply them to this situation if necessary.

Legal responses

A range of civil and criminal justice options are available to support survivors of domestic abuse. Civil justice options tend to be protective, whereas criminal justice is used to punish and deter people from committing further offences. There is no specific crime that covers the range of physical or sexual violence within a domestic abuse context, and the law responds to these through existing criminal offences.

The offence of controlling and coercive behaviour in intimate or family relationships (Serious Crime Act 2015) carries a maximum sentence of five years' imprisonment, a fine, or both. For the offence to apply, the controlling and coercive behaviour must take place 'repeatedly or continuously'; the behaviour must have a 'serious effect' on the victim; the behaviour must be such that the perpetrator knows or 'ought to know' that it will have a serious effect on the victim; and the perpetrator and victim have to have been personally connected when the incidents took place. See Home Office (2015) for further details.

Whatever the crime is, justice options should be offered to everyone equally; Clarke, Williams and Wydall (2016) found that in two thirds of cases of domestic violence towards older people, there was no evidence that criminal or civil justice options were discussed, meaning that older survivors' access to justice was not being supported.

Practitioners have a role to play in supporting access to justice through:

- advising people about their legal options, or knowing who to signpost them to in order to do so

- working with police to gather and record evidence which may be used to make a case in court

- ensuring the availability of support throughout the process of seeking justice.

Civil justice options – protective or preventative measures which can help to give a survivor some 'breathing space' away from the perpetrator – can enable a survivor to consider, free of control or coercion, their next steps in safety planning. These include:

- Domestic Violence Protection Notices and Orders (Crime and Security Act 2010)

- Forced Marriage Protection Orders (Anti-social Behaviour Crime and Policing Act 2014)

- FGM Protection Orders (Female Genital Mutilation Act 2003)

- Restraining orders and injunctions (Domestic Violence, Crime and Victims Act 2004).

The domestic violence disclosure scheme (Clare's law) gives people a 'right to ask' police if their partner has a history of perpetrating domestic violence (Home Office 2016).

The Care Act (2014) guidance (para.14.54) states that people are entitled to an advocate to support them through a safeguarding inquiry if they have 'substantial difficulty' in being involved in the process. Survivors can access independent advocacy support from a local domestic abuse service; advocates may need to work jointly where necessary, to ensure that the right expertise is available for the person's case.

However, case law (*DL v A Local Authority and Others* [2012]) set a precedent for working with people who are experiencing coercive and controlling behaviour. The case involved a local authority bringing proceedings to protect two older parents, one of whom lacked mental capacity, from their son who was allegedly threatening and bullying them. The judgement outlined that high levels of coercion may impair a person's capacity to make a decision, meaning that the inherent jurisdiction of the High Court can be used to protect people who do not lack mental capacity to make relevant decisions, but are experiencing constraint, coercion or undue influence.

Practitioners need to use assessment skills to gauge whether the person is making a capacitated decision in relation to their situation. In extreme cases where a person is experiencing high levels of coercive control, refusing any support and at very high risk of serious injury or death, an application to invoke the Inherent Jurisdiction of the High Court can be made in order to protect life (see Chapter 8).

Multi-agency working

Effective multi-agency working is recognised as crucial and challenging in situations of both domestic abuse and safeguarding adults. An analysis of Domestic Homicide Reviews highlighted multi-agency working as a key factor in providing a good response (Sharp-Jeffs and Kelly 2016). Each agency in the social care and health system has a role in coordinating a response. In addition, key partners include police, housing, children's social care, and domestic abuse services.

The role of the person leading the safeguarding inquiry may be to coordinate a response, being sure to keep the wellbeing of the person at the centre.

Practice tips

- Cultivate good relationships with and local knowledge of specialist workers in a range of agencies, and providers of domestic abuse services which are accessible to people with different social care needs.

- Be able to work within locally agreed policies and procedures, as well as knowing the broader policy and legal context for working with survivors of domestic abuse.

- Advocate for the survivor being worked with, taking time to understand their perspective and using a strengths-based and person-centred approach.

Summary and conclusions

Adult social care practitioners have a key role to play in supporting people with care and support needs who are experiencing domestic abuse, in both detecting coercive control and responding to it. The evidence shows that people with care and support needs are at higher risk of domestic abuse, meaning that health and social care practitioners should use safe enquiry when discussing relationships with people who use services. Where practitioners are leading safeguarding inquiries related to domestic abuse, working with people in a strengths-based, and needs and outcomes focused, way can support people to regain control over their lives.

References

Clarke, A., Williams, J., and Wydall, S. (2016) 'Access to justice for victims/survivors of elder abuse: A qualitative study.' *Social Policy and Society 15*, 207–220.

Crenshaw, K. (1993) 'Mapping the margins: Intersectionality, identity politics and violence against Women of Color.' *Stanford Law Review 43*, 1241–1299.

DAIP (1984) *Power and Control Wheel.* Available at www.theduluthmodel.org/training/wheels.html, accessed on 20 April 2017.

Davies, E. (2015) 'Survivor-led ethics in multi-agency work.' *DVRCV Advocate 1*, Autumn/Winter. Available at www.dvrcv.org.au/sites/default/files/Survivor-led_ethics_in_multi-agency_work_DVRCV_AUTWIN2015_davis.pdf, accessed on 20 April 2017.

DeafHope (n.d.) *Power and Control Wheel.* Available at www.deaf-hope.org/domestic-violence/power-and-control-wheel, accessed on 20 April 2017.

Department of Health (2016) *Care and Support Statutory Guidance.* London: DH.

Hague, G., Thiara, R., Magowan, P., and Mullendar, A. (2008) *Making the Links: Disabled Women and Domestic Violence.* Bristol: Women's Aid.

HM Government (2014) *Multi-Agency Practice Guidelines: Handling Cases of Forced Marriage.* Available at www.gov.uk/government/uploads/system/uploads/attachment_data/file/322307/HMG_MULTI_AGENCY_PRACTICE_GUIDELINES_v1_180614_FINAL.pdf, accessed on 20 April 2017.

Home Office (2015) *Controlling or Coercive Behaviour in an Intimate or Family Relationship: Statutory Guidance Framework.* London: The Home Office. Available at www.gov.uk/government/uploads/system/uploads/attachment_data/file/482528/Controlling_or_coercive_behaviour_-_statutory_guidance.pdf, accessed on 20 April 2017.

Home Office (2016) *Domestic Violence Disclosure Scheme (DVDS) One Year On – Home Office Assessment of National Roll-Out.* Available at www.gov.uk/government/uploads/system/uploads/attachment_data/file/505434/2016-03-08_DVDS_report_final_.pdf, accessed on 20 April 2017.

Home Office and Department for Education (2015) *Mandatory Reporting of Female Genital Mutilation: Procedural Information.* Available at www.gov.uk/government/publications/mandatory-reporting-of-female-genital-mutilation-procedural-information, accessed on 20 April 2017.

Home Office and FCO (2016) *Forced Marriage Unit Statistics 2015.* Available at www.gov.uk/government/uploads/system/uploads/attachment_data/file/505827/Forced_Marriage_Unit_statistics_2015.pdf, accessed on 20 April 2017.

Johnston, J.R. (2006) 'A child-centered approach to high-conflict and domestic-violence families: Differential assessment and interventions.' *Journal of Family Studies 12*, 1, 15–35.

Kelly, L., and Westmarland, N. (2015) *Domestic Violence Perpetrator Programmes: Steps Towards Change. Project Mirabal Final Report.* London and Durham: London Metropolitan University and Durham University.

Knight, L., and Hester, M. (2014) 'Domestic abuse and dementia: What are the characteristic features and patterns of longstanding domestic abuse following the onset of dementia?' *Safe*, Winter 2014, 10–14.

Lawson, J., Lewis, S., and Williams, C. (2014) *Making Safeguarding Personal: Guide 2014.* London: Local Government Association.

Laxton, C. (2014) *Virtual World, Real Fear: Women's Aid Report into Online Abuse, Harassment and Stalking.* Bristol: Women's Aid.

LGA and ADASS (2015) *Adult Safeguarding and Domestic Abuse – A Guide to Support Practitioners and Managers.* London: Local Government Association.

Magowan, P. (2004) *The Impact of Disability on Women's Experiences of Domestic Abuse: An Empirical Study into Disabled Women's Experiences of, and Responses to, Domestic Abuse.* ESRC/PhD research. Nottingham: University of Nottingham.

McCarthy, M., Hunt, S., and Milne-Skilman, K. (2015) '"I know it was every week, but I can't be sure if it was every day": Domestic violence and women with learning disabilities.' *Journal of Applied Research in Intellectual Disabilities 30*, 2, 269–282.

McGarry, J., and Simpson, C. (2011) 'Domestic abuse and older women: Exploring the opportunities for service development and care delivery.' *The Journal of Adult Protection 13*, 6, 294–301.

Munro, E. (2011) *The Munro Review of Child Protection: Final Report. A Child-Centred System.* London: TSO.

NICE (2014) *Domestic Violence and Abuse: Multi-Agency Working.* Public Health Guideline [PH50]. Available at www.nice.org.uk/guidance/ph50, accessed on 20 April 2017.

Research in Practice (2016) *Serious Case Reviews.* Available at http://seriouscasereviews.rip.org.uk, accessed on 20 April 2017.

Rich, K. (2014) '"My body came between us": Accounts of partner-abused women with physical disabilities.' *Affilia: Journal of Women and Social Work 29*, 4, 1–16.

Robbins, R., Banks, C., McLaughlin, H., Bellamy, C., and Thackray, D. (2016) 'Is domestic abuse an adult social work issue?' *Social Work Education: The International Journal 35*, 2, 131–143.

Robbins, R., McLaughlin, H., Banks, C., Bellamy, C., and Thackray, D. (2014) 'Domestic violence and Multi-Agency Risk Assessment Conferences (MARACs): A scoping review.' *The Journal of Adult Protection 16*, 6, 389–398.

Rogers, M. (2016) 'Breaking down barriers: Exploring potential for social care practice with trans survivors of domestic abuse.' *Health and Social Care in the Community 24*, 1, 68–76.

Sharp-Jeffs, N., and Kelly, L. (2016) *Domestic Homicide Review (DHR) Case Analysis: Report for Standing Together.* London: Standing Together and London Metropolitan University.

Smith, K. (ed.), Osborne, S., Lau, I., and Britton, A. (2012) *Homicides, Firearm Offences and Intimate Violence 2010/11: Supplementary Volume 2 to Crime in England and Wales 2010/11.* London: The Home Office.

Southend Safeguarding Adults Board (2011) *Mr and Mrs A (Mary Russell) Serious Case Review: Executive Summary.* Southend: Southend Safeguarding Adults Board. Available at http://withscotland.org/download/mr-mrs-a, accessed on 20 April 2017.

Stanley, N. (2011) *Children Experiencing Domestic Violence: A Research Review.* Dartington: Research in Practice.

Stark, E. (2007) *Coercive Control: How Men Entrap Women in Personal Life.* New York: Oxford University Press.

Thiara, R. (2015) *'Losing Out on Both Counts': Disabled Women and Domestic Violence.* Presentation for safelives.org.uk. Slides available at www.safelives.org.uk/sites/default/files/resources/Disabled%20Women%20and%20DV%20-%20FINAL%20-%20SafeLives%202016%20-%20Ravi%20Thiara.pdf, accessed on 20 April 2017.

Trevillion K., Oram S., Feder G. and Howard L.M. (2012) 'Experiences of Domestic Violence and Mental Disorders: A Systematic Review and Meta-Analysis.' *PLoS ONE* 7, 12, e51740. doi:10.1371/journal.pone.0051740

Walter-Brice, A., Cox, R., Priest, H., and Thompson, F. (2012) 'What do women with learning disabilities say about their experiences of domestic abuse within the context of their intimate partner relationships?' *Disability and Society 27*, 4, 503–517.

Women's Aid (2015) *Change that Lasts.* Available at www.womensaid.org.uk/our-approach-change-that-lasts, accessed on 20 April 2017.

Chapter 12

Palermo to Croydon

MODERN SLAVERY AND HUMAN TRAFFICKING – SEEKING
BEST PRACTICE ON A NEW FRONTIER OF SAFEGUARDING

Antony Botting, Tish Elliott and Sean Olivier

'Captivity is the greatest of all evils that can befall one.'

Miguel De Cervantes (De Cervantes 1992)

Introduction

This chapter provides a brief introduction to modern-day slavery as a safeguarding concern, drawing from the experiences of survivors of modern slavery and human trafficking over the last decade. It outlines current legislation, referral systems and specialist services, including strategies developed by a local authority in the UK capital (Croydon Council) in seeking to combat this issue. It introduces key factors that practitioners can consider when working with people who may be victims of human trafficking or modern-day slavery (MDS), or those who are potentially vulnerable.

> From the very first beating when I was choked to the point of unconsciousness until the day he pulled the trigger on the miraculously unloaded gun in my mouth, I knew obedience meant survival… I had to continue this life of being obedient to him so my family wouldn't get hurt. (Shamere McKenzie, a college student, survivor of sexual slavery)[1]

Such narratives illustrate the powerful hold that threatening behaviours have over victims and why many victims of slavery are bound by what is often referred to as 'invisible shackles'. Survivors' accounts highlight the extreme risk posed by the crime of MDS and the harrowing level

---

1   Available at www.endslaverynow.org/learn/modern-slave-narratives.

of deprivation which victims can be subject to. We consider what can be done to help gain traction in the understanding of professionals tasked (now by law) with combating what is both a criminal matter and a social care one.

Modern slavery, human trafficking and human smuggling

There are more people in slavery today than at any point in history.[2]

Modern slavery is a severe infringement of human rights where, through physical means or through threat of penalty, the perpetrator secures compliance in order to hold the victim captive and benefit from the victim's suffering. Slavery does not necessarily involve the forced movement of people, although many cases do involve some form of human trafficking.

Human trafficking is generally described in terms of three stages: *recruitment, transportation* and *exploitation*. It may or may not mean the crossing of borders – a victim may be moved from one town to another or even from one street to the next.

The international legal framework which defines human trafficking is the Protocol to Prevent, Suppress and Punish Trafficking in Persons, Especially Women and Children (Article 3, United Nations 2000), otherwise known as the Palermo Protocol:

> 'Trafficking in persons' shall mean the recruitment, transportation, transfer, harbouring or receipt of persons, by means of the threat or use of force or other forms of coercion, of abduction, of fraud, of deception, of the abuse of power or of a position of vulnerability or of the giving or receiving of payments or benefits to achieve the consent of a person having control over another person, for the purpose of exploitation.
>
> 'Exploitation' shall include, at a minimum, the exploitation of the prostitution of others or other forms of sexual exploitation, forced labour or services, slavery or practices similar to slavery, servitude or the removal of organs. (United Nations 2000, p.2)

---

2   *Global Slavery Index* (2016). In 2016, 45.8 million people were estimated to be in some form of modern slavery in 167 countries; see www.globalslaveryindex.org/findings.

Thus for a person to have been a victim of trafficking there will have been three elements: an *act*, achieved by *means* of force, deception or coercion, for the *purpose* of exploitation (Home Office 2015a).

Contemporary slavery is referred to broadly as 'modern-day slavery', which focuses more on the exploitation and the means used to coerce the victim, rather than focusing on the element of movement. Modern slavery, including sexual exploitation, domestic servitude and compulsory labour, involves both *means* and *service* (Reed 2016):

- *Means:* of being held, which may be physical or threat of penalty, abuse of power or exploiting vulnerability, and

- *Service:* as a result of the 'means' whereby an individual provides a service for the benefit of the perpetrator, which may include begging, sexual service, manual labour or domestic service.

High demand for inexpensive labour and commercial sex are predominant causes of modern slavery, alongside poverty and the vulnerability of marginalised people.

Human trafficking is often confused with human smuggling (for similarities and differences see Figure 12.1). Smuggled migrants are viewed as voluntary, active participants in the process of movement, dependent on the smuggler for the duration of the journey, but otherwise 'independent' in the eyes of the law. They may be aware of the conditions of their travel and on arriving at their destination are seen as free to go, even though their plight and the situation they are fleeing may be a high-level indicator to the contrary.

According to UK law (Immigration Act 1971), in cases of human smuggling a crime is committed against the state by the smuggler. It is possible for those being smuggled to become victims of trafficking, if during their journey they are unable to pay for a section of their journey or they fall into the hands of a trafficker (British Red Cross 2016).

In cases of human trafficking, control methods such as restriction of movement, deprivation of documentation and debt bondage may be used to achieve the ultimate objective which is the intended exploitation of the individual. In these cases, the victim is treated as a commodity and, unlike smuggling, their movement is a crime against the individual (British Red Cross 2016).

Practitioners in the public, private and third sector may see symptoms of slavery at any of the stages of recruitment, transportation and exploitation, though it would be rare for any one agency or person to be able to identify the crime in its entirety (Home Office 2015a). Some high-profile cases have found victims held captive in the same location, undiscovered for years.

Trafficking   Smuggling

Figure 12.1 Trafficking and smuggling: similarities and differences.[3]

In the case of the Connors family (*Crown Prosecution v Patrick Joseph Connors, Patrick Dean Connors, William Connors and Lee Carbis*), Cardiff Crown Court heard that:

> vulnerable men – many of them homeless and addicted to alcohol or drugs – were recruited in soup kitchens and outside jobcentres and promised cash payments, food and lodging in return for work… But once there they were forced to work for nothing…for up to 19 hours a day and were routinely abused, underfed and housed in filthy sheds and horseboxes. (Topping 2012)

---

3   Copyright. Reprinted by permission of the International Organization for Migration (IOM). Permission is granted for this material to be shared for non-commercial, educational purposes, provided that this copyright statement appears and that the recorded piece is not edited in any way and is always shown in its entirety. Available at www.blueblindfold.gov.ie/website/bbf/bbfweb.nsf/page/humantrafficking-traffickingsmuggling-en.

Those rescued were in poor health, one with scurvy, an indicator of the common health concerns experienced by victims of slavery held in distressingly inhumane conditions.

Modern slavery is something of a 'shape shifter'. It morphs into other categories and crosses boundaries. It can lead a practitioner to think that what they are reading, observing or experiencing is domestic violence, a labour dispute, child sexual exploitation or other form of coercion and control. More dangerously, practitioners may simply not see what they are looking at as slavery or trafficking. They may be forgiven for failing entirely to see these signs of abuse, often described as the 'invisible shackles' of modern slavery.

Haughey (2016) provides specific examples of what she describes as the 'invisible handcuffs of psychological imprisonment':

- removal and detention of travel and identification documents

- confiscation of mobile phones

- denial of unfettered access to communication with family or friends

- accompanying the victim at all times outside of the premises

- deprivation of money

- threats made about family or friends if the victim fails to comply with the criminal's directions

- victims of forced labour reluctant to report the offending they are being subjected to or even acknowledge its existence

- many victims trafficked to the UK considering the appalling conditions of their servitude in this country to be preferable to the alternatives in their country of origin.

UK legal and political developments

In response to the Palermo Protocol, the UK government introduced the National Referral Mechanism (NRM) in 2009 as a tool to be used by 'first responder' organisations, such as local authorities, the police and some non-statutory organisations, to refer suspected victims of modern slavery or human trafficking for determination as to whether such exploitation has taken place.[4]

For suspected adult victims who consent to enter into the NRM process and to receive support, a safe support and accommodation option can be made available through specialist organisations such as the Salvation Army (a UK charity) which has a government contract to provide support to suspected victims of modern slavery. The charity would make contact with the suspected victim and arrange a placement, perhaps with an appropriate subcontracting organisation. This placement is usually at least 100 miles away from the area where the alleged crime took place, to help prevent the survivor of slavery being re-trafficked. A growing number of organisations offer specialist support to victims (see useful website links listed at the end of the chapter).

The number of NRM referrals has been increasing steadily every year; 1002 people (including adults and minors) were referred from April to June 2016 alone, 925 of these being referred in England, a 12 per cent increase on the previous quarter (National Crime Agency 2016).[5] These potential victims were from 70 different countries, with the most common nationalities being Albanian, Vietnamese and British. Labour and sexual exploitation were the most prominent, with 312 and 231 adult cases respectively. The third most common form amongst adults was domestic servitude, with 89 cases reported.

The Modern Slavery Act (2015) consolidates previous offences relating to trafficking and slavery, creates two new civil orders to prevent slavery, and increases the maximum sentence for the crime of human trafficking to life imprisonment, also offering a statutory defence for victims to prevent their criminalisation and strengthen their protection. This established the first UK Independent Anti-Slavery Commissioner and placed a duty on large businesses, including supermarket chains, to play a part in eradicating slavery from global supply chains. The Haughey Review of the Modern Slavery Act (2016) recognises it as 'an important milestone in the fight against slavery and for social justice'.

---

4   See www.gov.uk/government/publications/human-trafficking-victims-referral-and-assessment-forms.

5   In addition to the referrals in England, 10 referred from Northern Ireland, 34 from Scotland and 33 from Wales. Of the 1002 total: 50 per cent were females, 49 per cent males and 1 per cent transgender; 66 per cent adults and 34 per cent minors.

Importantly, the Act also established a new statutory duty for first responder organisations to report all suspected cases of trafficking to the Modern Slavery Human Trafficking Unit (MSHTU), which is part of the National Crime Agency.[6] Operational advice and guidance on any human trafficking and slavery-related matter can be sought from the MSHTU on their website or helpline. Practitioners can also seek guidance and advice from the UK Modern Slavery Helpline and Resource Centre.[7]

Where there are suspected child cases of trafficking, an NRM referral should *always* be completed whether or not consent is given, whereas adult victims need to give consent. When a suspected adult victim does not wish to enter into the process, a Duty to Notify form (Home Office 2016) should be completed and forwarded to the Home Office.[8]

The main differences between the NRM and Duty to Notify form are that the NRM leads to an official determination as to whether a person has been a victim of trafficking and also may lead to a criminal investigation and prosecution of the perpetrator, whilst the Duty to Notify form triggers neither of these things. Instead, it provides intelligence in relation to potential trafficking activity to central government.

Current landscape and challenges moving forward

As a result of their treatment, their background and/or their pre-existing vulnerabilities, victims are not always willing or able to cooperate with the authorities. The result is that many victims are in effect 'held in plain sight' – having the appearance of living in society but in fact having little or no freedom. (Haughey 2016)

The Care Act (2014, s.42) places a responsibility on local authority social workers to enquire into allegations of abuse or neglect (see Chapter 8), which now specifically includes modern slavery, although this is not a matter for local authority practitioners to address alone.

---

6   See www.nationalcrimeagency.gov.uk/about-us/what-we-do/specialist-capabilities/uk-human-trafficking-centre.

7   See www.unseenuk.org/about/projects/uk-modern-slavery-helpline-and-resource-centre.

8   See www.gov.uk/government/publications/duty-to-notify-the-home-office-of-potential-victims-of-modern-slavery.

The Care Act (2014) allows the enquiry task to be delegated by the local authority to partner agencies. As such, a nurse at a hospital who has a relationship of trust with a suspected victim could conduct the fact-finding, following local inter-agency procedures accordingly (Department of Health [DH] 2016, para.14).

When any concern is raised it is important that practitioners assess whether or not the adult has care and support needs; and if so, the practitioner should, in the interest of being cautious, consider providing a Care Act (2014) Section 42 safeguarding response until this is proved otherwise. Without such a cautious approach there is a risk of under-reacting to a person's needs and not sufficiently reducing or removing the risk.

The response must be a multi-professional one, with the first responder leading colleagues on how to quickly create a network around the person concerned. A network meeting helps to decide what the risks and needs are. From this point more concrete actions can be set in place in the form of a safety plan, and the situation should be more accurately risk-assessed drawing from information held by all parties and shared as appropriate. A full list of 'First Responder' agencies is available on the National Crime Agency website.[9]

In summary, the tasks that a first responder could undertake once a suspected adult victim has come to their attention are the following:

- Consider the person's immediate safety (including the possible need for health appointment and police presence).

- Gain the salient features of their narrative, including the adult's desired outcomes.

- Inform them of the processes (NRM, safeguarding, police enquiry) and sequence of likely events/appointments.

- Create a multi-disciplinary network around the person (likely to include the Home Office, police, health workers, social workers and advocates), perhaps in a formal planning/network meeting.

- Complete either the NRM (if consent is given) or the MS1 Duty to Notify forms.

---

9   See www.nationalcrimeagency.gov.uk.

- If the adult has agreed, link them to the third sector partners who manage specialist human trafficking and modern slavery welfare and accommodation and ensure that logistical arrangements are made.

- Consider continuity of care and protection planning if the person leaves the first responder agency's geographical area.

Domestic abuse and modern slavery

In 2014 a young man, originally from Nigeria, was rescued after 24 years of being enslaved by a couple in the UK when he saw media reports about modern-day slavery and contacted the Hope for Justice charity. The perpetrators were found guilty of holding a person in slavery or servitude (*Metropolitan Police v Emmanuel and Antan Edet*, reported by Proto 2015).

Domestic abuse can be intrinsically linked to human trafficking and modern slavery when the type of abuse of the victim is for the purposes of domestic servitude and sexual exploitation. The Serious Crime Act (2015, s.76) created a new offence of controlling or coercive behaviour in intimate or familial relationships (Home Office 2015b), which includes FGM, forced marriage and honour-based violence (see Chapter 11).

Like domestic abuse, human trafficking and modern slavery are largely hidden crimes which require practitioners to remain alert to possible indicators and to maintain a healthy scepticism about explanations which may be given by potential perpetrators. A situation which appears to be one of domestic abuse may exhibit indicators suggesting that human trafficking and/or enslavement may also have taken place. The victim may be coerced into a seemingly loving relationship but go on to suffer sexual exploitation by their partner/ trafficker, and be forced to provide sexual services to others for the financial benefit of the abusive partner.

Given that both domestic abuse and modern slavery are additional categories of abuse in the Care Act (2014), the importance of responding to such complexities with a Section 42 inquiry is vital.

The following case studies are fictional, drawing from an amalgamation of different survivor experiences to support learning from practice.

CASE STUDY 1: DOMESTIC SERVITUDE

A practitioner visits an older man in his home. He lives with his family along with their lodger, who has come to the UK from Nigeria to live with them. They attend the same church and the family paid for his flight to the UK. The lodger says he has a small room in the basement of the house, staying there rent free. As a part of the arrangement he cares for the host family's elderly relative. He works part time in a restaurant and is attending a course to learn English. During the conversation he mentions that he is saving as he does not yet have any funds to return home.

It transpires his caring role often entails long anti-social hours and waking night care. He receives some payment for this but it is well below minimum wage for the hours. He appears happy and says he comes and goes, often doing the shopping for the whole family. He has access to his own money as well as that of the person for whom he cares.

On the one hand the arrangement is working well and the relationship appears to be symbiotic. The practitioner did not enquire as to the lodger's immigration status as this was not the purpose of the visit, but is aware that a migrant worker on an informal arrangement may not be aware of his rights, or perhaps lacks the formal right to work and subsequently may feel indebted to the family for the free accommodation and flight. If he did need to raise any concerns he may not feel able to do so. The practitioner has not seen the accommodation and returns to the office feeling unsettled.

The lodger does not have care and support needs and a safeguarding inquiry under Section 42 (Care Act 2014) is not required on current evidence available. The practitioner could, however, consider contacting the Gangmasters and Labour Abuse Authority[10] for advice, who oversee the labour market across all sectors of UK industry.

In 2014, a young woman with learning disability was freed from domestic servitude having been kept at a couple's home in Nottingham for five months, resulting in their prosecution for

---

10   Previously the Gangmasters Licensing Authority (GLA), recently renamed; see www.gla.gov.uk.

forced labour. She had been taken to their home by someone she met online, made to sleep on the kitchen floor or in a duck pen, and subjected to daily beatings, threats and intimidation (*Crown Prosecution vs Pascoe and Jepson* [2015]). Now a survivor, she was commended for her courage in supporting the police in the prosecution.

When supporting a person who may be a victim of MDS, it is vital to focus on the exploitation, and the support which can be provided, rather than issues relating to their immigration status or any crime which they may appear to have committed whilst in slavery. The Modern Slavery Act (2015) sets out a defence for crimes which may have been committed by victims of MDS whilst under duress from their trafficker. As such, care should be taken by the professional network to avoid *moral* responses which may criminalise the victims of slavery. All practitioners need to be aware of the indicators of labour exploitation and of their duty of care in this respect.

CASE STUDY 2: DOMESTIC ABUSE, TRAFFICKING AND SLAVERY

A young woman, a migrant with a right to work in the UK, presents at a local domestic abuse drop-in centre for survivors. She tells of meeting a male friend online, and that they moved to the UK to seek work and ended up living together as partners. She has care and support needs due to a physical disability, and has mental capacity to understand the risks which are salient in her situation. She describes how their relationship has been characterised by financial abuse culminating in his control of her due to her physical dependency, and more recently of physical violence.[11] When asked for her desired outcomes, the young woman requests help to return to her family back home and for no further action to be taken.

In this situation a response would be conducted under s.42 (Care Act 2014). A joint interview of the victim at the domestic abuse centre by a specialist abuse advocate as well as a safeguarding social worker would offer an opportunity for

---

11   See case studies 'Maria' and 'Emma': www.coercivecontrol.ripfa.org.uk.

the victim's narrative to be explored with a full chronology to establish if potential trafficking was involved. Was the online friendship and passage into the UK an act of 'kindness' by a friend or a conduit for the young woman to then be financially exploited and domestically abused?

This shows the value of establishing the length and breadth of the issue and matters which may predispose the risk, otherwise such cases may be treated as a domestic abuse case alone. Practitioners are encouraged to look at the motivating factors of the person thought to be causing the harm and examine the full context when formulating a plan to support the person who has been harmed. What appears to the woman to be a friendship which then becomes an abusive intimate relationship may well, with a more critical view, be the outcome of a perpetrator's plan to initially befriend her and then abuse her. However, she may identify as a victim of domestic abuse, but not of trafficking. As an adult with capacity, her wishes and desired outcomes need to be respected.

In such a situation the practitioner should consider the Duty to Notify procedures (Home Office 2016). Such cases may also be taken to a local Multi-Agency Risk Assessment Conference (MARAC) working in parallel with MDS procedures.[12]

CASE STUDY 3: SEXUAL EXPLOITATION

A nurse at a walk-in sexual health clinic notices that a female patient has frequent appointments, arriving at times with intimate bruising. She is always accompanied by an older female. The nurse is uncertain of their relationship and feels that the patient is intimidated by the older female. Explanations for the bruising are brief and not always consistent with the nature of the injuries. All staff have attended MDS training and have recorded that the patient does not appear free to speak. Staff report their concerns to the Trust's Safeguarding Lead as possible sexual exploitation. A Trust-wide 'red flag' is placed on the client's file prompting all staff to link presenting issues to these concerns.

---

12   See www.safelives.org.uk/practice-support/resources-marac-meetings.

When the patient next arrived for sexually transmitted infection testing, staff managed to see her briefly in private. The patient acknowledged that she did not feel fully in control of aspects of her life, her narrative suggesting she was being coerced into sexual practices. With the client's consent, immediate police and MDS reporting was initiated on the day and a place of safety sought.

The Sophie Hayes Foundation provides further victim narratives on the subject of sexual exploitation[13] which illustrate how a seemingly healthy relationship can 'morph' into trafficking for the purposes of sexual exploitation. Local authorities need to develop organisational strategies to tackle MDS, to consider local, national and international actions to interrupt 'supply chains', and ensure that all staff are aware of specialist MDS agencies.

Professional development

This section signposts practitioners to further areas for development when working with safeguarding situations of this nature.

Eliciting the desired outcome

Eliciting the person's desired outcomes and their own views as to what they wish to happen is fundamentally important, congruent with person-centred outcomes and practice, and in line with guidance on Making Safeguarding Personal (see Chapters 1 and 5).

In MDS cases there are particular issues that make eliciting the desired outcomes difficult. The practitioner should not assume that the person's original stated desires are going to remain their viewpoint. Victims may not realise all their options when initially interviewed, so the topic should be revisited at various points along the process to ensure that the person feels as in control as it is possible to be. Lastly, the timing of intervention is significant. While immediate steps are taken to make a person safe, as Kate Garbers states, 'just because it is an opportune time for us to offer assistance and support, it doesn't mean that it is the right time for them' (Garbers 2016), thus a *slow burn* approach to building confidence and trust should be taken.

---

13   See https://sophiehayesfoundation.org/about.

If a person refuses the NRM process, then first responders need to work to negotiate what level of input the person will accept.[14] This may not be direct assistance initially but may simply be an agreement to return for a second interview (and at the same time, allow both trust and a relationship to build). A victim may only agree to enter the NRM process after several interactions with a practitioner. If people have care and support needs then joint work needs to be carried out (including with the Home Office) to ensure that any support required can still be received during the period of reflection (45 days). Under certain circumstances it may be considered better for the person not to be dispersed to another town but rather to remain close to where their support needs can be met.

Joint working and pre-planning

Practitioners may need to undertake joint work closely and very quickly. If a survivor comes to the attention of practitioners as a result of being freed, they will require immediate medical attention as well as accommodation planning. Second, police will need to be involved, and this may create anxiety for the person concerned. Practitioners need to approach this sensitively and balance the desires of the person with the need to prosecute those involved in slavery and the wider public interest of those who are also at risk. Such matters are police-led and may involve raids on illegal premises. Practitioners will need to ensure that their own supervision and opportunities for debrief are in place.

Communication considerations

Practitioners will frequently be working with people who have limited understanding of English, so interpreters should be offered to the person, with the same interpreter throughout the process wherever possible, to help build trust in interviews. Give careful consideration to possible family relationships or community connections with interpreters, including potential links to the abuser(s); also to gender and privacy, especially if the nature of the disclosure is intimately traumatic. This principle applies to all those with communication

---

14   In Croydon (London borough) only 50 per cent of clients who were seen as victims of MDS agreed to be referred to the NRM service.

needs where reasonable adjustments are required, and may include asking a professional signer or speech therapist for assistance (Equality Act 2010, s.20).

The 'one chance' and 'clear the schedule' principles

Some circumstances require practitioners' undivided and immediate attention. For example, in the prevention of forced marriage (see Chapter 11), practitioners are advised that they must recognise the 'one chance' rule (HM Government 2014), meaning that a practitioner may only get one opportunity to help the person. If the practitioner is not alert to what is occurring and is not aware of his or her options, that opportunity can be lost. Given that such cases will likely require intense work and the NRM can take several days to produce a decision, workers will need the flexibility to 'clear their schedules' to enable them to dedicate that time to helping the person.

Mental capacity and advocacy considerations

As early as possible, ideally in the first interview, the practitioner would assess mental capacity (Home Office 2007) or seek the opinion of a trained Mental Capacity Act professional (see Chapter 7). If the person lacks capacity to make a specific decision as a result of an impairment of their mind or brain, then the Best Interests process would be followed and an advocate appointed. An assessment may need to be conducted again during the process (even several times), given that any mental capacity assessment is 'moment-specific'.

Should a person appear to have capacity, but practitioners feel that the person is making unwise decisions due to being under 'undue influence' (Home Office 2015b), then workers can attempt to draw together evidence demonstrating that the person has capacity but that they are making decisions placing them at harm due to 'invisible shackles' (such as fear of going to prison, being deported or threats made being enacted by the abusers), believing that no positive changes can ever be made. Such arguments are best supported by recording a chronology of occasions when the person was planning to take action to keep themselves safe, but later changed their plan after influence from the perpetrators. This provides a basic cause-and-effect argument to help demonstrate to a court the exact nature of the influence which is keeping the person in slavery, including the victim being coerced into dependence on the abuser.

Cases of people who have capacity but who are making unwise decisions due to coercion or undue influence could be considered to be brought before the High Court to request use of their power of Inherent Jurisdiction. A practitioner would require the help of the local authority's legal team for such an argument. Examples may include an abuser targeting a person who is alcohol or drug dependent and, once enslaved, keeping this person supplied with alcohol/drugs to increase their dependence on the perpetrator and lessen their chances of trying to leave.

Repatriation considerations

In the past, local authorities have funded expenses for repatriation; however, the combination of care and support needs and having been a recent victim of trafficking has its own challenges, and failure to adequately plan for their future protection may simply give rise to an increased chance of the person being targeted again. Trading Standards teams refer to 'target hardening' when helping victims of financial abuse to be more aware and educated over how a scam works, leading to a decreased chance of the person being re-victimised. Similar work can be conducted with survivors of modern slavery considering repatriation, or indeed those remaining in the UK.

Should a person wish to return to their country then arrangements should be made with them for the travel to take place. However, the duty of care extends as far as is reasonably possible. Practitioners should seek assurances on such issues as:

- who is meeting the person at the port of arrival and what the care and social plans will be from that point

- what accommodation will be available to them

- initial subsistence

- health considerations

- and, potentially, care needs assessment.

The Home Office has an Assisted Return Process for people who wish to return to their country of origin, though this precludes ongoing contact once the person has returned. Given the trafficking history, time should be taken to assess the risks of returning by exploring the details of their narrative to understand exactly how they were coerced into slavery and how this could be prevented from re-occurring. In *Life Beyond the Safe House* the authors suggest that 'case monitoring should be finalised only when it is believed that a victim is economically and socially capable, and able to live independently' (Beddoe, Bundock and Jardan 2015, p.20).

Best practice guide

Table 12.1 Key points to remember, and common pitfalls to avoid

Do	Don't
Do consider if the person is eligible for a Section 42 Care Act (2014) response (do they have care and support needs as now defined?).	Don't ignore non-statutory partners who can assist in making a safe enquiry, safety planning and service delivery.
Do work jointly with the Home Office.	Don't allow suspected MDS cases to drift.
Do make urgent safety plans if required; have safeguarding discussions.	Don't confuse the NRM, Duty to Report and Section 42 safeguarding process. These are separate but parallel – one can help strengthen the other but must not be done instead of the other.
Do consider if the victim(s) require a package of care, and plan for needs post the NRM period.	
Do remember the five principles of the Mental Capacity Act (2005) and that adults with capacity have a right to make an unwise decision.	Don't rely on the original assessment – repeat the assessment as the situation progresses.
Do consider whether a person has capacity but may be under 'undue influence'. Use specialist services, including professional translators/signers, and consult with MDS experts.	Don't ignore the possibility of family interpreters or anyone known to the victim being part of the abuse network.
	Don't be defined by category – assess holistically in all areas that require attention.
Do hold in mind that people who decline help may be controlled and coerced, and that this may be a police matter which itself creates further fear.	Don't use a Duty to Notify form for under-18s – all suspected MDS cases involving minors must be referred to Children's Safeguarding services and into the NRM process, with or without consent.
Do report all suspected adult cases to the UK Human Trafficking Centre via the NRM for those who consent, or via the MS1 Duty to Notify form for those who do not.	

Conclusion

This chapter has shown how new political and legislative developments have led to specialist provision and guidance that should give rise to more concrete practices and clear local policies on MDS as a core part of adult safeguarding work. It is hoped that this brief account of complex work will support practitioners to be better able to recognise the possible indicators of human trafficking and modern slavery, to take decisive action to combat this and to provide appropriate, relevant support to survivors. A number of local authorities have appointed Slavery Safeguarding Leads or established Anti-Slavery Committees to support this work, though we would encourage all practitioners to develop their knowledge and skills in this crucial aspect of adult safeguarding. Familiarity with the NRM process is central to the response in the context of rising situations coming to light of people being trafficked, enslaved, coerced and controlled, at times to the extent of no longer understanding any concept of consent.

References

Beddoe, C., Bundock, L., and Jardan, T. (2015) *Life Beyond the Safe House: For Survivors of Modern Slavery in London.* London: Human Trafficking Foundation. Available at www.humantraffickingfoundation.org/sites/default/files/Life%20Beyond%20the%20Safe%20House_0.pdf, accessed on 21 April 2017.

British Red Cross (2016) *Humanity at a Crossroads: Migrants' Journeys on the Central Mediterranean Route.* London: British Red Cross. Available at www.redcross.org.uk/~/media/BritishRedCross/Documents/About%20us/Migration%20Report.pdf, accessed on 21 April 2017.

De Cervantes, M. (1992) *Don Quixote.* Hertfordshire: Wordsworth.

Department of Health (2016) *Care and Support Statutory Guidance.* London: DH.

Garbers, K. (2016) *Modern Slavery: Would You Spot the Signs of the 'Unseen Crime'?* Community Care. Available at www.communitycare.co.uk/2016/03/23/modern-slavery-can-social-workers-spot-signs-unseen-crime, accessed on 21 April 2017.

Global Slavery Index (2016) Available at www.globalslaveryindex.org, accessed on 21 April 2017.

Haughey, C. (2016) *The Modern Slavery Act 2015 Review: One Year On.* London: Home Office. Available at www.gov.uk/government/uploads/system/uploads/attachment_data/file/542047/2016_07_31_Haughey_Review_of_Modern_Slavery_Act_-_final_1.0.pdf, accessed on 21 April 2017.

HM Government (2014) *The Right to Choose: Multi-Agency Statutory Guidance for Dealing with Forced Marriage.* London: Cabinet Office.

Home Office (2007) *Mental Capacity Act 2005: Codes of Practice.* London: The Stationery Office.

Home Office (2015a) *Modern Slavery Offenders – Evidence Review.* Cited by Devon and Cornwall Police, Peninsula Overview of Modern Slavery (July 2015).

Home Office (2015b) *Controlling or Coercive Behaviour in an Intimate or Family Relationship: Statutory Guidance Framework.* Available at www.gov.uk/government/uploads/system/uploads/attachment_data/file/482528/Controlling_or_coercive_behaviour_-_statutory_guidance.pdf, accessed on 21 April 2017.

Home Office (2016) *Duty to Notify the Home Office of Potential Victims of Modern Slavery Guidance for Specified Public Authorities.* Available at www.gov.uk/government/publications/duty-to-notify-the-home-office-of-potential-victims-of-modern-slavery, accessed on 21 April 2017.

National Crime Agency (2016) *National Referral Mechanism Statistics.* Available at www.nationalcrimeagency.gov.uk/publications/national-referral-mechanism-statistics, accessed on 21 April 2017.

Proto, L. (2015) 'Couple convicted of keeping Nigerian man as slave for 24 years.' *Evening Standard.* Available at www.standard.co.uk/news/crime/couple-convicted-of-keeping-nigerian-man-as-slave-for-24-years-a3116931.html, accessed on 21 April 2017.

Reed, A. (2016) *Anti-Trafficking and Modern Slavery.* Territorial Director of Anti Trafficking & Modern Slavery with The Salvation Army, Keynote Speech. Forum for Race Equality and Diversity Awareness, Plymouth University 'Learning Together' event, 21 April 2016. Unpublished.

Topping, A. (2012) 'Four face jail after first convictions under new "slavery" laws.' *Guardian.* Available at www.theguardian.com/uk/2012/jul/11/four-face-jail-slavery-law-convictions, accessed on 21 April 2017.

United Nations (2000) *Protocol to Prevent, Suppress and Punish Trafficking in Persons, Especially Women and Children.* Supplementing the United Nations Convention against Transitional Organised Crime.

Useful website links

Anti Trafficking Consultants – Ann's Story
www.antitraffickingconsultants.co.uk/anns-story

End Slavery Now – Modern Slave Narratives
www.endslaverynow.org/learn/modern-slave-narratives

Gangmasters Licensing Authority – The Gangmasters and Labour Abuse Authority
www.gla.gov.uk/who-we-are/our-aims-and-objectives/the-gangmasters-and-labour-abuse-authority

Home Office – Duty to notify the Home Office of potential victims of modern slavery
www.gov.uk/government/publications/duty-to-notify-the-home-office-of-potential-victims-of-modern-slavery

Hope for Justice
http://hopeforjustice.org

Human Trafficking Foundation
www.humantraffickingfoundation.org

The Salvation Army – Modern Slavery
www.salvationarmy.org.uk/human-trafficking

Stronger Together – Tackling Modern Slavery in Supply Chains
http://stronger2gether.org

Unchosen – The Power of Film to Fight Modern Slavery
www.unchosen.org.uk

International Organization for Migration UK
http://unitedkingdom.iom.int
http://unitedkingdom.iom.int/sites/default/files/doc/ct/IOM_UK_Counter-
    Trafficking_Directory.pdf

Unseen – UK Modern Slavery Helpline and Resource Centre
www.unseenuk.org/about/projects/uk-modern-slavery-helpline-and-resource-centre

Chapter 13

Safeguarding Adults at Risk of Financial Scamming

Sally Lee, Rebecca Johnson,
Lee-Ann Fenge and Keith Brown

Introduction

Fraud and financial scamming have grown into global concerns, increasingly enabled by the extensive reach of the internet and the anonymity this offers to criminals. The full scale of scamming is unknown, but research suggests that the problem is enormous: 'there were an estimated 5.1 million incidents of fraud, with 3.8 million adult victims in England and Wales' (Office of National Statistics 2015), with many more being targeted.

This chapter focuses on financial scams, which are described as financial crime and abuse to emphasise that they are illegal, criminal activities. However, it is also important to recognise that legitimate companies and charities can behave unscrupulously, often encouraged by ambitious targets, and whilst not a scam this behaviour is unlawful and abusive. Research and personal accounts from victims are drawn on to identify circumstances and personal attributes leading people to be at risk from scams, and explore the consequences of scamming for individuals and their networks. Preventative measures are suggested which practitioners can use to protect the people with whom they work. An example of good practice is provided.

The increasing prevalence of financial scams poses a serious risk to people who are being purposefully targeted; specifically those whose circumstances create vulnerability through, for example, poverty, social isolation or bereavement. In addition there is a growing population of older people living alone who retain control of their financial affairs but whose deteriorating cognitive skills reduce their financial literacy, increasing their vulnerability (Olivier *et al.* 2015). The growth in the range and scope of financial scams means that health and social care professionals are increasingly becoming involved with victims as the circumstances which lead to both social care needs and financial vulnerability intersect.

Financial Crime Against Vulnerable Adults, the 2011 report by the Social Care Institute for Excellence (SCIE), highlights the diversity of financial crime and multifaceted solutions required: 'Prevention and responses need to take into account the nature of the perpetrator, the detail of the crime and the level of vulnerability of the adult' (SCIE 2011b, p.5).

First, practitioners need to appreciate the scope of financial abuse and the circumstances leading to someone being targeted by a scam. They need 'in-depth knowledge and understanding of mass marketing fraud (and other forms of scamming) including how perpetrators set up scams and sustain victims' involvement in them' (Olivier *et al.* 2015, p.360).

Second, practitioners need to work in partnership with people, families, carers and communities to ensure they are alert to scams and empowered to protect themselves.

The Care Act (2014), underpinned by the wellbeing principle, compels practitioners to meet this practice challenge (see Appendix). It states that local authorities, practitioners and social care providers have a duty to safeguard people who have care and support needs and who are unable to protect themselves from abuse or neglect because of those support needs. This duty also applies to people who self-fund their care services or receive NHS-funded services. Local authorities may also:

> choose to undertake safeguarding inquiries for people where there is not a Section 42 duty, if the local authority believes it is proportionate to do so, and will enable the local authority to promote the person's wellbeing and support a preventative agenda. (Department of Health [DH] 2016, para.14.44)

This could be helpful in cases where an individual does not have care and support needs but is nonetheless at risk from scamming – including being at risk of developing care and support needs.

Financial abuse is defined within the Care Act (2014, s.42(3)) as:

- having money or other property stolen

- being defrauded

- being put under pressure in relation to money or other property

- having money or other property misused.

Financial scams primarily fall into the second and third points of this definition, and this chapter provides practitioners with an understanding of: the scope, scale and different types of financial scams; why people respond to scams and who is most at risk; the impact of financial scams on individuals and their network of support; and what can be done to scam involvement and assisting victims once they have been scammed.

What is financial scamming?

Scams are fraudulent criminal activity defined in the Fraud Act (2006). Fraud is committed in three specific ways, with different scams falling into each category:

(a) Fraud by false representation

(b) Fraud by failing to disclose information

(c) Fraud by abuse of position.

(Fraud Act 2006, Chapter 35(1))

Further legal protection is offered by the Consumer Protection from Unfair Trading Regulations (2008) which makes misleading actions or omissions by traders a criminal offence. That is, if a trade, business or service interaction is untruthful, is likely to deceive, leads to a person engaging in a transaction they would not normally do, or hides or leaves out crucial information (Age UK 2015). This includes unscrupulous behaviour by legitimate traders, for example repeated sales of the same product to someone who has forgotten they have already made the purchase. Schedule 1 of the Regulations sets out specific banned practices of relevance to scams, such as:

> Creating the false impression that the consumer has already won, will win, or will on doing a particular act win, a prize or other equivalent benefit, when in fact either:

there is no prize or other equivalent benefit, or

taking any action in relation to claiming the prize or other equivalent benefit is subject to the consumer paying money or incurring a cost which includes 'persistent unwanted solicitation by phone or email and pretending that a prize has been won'.

(Office of Fair Trading 2008)

Banned practices also include the use of aggressive selling techniques which are often characteristic of scams.

Scams have been defined as 'a misleading or deceptive business practice where you receive an unsolicited or uninvited contact (for example by email, letter, phone or ad) and false promises are made to con you out of money' (Office of Fair Trading 2006, p.12).

Concerns have also been raised about techniques used by charities to raise funds, including frequent and aggressive contact with individuals who may be in vulnerable circumstances. The use of such techniques can impact significantly on individual wellbeing (Fundraising Standards Board 2016).

Scams are constantly evolving as fraudsters take advantage of the opportunities created through new technologies, whilst also adapting to the detection and intervention of international law enforcement agencies (Whitty 2013).

Practitioners need to be alert to vulnerabilities created by people's circumstances, maintaining awareness of the types of scam an individual may respond to. For example, those living in poverty may be drawn into 'get rich quick' schemes. People with deteriorating cognitive function who can no longer discern between personal post and scam mail may feel obliged to respond to all correspondence with equal emotional and financial commitment.[1]

Why do people respond to scams?

Most people will have received some form of scam approach, either via post, phone call or email. However, many decide not to respond. Psychology theories of human behaviour illuminate why some people respond, which includes the complex interplay of a person's life history, circumstances and personality.

---

1   See the Think Jessica campaign at www.thinkjessica.com for a personal account.

Research by Fischer, Lea and Evans (2013) suggests that there are four key psychological processes encouraging individuals to respond to scams:

1. *Urgency and scarcity:* encouraging victims to rush decisions by increasing the time pressure on an offer and enhancing the value of an offer by increasing the perceived scarcity.

    Scam response can be triggered by emotions such as hope, excitement or fear. The use of persuasive marketing techniques lures victims, encouraging them to make quick decisions appealing to emotional rather than reasoned decision making. An inability to control one's impulses under high stakes may increase scam involvement (Knutson and Samanez-Larkin 2014). This is the case when a victim might suspect the validity of the offer, but they proceed because the size of the prize makes the risk worthwhile, have already invested so much (Whitty 2013), or believe their turn for a pay-out is coming. Lottery wins and prize draws are typical of this kind of scam (Olivier *et al.* 2015).

    Encouragement to make quick judgements, without full reasoning, draws on heuristic decision making leading to increased unwise decisions (Fischer *et al.* 2013). Decisions are made relying on imperfect information or mental shortcuts such as 'rule of thumb' or 'common sense' (Dietrich 2010). Criminals are aware of the psychological processes involved in decision making and exploit these. Practitioners working with scam victims need to understand these processes and have clear evidence to challenge the mental shortcuts and assumptions made by victims who may be reluctant to admit or recognise they have been scammed.

2. *Social influence and consistency:* establishing 'similarity' with victims and maintaining consistent contact.

    Grooming is a universal characteristic of scams to promote trust and make the offer seem appealing and persuasive. Scams attempt to create a transaction with a victim; they are a form of marketing which has a high degree of enterprise and mirrors skills found amongst legitimate marketing sales activities.

3. *Acceptance of trust cues:* scammers may imitate authority and use personal interaction to build trust with victims.

    Socialised perceptions of 'correct' or 'trusting' behaviour may lead to an individual responding to scams. 'The social rules of reciprocation may lead to scam response often producing a "yes" response to a request that, except for an existing feeling of indebtedness, would have surely been refused' (Cialdini 1984, p.21, cited in Olivier *et al.* 2015, p.361).

    The language used, often presented in 'official'-looking formats, acts as both a lure and then a hook to sustain the scam, taking advantage of reciprocity from the victim. This enables increasing demands to be made whilst the scammer strengthens the 'relationship', making the victim feel 'special and personally selected' (Lea and Webley 2006, p.21). Olivier *et al.*'s (2015) work illustrates the false friendship scammers develop with their victims in the case study of a bereaved individual and a clairvoyance scam. Phone contact between the bereaved person and the scammers led the victim to feel supported, but this came at a financial and emotional cost as the scammer's demands increased.

4. *Incentive:* using high incentives invokes responses in victims, preventing them from judging risk in the same way and leading to flawed decision making.

    Langenderfer and Shrimp's (2001) research into vulnerability linked to gullibility and scepticism suggests that the closer the reward appears to the victim (seemingly handwritten personal messages as an additional note to a typewritten letter), and the more the scam appeals to basic needs, the greater the emotional response will be. In these circumstances emotions tend to override reason. The potential of a large reward being tantalisingly close influences risk-taking, and this is exploited further by an individual's predisposition to trust others (Fischer *et al.* 2013). Criminals exploit such characteristics as trust, politeness and reciprocity through 'visceral triggers to make the victim focus on huge prizes or benefits and imagined positive future emotional states' (Whitty 2013, p.667). Criminals also add legitimacy to disguise the scam, making discerning between a scam and a genuine offer more difficult (Olivier *et al.* 2015).

Personal and social characteristics which increase vulnerability to scams

Everyone is vulnerable to financial scams; however, research indicates that age, social isolation, loneliness and cognitive impairment are key factors which make people especially vulnerable (Fischer *et al.* 2013). These factors coincide with some indicators of social care needs.

A number of factors linked to old age increase the risk of being scammed:

- Age-related deterioration in health and mobility, reduced contact with family and friends and bereavement create greater risk of social isolation and loneliness (Holt-Lunstad *et al.* 2015).

- Older people spend more time at home during the day and are therefore exposed to more frequent unsolicited telemarketing calls (Lee and Geistfeld 1999). They may have more time to answer telephone calls, listen to the caller and feel it is impolite to cut the call off.

- Older people may have more savings, making them appear to be an attractive target for scammers (Age UK 2015).

- Age-related cognitive impairment can lead to a lack of insight and overconfidence in financial knowledge (Olivier *et al.* 2015).

- Psychological wellbeing, memory and cognitive function, including problem solving, risk assessment, decision making and concentration, are reduced (Timpe *et al.* 2011).

- Older people have been found to have lower financial literacy levels, leaving them ill-equipped to make financial judgements and decisions (Lusardi 2009).

- In the UK the population aged over 65 is predicted to increase from 9.7 million in 2015 to 13.2 million by 2030 (POPPI 2015). It is therefore likely that scamming will become a bigger problem over time.

Loneliness is an under-recognised social problem which can increase an individual's risk of being targeted and responding to a scam, and over one million older people said they always or often feel lonely (Age UK 2014). The number of people aged over 65 and living alone is forecast to increase from 3.5 million to 4.4 million by 2025 (POPPI 2015), although this may not necessarily lead to increased loneliness or social isolation.

Social isolation and loneliness are distinctly different and are experienced in different ways. Social isolation is an objective term describing an absence of contact with others, whereas loneliness is a subjective term describing how a person feels about their level of contact with others. People who are socially isolated from the community are more likely to feel lonely, but people who feel lonely may not be socially isolated. Loneliness is more prevalent and can have bigger implications on health and wellbeing (Luo *et al.* 2012).

Social support and connection with people is related to health, wellbeing and quality of life (Helliwell, Layard and Sachs 2015). Absence of such connections can lead to people seeking them elsewhere, which is why strong relationships can form between the individual and scammer (Kang and Ridgway 1996). This sense of connection is strengthened by the frequency of contact, and the frequency is valued more highly than the quality of contact. As a result, socially isolated older people are more likely to respond to telemarketing phone calls, doorstep sales and scam mail (Lee and Geistfeld 1999), leading to greater vulnerability to financial scams and manipulations (Lubben *et al.* 2015).

The prevalence of cognitive impairments, such as dementia, increases in old age. Dementia can affect a person's ability to make decisions, apply caution and judge risk in everyday circumstances (Alzheimer's Society 2014). A decline in cognition has been linked to a decline in financial literacy (Gamble *et al.* 2013), preventing people from understanding the consequences of their actions (Cohen 2008). When evaluative functions of the brain are affected by dementia, people are at increased risk due to inability to apply caution in decision making or distinguish genuine from bogus.

There are approximately 850,000 people living in the UK with dementia at present, which is 1 in 14 people aged over 65 (Alzheimer's Society 2016). This figure is predicted to rise to 1.1 million by 2021 (Alzheimer's Society 2014), making it likely that financial scamming will become a bigger problem.

The impact of scams

The financial detriment to victims varies in each case, depending on the type of scam and level of victim response. In some cases the detriment remains unknown because the victim has responded to scams for decades. In many cases the financial loss is severe enough to impact an individual's wellbeing and standard of living. Some victims have sold or re-mortgaged their home or taken out loans to fund scams or pay off debts. Victims may choose to go without basic needs such as food or heating to pay for scams. The financial loss can result in victims who would otherwise be self-funding relying on local authority-funded care services.

Financial scams can have a serious impact on health and wellbeing, causing long-lasting damage to an individual's quality of life. Victims report stress, anxiety and loss of self-esteem, whilst others find that their confidence and financial capability is eroded (Button, Lewis and Tapley 2009). Some victims deny involvement, feel shame or blame themselves. The impact on mental health can be particularly damaging (Whitty 2013); and scammers may isolate victims from their friends and family, compounding the psychological impact.

Scams are believed to be a key factor in the rapid decline of health in older people. A Home Office study found that older victims of doorstep crime and burglary decline in health faster than non-victims of a similar age (Donaldson 2003). It is important that practitioners who visit older people in their own homes are 'scam-aware' and are able to quickly assess the signs of scam involvement.

Guidance for practice

Agencies such as trading standards, adult social services, housing, the police and the financial sector may be the first to recognise scamming and be in a position to intervene (Gibson and Qualls 2012). The Care Act (2014) requires that services protect adults who are unable to protect themselves because of their health and care needs. Part of strategically planned protection includes agencies using the same information utilised by scammers to identify those vulnerable to scams and having discussions at the early stages of dementia or decline in health. In order to provide the most effective intervention it is necessary for society, communities and the individuals affected to recognise that there is a problem (SCIE 2011b).

Awareness of indicators of financial abuse includes:

- changes to physical wellbeing: weight loss, personal hygiene routines, self-neglect, physical agitation

- changes to emotional wellbeing: low mood, loss of interest in hobbies/activities

- reduced contact with family and friends

- change to financial situation: making uncharacteristic financial decisions or a sudden focus on money

- increase in post, telephone calls or emails.

Practitioners have a preventative role, working with individuals and their networks to protect themselves. The Financial Conduct Authority (2014) has produced guidelines which include the following advice that practitioners can provide to people they work with:

- Do not send advance payments or money to anyone unknown.

- Do not give banking details to anyone unknown.

- Check poor spelling and grammar and check the credentials of the sender.

- Get the Mail Preference Service from Royal Mail.

- Do not give your pin number to anyone.

- Get the Telephone Preference Service.

- Install a call blocker system.

- Do not pay for services in advance.

- Get all arrangements in writing prior to any service.

- Check all credentials.

- Do not deal with cold callers.

- Thoroughly research any offer.

Implication for practice

CASE STUDY

Mr Smith is in his early 80s. He lives alone, having been widowed three years earlier. He has a son and daughter, both of whom live at a distance. They visit Mr Smith regularly, also keeping in frequent phone contact. They would like him to move nearer to one or other of them, but he does not want to leave the marital home which holds so many memories.

Mr Smith has been in good health with no grounds to question his decision-making capacity; however, he recently fell and was not found for several hours. He sustained a broken hip and shoulder and has suffered from recurrent urinary tract infections since then. He receives a Direct Payment which he uses to purchase personal care, enabling him to continue living independently in his own home.

Carers have reported to the local social services department that Mr Smith is very agitated each morning, stating that he is expecting post and his recent fall and hospital admission had disrupted important correspondence. On further enquiry the carer realises that Mr Smith is in contact with several 'clairvoyants' and has been sending regular amounts of money to each one in the expectation of receiving the large windfalls promised. In addition he receives up to ten items of scam post daily ranging from catalogues to prize draws and international lotteries. He also discloses that he receives numerous phone calls each day, which he finds irritating now he cannot mobilise easily.

Mr Smith explains that the correspondence started after he responded to an advert for a free hearing aid just before his wife's death. Since his bereavement he says the regularity of the post has been a comfort, giving him focus and a routine which has included going to the post office to buy stamps. The personalised nature of the clairvoyants' letters is also very meaningful to him. However, since being in hospital and not being able to keep up with the post or the regular payments he was making, the letters have become intermittent and threatening. He has found this extremely upsetting as he had thought the clairvoyants were genuine friends. He has not told his family about the correspondence as he did not want to involve them in something he felt was so personal. Mr Smith discloses that he has boxes of letters carefully filed away. The carer discusses the situation with Mr Smith, who states that he feels harassed and distressed and wants the correspondence to stop. The carer explains that the social worker and care agency management will be notified and a safeguarding concern raised on the grounds of suspected financial abuse.

The practitioner visits Mr Smith and they discuss his view of the correspondence, its meaning and its value to him. Whilst together they contact trading standards and arrange a joint visit. Mr Smith states that he feels he has lost confidence in his personal judgement and blames himself for being 'duped'. He requires the reassurance that his experience is very common and that by providing information to the investigative officers he can help reduce the potential of it happening to others. The practitioner works with Mr Smith to develop his social networks and reduce the social isolation which had contributed to his maintaining the correspondence.

Mr Smith informs his family about his situation and he agrees to the installation of a telephone call blocker and arranging a Lasting Power of Attorney. Trading standards work with him, helping him understand how he was scammed and stopping the correspondence at source. He subsequently becomes a Mail Marshal, sending any further scam correspondence to them for investigation.

This case study illustrates balancing empowerment and the promotion of autonomy, which involves risk enablement and the ability to make unwise decisions, but also protection from harm.

The statutory safeguarding framework in ss.42–47 and 68 of the Care Act (2014) makes explicit reference to financial abuse (s.42(3)). Scamming, which depends on a response from the victim, raises the fundamental dilemma at the root of practice in adult social care.

Negotiating this balance is core to practice. The Care Act (2014) and Making Safeguarding Personal (Local Government Association and Association of Adult Directors of Social Services 2014) promote the centrality of the individual and the importance of maximising their ability to make informed decisions. This approach to safeguarding practice centres on giving people more control over, and supporting them to make choices about, their lives. Practitioners 'work with adults who may be at risk, to help them recognise potentially abusive situations and understand how they can protect themselves' (SCIE 2015).

Practitioners have to consider the protection of both the individual and the wider public interest. For example, the individual may value the contact they have with a scammer and want to maintain this, deeming it worth any financial loss, while the professional is aware that involvement in scams leads to further vulnerability and potential loss of assets with the financial proceeds of scamming potentially being used to fund other criminal activity. Similar to working with self-neglect, the building of a trusting relationship between practitioner and individual is crucial to making positive changes (SCIE 2011a). Olivier *et al.* (2015, p.369) recommend that practitioners take time to establish the 'length and breadth of the issue', that is, to understand how long the scam involvement has been going on, key life events affecting the individual during this period, their social connections and the psychological meaning of the scam to them. In cases where the utility of involvement in a scam is important to the victim, practitioners can work with the individual to find alternative sources of meaning, purpose and social capital (Olivier *et al.* 2015).

Core to all safeguarding work is the issue of mental capacity, defined by the Mental Capacity Act (2005). Assessment of an individual's capacity is crucial to negotiating risk and protection, with the outcome of the assessment guiding subsequent action (see Chapter 7).

Different challenges arise for practitioners working with people who retain the capacity to manage their financial affairs, yet choose to be involved in an abusive situation. The law enables people to make 'unwise decisions' (Principle 3 of the Mental Capacity Act) and practitioners seek to promote autonomy, but must also endeavour to protect and prevent harm. Some individuals lack insight or do not acknowledge the abusive nature of their experience, being convinced of the legitimacy of the scam. Or the individual may decide that the value gained through the sense of utility, social capital and contact offered by involvement is worth the financial loss (Olivier *et al.* 2015).

This illustrates the debate about capacity and vulnerability, where those deemed to have capacity can be left unsupported. Yet the courts recognise that 'between active decision makers and those certified as lacking mental capacity is a category of vulnerable adults who are open to exploitation' (Sofaer 2012).[2] Undertaking a balance sheet or risk assessment with the individual can be a helpful tool to explore their insight into the situation, and to understand the degree to which they are making informed decisions. It is also a means to help the person consider the pros and cons of their choices.

In addition, grooming, coercion or undue influence by scammers can cloud the individual's judgement, bringing their capacity into question. In such cases the Mental Capacity Act (2005) is not applicable; however, a local authority can apply to the courts 'to exercise its inherent jurisdiction to protect an adult with mental capacity...who is "reasonably believed" to be "under constraint" or "subject to coercion or undue influence", or for another reason "deprived of the capacity to make the relevant decision", or prevented from making a free choice, or from "giving or expressing a real and genuine consent"' (SCIE 2014). The aim of such action is to ensure that decisions are made freely rather than overriding the individual's choices, no matter how 'unwise' they might be. Also, trading standards and the police target perpetrators, and collaborative work between agencies is beneficial to all.

Conclusion

Financial scamming is a growing issue and it is vital that the groups of people most at risk are provided with the information and support to prevent harm occurring. Raising awareness and building social capital requires strategic measures such as the National Centre for Post-Qualifying Social Work and Professional Practice at Bournemouth University working with the Chartered Trading Standards Institute, National Trading Standards Scams Team and local authority Trading Standards Teams on a campaign to promote change to protect the people most at risk from scamming.[3]

This work requires a collaborative approach to identifying and protecting those at risk, including the police, trading standards, the financial sector and health and social care. The success of initiatives to combat involvement in scams must be focused on working in partnership with those at risk, to empower them to protect themselves.

---

2   See *DL v A Local Authority and Others* [2012] EWCA Civ 253 for case law illustrating how the Court of Appeal decided that statutes and precedents cannot be applied in ways which leave people with vulnerabilities at risk.

3   See www.ncpqsw.com.

References

Age UK (2014) *Evidence Review: Loneliness in Later Life*. London: Age UK.

Age UK (2015) *Only the Tip of the Iceberg: Fraud Against Older People*. London: Age UK.

Alzheimer's Society (2014) *Dementia UK: Update* (Second edition). London: Alzheimer's Society. Available at www.alzheimers.org.uk/dementiauk, accessed on 25 April 2017.

Alzheimer's Society (2016) *Demography* [Online]. Available at www.alzheimers.org.uk/info/20091/what_we_think/93/demography, accessed on 25 April 2017.

Button, M., Lewis, C., and Tapley, J. (2009) *Fraud Typologies and Victims of Fraud: Literature Review*. London: National Fraud Authority.

Cialdini, R.B. (1984) *The Psychology and Influence of Persuasion*. New York: Quill William Morrow.

Cohen, C. (2008) 'Editorial: Consumer fraud and dementia – Lessons learned from conmen.' *Dementia: The International Journal of Social Research and Practice 7*, 3, 283–285.

Department of Health (2016) *Care and Support Statutory Guidance*. London: DH.

Dietrich, C. (2010) 'Decision making: Factors that influence decision making, heuristics used, and decision outcomes.' *Inquiries Journal/Student Pulse [Online] 2*, 2, 1–3. Available at www.inquiriesjournal.com/a?id=180, accessed on 25 April 2017.

Donaldson, R. (2003) *Experiences of Older Burglary Victims* [Online]. Available at http://webarchive.nationalarchives.gov.uk/20110220105210/rds.homeoffice.gov.uk/rds/pdfs2/r198.pdf, accessed on 25 April 2017.

Fischer, P., Lea, S., and Evans, K. (2013) 'Why do individuals respond to fraudulent scam communications and lose money? The psychological determinants of scam.' *Journal of Applied Social Psychology 43*, 10, 2060–2072.

Fundraising Standards Board (2016) *FRSB Investigation into Charity Fundraising Practices Instigated by Mrs Olive Cooke's Case* [Online]. Available at https://www.fundraisingregulator.org.uk/investigations/frsb-investigation-charity-fundraising-practices-instigated-mrs-olive-cookes-case/.

Gamble, K.J., Boyle, P., Yu, L., and Bennett, D.A. (2013) *Aging, Financial Literacy, and Fraud* [Online]. Available at http://arno.uvt.nl/show.cgi?fid=132378.

Gibson, S., and Qualls, S. (2012) 'A family systems perspective of elder financial abuse.' *Journal of the American Society on Aging 36*, 3, 26–29.

Helliwell, J., Layard, R., and Sachs, J. (eds) (2015) *World Happiness Report 2015* [Online]. New York: Sustainable Development Solutions Network. Available at http://worldhappiness.report/wp-content/uploads/sites/2/2015/04/WHR15.pdf, accessed on 25 April 2017.

Holt-Lunstad, J., Smith, T.B., Baker, M., Harris, T., and Stephenson, D. (2015) 'Loneliness and social isolation as risk factors for mortality: A meta-analytic review.' *Perspectives on Psychological Science 10*, 2, 227–237.

Kang, Y., and Ridgway, N. (1996) 'The importance of consumer market interactions as a form of social support for elderly consumers.' *Journal of Public Policy & Marketing 15*, 1, 108–117.

Knutson, B., and Samanez-Larkin, G. (2014) *Individual Differences in Susceptibility to Investment Fraud*. Available at www.saveandinvest.org/sites/default/files/Individual-Differences-in-Susceptibility-to-Investment-Fraud.pdf, accessed on 25 April 2017.

Langenderfer, J., and Shimp, T. (2001) 'Consumer vulnerability to scams, swindles and fraud: A new theory of visceral influences on persuasion.' *Journal of Psychology and Marketing 18*, 7, 763–783.

Lea, S.E.G., and Webley, P. (2006) 'Money as tool, money as drug: The biological psychology of a strong incentive.' *Behavioural Brain Sciences 29*, 2, 161–209.

Lee, J., and Geistfeld, L. (1999) 'Elderly consumers' receptiveness to telemarketing fraud.' *Journal of Public Policy and Marketing 18*, 2, 208–217.

Local Government Association and Association of Adult Directors of Social Services (2014) *Making Safeguarding Personal* [Online]. Available at https://www.cumbria.gov.uk/elibrary/Content/Internet/327/949/4246511249.pdf.

Lubben, J., Gironda, M., Sabbath, E., Kong, J., and Johnson, C. (2015) *Social Isolation Presents a Grand Challenge for Social Work*. American Academy of Social Work and Social Welfare Working Paper No. 7. Available at http://aaswsw.org/wp-content/uploads/2015/03/Social-Isolation-3.24.15.pdf, accessed on 25 April 2017.

Luo, Y., Hawkley, L., Waite, L., and Cacioppo, J. (2012) 'Loneliness, health, and mortality in old age: A national longitudinal study.' *Social Science and Medicine 74*, 6, 907–914.

Lusardi, A. (2009) 'Financial literacy and financial decision-making in older adults.' *Journal of the American Society of Aging 36*, 2, 25–32.

Office of Fair Trading (2006) *Research on Impact of Mass Marketed Scams: A Summary of Research into the Impact of Scams on UK Consumers*. London: Office of Fair Trading.

Office of National Statistics (2015) *Measuring National Wellbeing: Insights into Loneliness, Older People and Wellbeing* [Online]. Available at www.ons.gov.uk/peoplepopulationandcommunity/wellbeing/articles/measuringnationalwellbeing/2015-10-01/pdf, accessed on 25 April 2017.

Olivier, S., Burls, T., Fenge, L.A., and Brown, K. (2015) '"Winning and losing": Vulnerability to mass marketing fraud.' *The Journal of Adult Protection 17*, 6, 360–370.

POPPI (2015) *Living Alone* [Online]. Available at www.poppi.org.uk/index.php?pageNo=324&PHPSESSID=jlmbne15imnjge3ed4irkbue23&sc=1&loc=8640&np=1, accessed on 25 April 2017.

Social Care Institute for Excellence (2011a) *Report 46. Self-Neglect and Adult Safeguarding: Findings from Research* [Online]. Available at www.scie.org.uk/publications/reports/report46.asp, accessed on 25 April 2017.

Social Care Institute for Excellence (2011b) *Report 49. Assessment: Financial Crime against Vulnerable Adults*. London: SCIE. Available at www.scie.org.uk/publications/reports/report49.asp, accessed on 25 April 2017.

Social Care Institute for Excellence (2014) *Context of the Mental Capacity Act 2005 (MCA) in Gaining Access to an Adult Suspected of Being at Risk of Neglect or Abuse: A Guide for Social Workers and their Managers in England* [Online]. Available at www.scie.org.uk/care-act-2014/safeguarding-adults/adult-suspected-at-risk-of-neglect-abuse/law/mca2005.asp, accessed on 25 April 2017.

Social Care Institute for Excellence (2015) *Care Act 2014: Adult Safeguarding Practice Questions* [Online]. Available at www.scie.org.uk/care-act-2014/safeguarding-adults/adult-safeguarding-practice-questions/index.asp, accessed on 25 April 2017.

Sofaer, M. (2012) *Can the Court Protect Vulnerable Adults who have Capacity?* [Online]. Available at www.familylawweek.co.uk/site.aspx?i=ed101172, accessed on 25 April 2017.

Timpe, J.C., Rowe, K.C., Matsui, J., Magnotta, V.A., and Denburg, N.L. (2011) 'White matter integrity, as measured by diffusion tensor imaging, distinguishes between impaired and unimpaired older adult decision-makers: A preliminary investigation.' *Journal of Cognitive Psychology 23*, 6, 760–767.

Whitty, M. (2013) 'The scammers' persuasive techniques model: Development of a stage model to explain the online dating romance scam.' *British Journal of Criminology 53*, 4, 665–684.

How to Practise Safeguarding Well

Adi Cooper

A number of common themes running through the chapters of the book are highlighted in this conclusion. These are intended as a prompt for practitioners, as a reminder about what is important, in order to practise adult safeguarding well. Safeguarding adults is fundamentally a partnership endeavour – partnership with a person at risk of abuse or neglect, as well as with carers, practitioners or partners – as evidenced by one of the six safeguarding principles (Department of Health [DH] 2016, para.14.13). These key messages therefore apply to adult safeguarding work in relevant agencies and organisations and across many professional and sector boundaries.

Adult safeguarding practice is complex territory: practitioners need knowledge, skills and professional curiosity. It is also constantly changing, as understanding about 'what works' for people at risk of abuse or neglect develops, which then informs adult safeguarding practice. The first key message for practitioners is to continue to learn, from all sources, including their practice. This learning can be formal or informal, with colleagues or across multi-agency teams, through studying, or reflecting on casework. The diverse contributions from the authors within this book can be used to prompt discussion and debate. There are a wide range of methods and approaches that can support people at risk of abuse or neglect to achieve resolution and recovery: authors have described some of these in their chapters (see Chapters 1–5), and there are more that can be helpful which haven't been included (White 2015). Crucially, learning may also include being open to different ways of thinking about what might be helpful to the person or people that practitioners support in their day-to-day work.

Learning is also essential from the messages emerging from Safeguarding Adults Reviews (SARs) or Serious Case Reviews, cited in several chapters (see Chapters 1, 9 and 10). The detailed analysis of these tragic events challenges everyone, whether practitioners, leaders or policy makers, to consider what needs to improve in terms of adult safeguarding practice, systems and processes. Here, the Safeguarding Adults Boards have a critical leadership role to play, not only to ensure that the learning from SARs is disseminated, but also that there is change as a result which improves inter-agency adult safeguarding practice.

The second message for practitioners is about listening to what people tell us about their lives, using a person-centred approach, and ensuring that any agreed actions and interventions deliver their desired outcomes. This is fundamental to the Making Safeguarding Personal approach to practice (see Chapters 1 and 5). Doing this means the outcomes that people identify are more likely to be achieved, protection plans are more likely to be effective, and people are more likely to achieve resolution and recovery (Butler and Manthorpe 2016; Cooper *et al.* 2016; Lawson *et al.* 2014; Preston-Shoot and Cooper 2015). A strengths- or asset-based approach, whether 'signs of safety', 'narrative' or other, facilitates a person-centred way of working (see Chapters 2 and 5) and supports putting Making Safeguarding Personal into practice. This way of working has been positively received by practitioners (Lawson *et al.* 2014; Pike and Walsh 2015), and findings from a survey of social workers on the impact of the Care Act (2014) suggest that Making Safeguarding Personal is its 'biggest success' (Godden 2016). Fundamentally, Making Safeguarding Personal is about culture change, and this is ongoing; it is not yet fully implemented across all local authorities, let alone all partner agencies and organisations, so must be considered 'work in progress' (Cooper *et al.* 2016; Local Government Association 2016).

The Care Act (2014) has made adult safeguarding a formal statutory function, and the third key message is the need for practitioners to be legally aware; legal literacy has been a major theme throughout the book. The expectation is not that everyone has to be a lawyer, but that practitioners understand how to practise using all aspects of the legal framework available to them (see Chapter 8). Along with the range of other literacies that practitioners need (see Chapter 10), this can help with some of the ethical and moral dilemmas that exist:

regarding human rights, autonomy or risk enablement and duty of care, protection or risk mitigation. In particular, issues about risk and mental capacity are often challenging, so interpreting and applying the legal principles in adult safeguarding practice in these areas are critical (see Chapters 6 and 7). This requires confidence and competence in understanding and interpreting legal knowledge.

Fourth, there are ongoing challenges and issues confronting adult safeguarding practitioners which are mentioned throughout the book, for example working with families or carers who hinder access to people (see Chapter 9). There are the newer areas of safeguarding practice, including people who self-neglect, and those who are victims of domestic abuse, modern slavery or scamming (see Chapters 10–13). A common thread across all these areas is the likelihood that people may have contradictory and complex responses to offers of help and support: this is not unfamiliar in adult safeguarding practice, although may be new ground for some practitioners. Responding appropriately in these situations demands flexible and thoughtful consideration as well as knowledge, skills and respectful professional curiosity. The Making Safeguarding Personal approach still applies in these circumstances – working with someone who won't allow access (actually or metaphorically) requires personalised, strengths-based and outcome-orientated practice.

The final key message is that practice in this area is constantly changing. Although authors have captured current best practice to share through this book, there will be further change and improvement, as the evidence base for good practice in adult safeguarding grows. This should prompt practitioners to contribute to the development of best practice, to get involved in research and write about it.[1] Evidence-informed practice is a mix of research, practitioner expertise and the views and experience of people who use services and carers: this is how the evidence base can grow and learning can spread.[2]

As the Care Act (2014) becomes embedded, there are further challenges for adult safeguarding practice. Prevention, through early intervention to address the risks of abuse and neglect so that people can keep themselves safe, is a significant priority. Raising awareness and understanding of abuse and neglect, and how to access adult

---

1   For example, *Journal of Adult Protection* welcomes contributions from practitioners; see www.emeraldinsight.com/journal/jap.

2   See www.ripfa.org.uk/about-us/about-evidence-informed-practice.

safeguarding services, is an essential prevention activity. However, there are other areas to be explored. The extent of loneliness in society, especially of older people and adults with care and support needs, and its impact on mental, emotional and physical health, has been recognised at a policy level.[3] The impact of loneliness or social isolation on safeguarding as a causal factor is mentioned by authors in a range of areas, including scamming (see Chapter 13). Reducing social isolation to reduce vulnerabilities to different forms of abuse or neglect seems to be an obvious preventative priority.

Additionally, poor quality care can deteriorate into safeguarding risks, therefore there is a need to improve quality of care, the culture and competencies of care workers, and ensure that people are treated with dignity and respect. These areas must be a focus for future preventative safeguarding work. Using strengths- and asset-based approaches to build individual and community resilience, so people can keep themselves safe, is another safeguarding prevention priority. These are areas that practitioners recognise from their day-to-day work. To date, resources have not necessarily been invested in prevention and it has not always been a focus of safeguarding policy. However, the cost benefit of early intervention and prevention in safeguarding should be explored and piloted to provide a business case for investment of scarce time and resources.

In conclusion, clearly this book does not have all the answers, neither is it exhaustive in terms of the broad remit of safeguarding adults: it is a contribution to support the development of good practice in adult safeguarding. This book has attempted to capture best practice at this point in time, but it is a changing environment as we learn more, make mistakes and see new areas of risk and vulnerabilities emerge. The overall ambition continues to be that practitioners deliver good adult safeguarding practice in a way that best meets the needs of the people that they are working with. Keeping this in mind, the authors have offered their contributions to support good practice in adult safeguarding.

---

3   See www.campaigntoendloneliness.org.

References

Butler, L., and Manthorpe, J. (2016) 'Putting people at the centre: Facilitating Making Safeguarding Personal approaches in the context of the Care Act 2014.' *The Journal of Adult Protection 18*, 4, 204–213.

Cooper, A., Briggs, M., Lawson, J., Hodson, B., and Wilson, M. (2016) *Making Safeguarding Personal Temperature Check.* London: ADASS.

Department of Health (2016) *Care and Support Statutory Guidance.* London: DH.

Godden, J. (2016) 'Report on the findings of the BASW England survey on members' experiences of implementation of the Care Act.' *Professional Social Work Magazine*, September 2016, British Association of Social Workers.

Lawson, J., Lewis, S., Williams, C., and Cooper, A. (2014) *Making Safeguarding Personal: Report of Findings.* London: Local Government Association.

Local Government Association (2016) *Care Act Stocktake 6.* Available at https://www.local.gov.uk/our-support/our-improvement-offer/care-and-health-improvement/care-and-support-reform/stocktake, accessed on 14 July 2017.

Pike, L., and Walsh, J. (November 2015) *Making Safeguarding Personal Evaluation Report.* London: Local Government Association.

Preston-Shoot, M., and Cooper, A. (eds) (2015) *Journal of Adult Protection* Special Issue: Making Safeguarding Personal. *Journal of Adult Protection 17*, 3, 153–165.

White, E. (2015) *Making Safeguarding Personal: A Toolkit for Responses* (4th edition). London: Local Government Association.

Appendix

This appendix provides a guide to the legislation most commonly referenced in this book or considered by the editors to be most useful to practitioners undertaking work in safeguarding adults.

It does not aim to provide a comprehensive overview of all legislation; for example, housing-related or environmental health legislation are not referenced here but can be found in detail in Chapter 10. References in this appendix also provide further information.

Table A.1 Common legislation

| Care Act (2014)

Web link:

www.legislation.gov.uk/
ukpga/2014/23/contents/
enacted

Care and Support Statutory Guidance
(2016)

Web link:

www.gov.uk/government/
publications/care-act-statutory-
guidance/care-and-support-
statutory-guidance | Sets out in one place local authorities' duties in relation to assessing people's needs (s.9), their eligibility for publicly funded care and support, and duties to cooperate (s.6(7)). Fundamentally for this book, it also sets out duties in respect of safeguarding adults and advocacy:

Safeguarding

The safeguarding duties under the Care Act (2014) are the following:

• Local authorities must lead a multi-agency local adult safeguarding system that seeks to prevent abuse and neglect and stop it quickly when it happens.

• Local authorities must make enquiries, or request others to make them, when they think an adult with care and support needs may be at risk of abuse or neglect and is unable to protect themselves, and they need to decide what action may be needed.

• Local authorities must establish Safeguarding Adults Boards, including the local authority, NHS and police, which will develop, share and implement a joint safeguarding strategy.

• Local authorities must carry out Safeguarding Adults Reviews when someone with care and support needs dies or is seriously injured as a result of neglect or abuse and there is a concern that the local authority or its partners could have done more to protect them.

• Local authorities must arrange for an independent advocate to represent and support a person who is the subject of a safeguarding inquiry or review, if required.

• Any relevant person or organisation must provide information to Safeguarding Adults Boards as requested.

The safeguarding principles enshrined in the *Care and Support Statutory Guidance* are:

Empowerment – People being supported and encouraged to make their own decisions and informed consent.

Prevention – It is better to take action before harm occurs.

Proportionality – The least intrusive response appropriate to the risk presented.

Protection – Support and representation for those in greatest need.

Partnership – Local solutions through services working with their communities. Communities have a part to play in preventing, detecting and reporting neglect and abuse.

Accountability – Accountability and transparency in delivering safeguarding.

Advocacy

Local authorities must arrange an independent advocate to facilitate the involvement of a person in their assessment, in the preparation of their care and support plan and in the review of their care plan, if two conditions are met:

• The person has substantial difficulty in being fully involved in these processes.

• There is no one appropriate available to support and represent the person's wishes. |

Criminal Justice Act (2003)	Disability Hate Crime is any criminal offence that is motivated by hostility or prejudice based upon the victim's disability or perceived disability.
	Where there is sufficient evidence, s.146 of the Criminal Justice Act (2003) provides that the court must state the hostility or prejudice as an aggravating factor at the sentencing stage. This includes:
	• physical attacks such as physical assault, damage to property, offensive graffiti and arson
	• threat of attack including offensive letters, abusive or obscene telephone calls, groups hanging around to intimidate, and unfounded, malicious complaints
	• verbal abuse, insults or harassment – taunting, offensive leaflets and posters, abusive gestures, dumping of rubbish outside homes or through letterboxes, and bullying at school or in the workplace.
Criminal Justice and Courts Act (2015) Web link: www.legislation.gov.uk/ukpga/2015/2/contents	Ss.20–25 and Schedule 4 create two new criminal offences of ill-treatment or wilful neglect applying to individual care workers and care provider organisations.
	S.20 makes it an offence for an individual to ill-treat or wilfully neglect another individual of whom he has the care by virtue of being a care worker.
	S.21 provides for a care provider to be guilty of an offence if someone who is part of the care provider's arrangements for the provision of care ill-treats or wilfully neglects an individual under the care provider's care; the way in which the care provider manages or organises its activities amounts to a gross breach of a relevant duty of care owed by it to the victim; and if that breach had not occurred the ill-treatment or wilful neglect would not have occurred or would have been less likely to occur.
Domestic Violence, Crime and Victims Act (2004) Web link: www.legislation.gov.uk/ukpga/2004/28/contents	Introduced a new offence of causing or allowing the death of a child or adult with care and support needs.
	The offence provides that members of a household who have frequent contact with a child or adult with care and support needs will be guilty if they caused the death of that child or adult with care and support needs or three conditions are met:
	• They were aware or ought to have been aware that the victim was at significant risk of serious physical harm from a member of the household.
	• They failed to take reasonable steps to prevent that person coming to harm.
	• The person subsequently died from the unlawful act of a member of the household in circumstances that the defendant foresaw or ought to have foreseen.
	S.32 created a Code of Practice which sets out the services and standards that must be provided to victims of crime. It states that victims of crime should be treated in a respectful, sensitive, tailored and professional manner without discrimination of any kind. They should receive appropriate support to help them, as far as possible, to cope and recover and be protected from re-victimisation. It is important that victims of crime know what information and support is available to them from reporting a crime onwards and who to request help from if they are not getting it.
Forced Marriage (Civil Protection) Act (2007) Web link: www.gov.uk/guidance/forced-marriage	S.1 enables the courts to make Forced Marriage Protection Orders (FMPOs) to prevent forced marriages from occurring and to protect those who have already been forced into marriage. S.120 of the Anti-Social Behaviour, Crime and Policing Act (2014) further amended the Family Law Act (by inserting s.63CA) making it a criminal offence to knowingly breach a FMPO.

Human Rights Act (1998) Web link: www.legislation.gov.uk/ ukpga/1998/42/contents	Puts the European Convention on Human Rights into UK statute. Article 2 is the right to life and places an obligation on the state, through its agents, to refrain from itself causing the deprivation of life. Public bodies must consider the right to life when making decisions that might put individuals in danger or affect life expectancy. It also requires public bodies to take appropriate preventative measures to safeguard a person if there is a reasonable cause for concern that their life is at risk. Article 3 prohibits torture, and 'inhuman or degrading treatment or punishment'. Public bodies are required to intervene to protect people against 'ill treatment that attains a minimum level of severity and involves actual bodily injury or intense physical harm or mental suffering. Where treatment humiliates or debases an individual showing lack of respect for or diminishing his or her human dignity or arouses feelings of fear, anguish or inferiority capable of breaking an individual's moral and physical resistance, it may be characterised as degrading and also fall within the prohibition of Article 3.' These rights are absolute, meaning that where a person can demonstrate that a public authority's actions or inaction would likely result in such treatment it is not possible for a local authority to argue that their actions are proportionate or justified. Article 5 is the right to liberty and security which protects the right of a person not to be arbitrarily deprived of their liberty. In many circumstances it is permissible for public bodies to interfere with this right, but they can only do so if they have legal powers (through legislation or a court order) and can demonstrate that the interference is necessary and proportionate. In April 2009 the Deprivation of Liberty Safeguards (DoLS) came into effect as an amendment to the Mental Capacity Act via the Mental Health Act (2007). The DoLS are intended to satisfy the procedural safeguards required by Article 5, for people who lack capacity to consent to restrictive care regimes residing in hospital or care homes by providing that any deprivation is kept under review. It may also be possible to obtain legal authority to deprive someone of their liberty under powers set out in the Mental Health Act or if the Court of Protection authorises this. Article 6 is the right to a fair trial, which not only protects a person who is charged with a criminal offence but also requires a public authority to offer a fair and public hearing if they are making a decision that has an impact upon a person's civil rights and obligations. Article 8 is the right to respect for private and family life, home and correspondence. The obligation on the state under Article 8 is to refrain from interfering with the right itself and also to take some positive measures if they know or ought to know that others are interfering with this right. Public bodies may only interfere with this right if they can show that the action they propose is lawful, necessary and proportionate to protect public safety, health and morals or the rights and freedoms of other people, prevent disorder or crime, and protect national security or the economy. The concept of a right to a private life encompasses the importance of personal dignity and autonomy and the interaction a person has with others. The right to family life is often engaged, for example, when measures are taken by the state to separate family members (Liberty 2016).

Health and Social Care Act (2008) (Regulated Activities) Regulations (2014) Web link: www.legislation.gov.uk/ ukdsi/2014/9780111117613/ contents	These regulations contain details of the standards that people registered to provide and manage health and care services have to observe. The law also makes requirements of the Care Quality Commission, and sets out the powers it has to regulate services and enforce compliance. From 1 April 2015, the Care Quality Commission took the lead role from the Health and Safety Executive (HSE) for patient and service user health and safety in health and adult social care in England. However, the HSE website contains useful guidance on sensible health and safety risk assessment in social care. The HSE advises: • concentrating on real risks where there is a realistic risk of harm • close liaison with the individual, carer and family when carrying out risk assessments to achieve outcomes that matter to them • how the risks flowing from an individual's choice can best be reduced by putting in place sensible controls • when organising group activities, how the most vulnerable can be protected without restricting the freedoms of the most capable.
Inherent jurisdiction of the High Court	'Inherent jurisdiction' is a term used to describe the power of the High Court to hear any case which comes before it unless legislation or a rule has limited that power or granted jurisdiction to some other court or tribunal to hear the case. This means that the High Court has the power to hear a broad range of cases including those in relation to the welfare of adults. If a person has capacity but cannot take a decision (freely) because of coercion, undue influence or constraint – or other circumstances – then an application can be made relying on the court's inherent jurisdiction. The inherent jurisdiction can be exercised for adults who are 'reasonably believed' to be 'under constraint' or 'subject to coercion or undue influence', or for another reason 'deprived of the capacity to make the relevant decision', or prevented from making a free choice, or from 'giving or expressing a real and genuine consent' (Social Care Institute for Excellence [SCIE] 2014).

Mental Capacity Act (2005)	The Mental Capacity Act (2005) provides a framework so that individuals who lack capacity are the focus of any decisions made, or actions taken, on their behalf. All decisions about mental capacity should be guided by the five Core Principles of the Mental Capacity Act. This means that an individual approach which centres round the interests of the person who lacks capacity, not the views or convenience of those caring and supporting that person, should prevail.
Web link: www.legislation.gov.uk/ ukpga/2005/9/contents	

	The five principles are the following:
	• Assume that a person has capacity unless it can be demonstrated otherwise.
	• Support people to make their own decisions wherever possible.
	• People can make 'unwise' decisions – making an unwise decision (e.g. to stay in an abusive relationship) does not mean someone lacks capacity.
	• Any decision made on behalf of someone who lacks capacity must be in their best interests.
	• Decisions made on behalf of someone who lacks capacity must reflect the least restrictive option.
	Gaining access
	If there is concern that a person may lack mental capacity in relation to a matter relating to their welfare or property and financial affairs, the Court of Protection has the power to make a declaration regarding their capacity and the lawfulness of any act done or yet to be done in relation to that person under s.15 of the Mental Capacity Act. This could include requiring another person to provide access to enable enquiries or assessment or for the provision of treatment, care and support. The court can also make an order or appoint a deputy to make decisions on the person's behalf under s.16(2) of the Mental Capacity Act.
	Offences
	S.44 of the Mental Capacity Act created an offence of ill-treating or wilfully neglecting a person who lacks capacity, or whom the offender reasonably believes to lack capacity. The offence may only be committed by certain persons who have a caring or other specified responsibility for the person who lacks capacity.

Mental Health Act (1983) (amended 2007) Web link: www.legislation.gov.uk/ ukpga/2007/12/contents	The Mental Health Act (MHA) allows people with a 'mental disorder' to be admitted to hospital, detained and treated without their consent for their own health and safety, or for the protection of other people.
	An important guiding principle is that the person must be as fully involved in planning treatment as possible, and their wishes should be taken into account. Family members and carers should also be involved. A person's 'nearest relative' (defined in s.26 of the MHA) has a statutory function and should be consulted; if the person who is unwell does not want them to be then they should be assisted to revoke this power.
	Another key guiding principle is that care and treatment should be provided in the least restrictive way possible – this means that, if possible, someone should be admitted to hospital without the constraints of the MHA applying to them.
	Gaining access
	If there is concern about a mentally disordered person: s.115 of the MHA provides the power for an approved mental health professional (approved by a local authority under the MHA) to enter and inspect any premises (other than a hospital) in which a person with a mental disorder is living, on production of proper authenticated identification, if the professional has reasonable cause to believe that the person is not receiving proper care.
	If a person is believed to have a mental disorder, and there is suspected neglect or abuse: under s.135(1) of the MHA, a magistrates court has the power, on application from an approved mental health professional, to allow the police to enter premises, using force if necessary and if thought fit, to remove a person to a place of safety if there is reasonable cause to suspect that they are suffering from a mental disorder and (a) have been, or are being, ill-treated, neglected or not kept under proper control, or (b) are living alone and unable to care for themselves (SCIE 2014).
	Offences
	S.127 of the MHA (1983) created an offence of ill-treating or wilfully neglecting a patient or a 'mental disordered patient' subject to guardianship under the MHA.
Modern Slavery Act (2015)	Provides the tools to enforce the law against modern slavery, ensure perpetrators receive suitable punishment and enhance support and protection for victims.
	Modern slavery appears in the Care Act (2014) safeguarding guidance (Chapter 14) statutory definitions of abuse.
	S.52 imposes an obligation on local authorities and police forces to notify the Secretary of State via the national referral mechanism www.nationalcrimeagency.gov.uk/about-us/what-we-do/specialist-capabilities/uk-human-trafficking-centre/national-referral-mechanism if they have reasonable grounds to believe a person may be a victim of human trafficking or slavery.

Police and Criminal Evidence Act (1984) Web link: www.legislation.gov.uk/ ukpga/1984/60/contents	S.17(1)(b) of the Police and Criminal Evidence Act (PACE) is a power of the police to enter and arrest a person for an indictable offence. *Gaining access* If there is risk to life and limb, s.17(1)(e) of PACE gives the police the power to enter premises without a warrant in order to save life and limb or prevent serious damage to property. This represents an emergency situation and it is for the police to exercise the power. The police have a common law power to prevent, and deal with, a breach of the peace. Although breach of the peace is not an indictable offence, the police have a common law power to enter and arrest a person to prevent a breach of the peace (SCIE 2014).
Serious Crime Act (2015) Web link: www.legislation.gov.uk/ ukpga/2015/9/contents/enacted	The Serious Crime Act (2015) introduces measures to enhance the protection of vulnerable children and others, including by strengthening the law to tackle female genital mutilation (FGM) and domestic abuse: • S.76 criminalises patterns of repeated or continuous coercive or controlling behaviour against an intimate partner or family member. • S.72 introduces a new offence of failing to protect a girl from risk of FGM. • S.74 introduces a duty on health care professionals, teachers and social care workers to notify the police of known cases of FGM carried out on a girl under 18.

References

Liberty (2016) www.liberty-human-rights.org.uk.

Social Care Institute for Excellence (2014) *Gaining Access to an Adult Suspected of Being at Risk of Neglect or Abuse: A Guide for Social Workers and their Managers in England.* Available at www.scie.org.uk/care-act-2014/safeguarding-adults/adult-suspected-at-risk-of-neglect-abuse, accessed on 25 April 2017.

Further reading

Braye, S., and Preston-Shoot, M. (2016a) *Practising Social Work Law* (4th edition). Basingstoke: Palgrave.

Braye, S., and Preston-Shoot, M. (2016b) *Legal Literacy: Practice Tool.* Totnes: RiPfA.

Author Biographies

Dan Baker

Dan Baker is the Mental Capacity Act (2005) Lead Officer for Central Bedfordshire Council, responsible for providing practice guidance to adult social care practitioners and management whilst overseeing the Deprivation of Liberty Safeguards. Having worked in various adult social care fields, at practitioner and team management levels, he is an experienced social worker and Best Interests Assessor, with particular experience in responding to complex adult safeguarding situations (including Court of Protection and High Court applications). Previously writing for *Community Care Inform*, he seeks to embed the Mental Capacity Act principles and promote its empowering potential.

Fiona Bateman

Fiona Bateman is a public law solicitor with expert knowledge of health and social care law and safeguarding responsibilities. She has over 13 years' experience representing local authorities and advising on implications of case law, legislative and policy developments. Fiona was recognised for innovation in organisational change as a finalist for the Local Government's Young Lawyer of the Year in 2013. Fiona has designed and delivered social care legal framework training since 2006. Since 2014 she has worked as an Independent Chair to Safeguarding Adults Boards, also undertaking Serious Case and Safeguarding Adults Review work.

Antony Botting

Antony Botting is Modern Slavery Project Lead for Croydon Council and has over ten years' experience working in local government. He has led the development of Croydon's multi-agency processes in relation to suspected cases of adult and child trafficking, and has facilitated a programme of multi-agency awareness-raising for practitioners in Croydon. Antony holds a Masters degree in International Law and Politics, and a LLB Law with European Legal Studies from the University of Hull.

Suzy Braye

Suzy Braye is Emerita Professor of Social Work at the University of Sussex. She works as an independent consultant and trainer in adult social care, and as a lead reviewer undertaking Safeguarding Adults Reviews. Her professional background is in social work practice and management, and a key focus of her current work is to support organisations in engaging with research evidence that informs policy and practice. As a social work researcher she has written widely on the relationship between law and social work, and on adult safeguarding and self-neglect. She is the editor of the *European Journal of Social Work*.

Keith Brown

Professor Keith Brown holds academic and professional qualifications in social work, nursing, teaching and management. He has worked in university and local authority education and training for over 25 years, and is currently Director of the National Centre for Post-Qualifying Social Work and Professional Practice and Director of the Institute of Health and Social Care Integration at Bournemouth University. He received the Linda Ammon memorial prize in 2005, for making the greatest contribution to education and training in the UK. He sits on the Department of Health Adult Safeguarding Advisory Board, the Joint Department of Health and Ministry of Justice National Mental Capacity Leadership forum and the Home Office Joint Financial task force.

Sarah Carr

Dr Sarah Carr is Associate Professor of Mental Health Research at Middlesex University London. She uses her experience of mental distress and service use to inform her work. Sarah previously worked for the Social Care Institute of Excellence as a Senior Research Analyst. She is Vice Chair of the National Survivor User Network and on the editorial board of *Disability and Society*. Sarah is a Fellow of the Royal Society of Arts, Honorary Senior Lecturer at the School for Social Policy, Birmingham University, and Visiting Fellow at the School of Social Policy and Social Work at the University of York.

Adi Cooper

Dr Adi Cooper OBE is Independent Chair of two Safeguarding Adults Boards, Co-Chair of the Association of Directors of Adult Social Services Safeguarding Adults Policy Network, the Care and Health Improvement Advisor for London (and safeguarding adults lead) for the Local Government Association, and is Visiting Professor at the University of Bedfordshire. Working in adult social care for over 25 years, she was the Director of Adult Social Services, Housing and Health for Sutton Council for nine years. She has contributed to adult safeguarding national policy development, service improvement, Care Act (2014) guidance, and the Making Safeguarding Personal programme.

Tish Elliott

Tish Elliott is a social worker and practice educator with over 30 years' experience of working for Devon local authority, primarily in safeguarding practice and workforce development. In her current social work lecturer role at the University of Plymouth, Tish has worked collaboratively with other stakeholders (service users, carers, students, practitioners and academics) to develop local Standards for the Promotion of Race Equality, Social Justice and Human Rights in social work practice, and has co-led training events on tackling Modern Slavery, Human Trafficking and Female Genital Mutilation. She is an Associate of Research in Practice for Adults, part of the Dartington Hall Trust.

Lee-Ann Fenge

Dr Lee-Ann Fenge is Deputy Director of the National Centre for Post-Qualifying Social Work at Bournemouth University. Her research interests concern inclusive research methodologies for engaging with seldom-heard groups, adult safeguarding and developing inclusive practice with older people. She teaches on post-qualifying programmes and supervises a number of doctoral students.

John Gunner

John Gunner was a leading mediator and restorative justice practitioner with experience spanning civil, workplace, community and criminal cases for 20 years. He was founding Vice Chair (Chair 2016) of the UK National Mediation Providers Association and twice-running, award-winning pioneer of *Telephone Mediation*, a SKY TV series. He was Visiting Lecturer at the University of Hertfordshire School of Law. He advised several governments on dispute resolution and legal policy.

Trish Hafford-Letchfield

Dr Trish Hafford-Letchfield is Professor of Social Care at Middlesex University where she provides inter-professional leadership education for people working in public and community services and teaches on research methods, social policy and adult social care. As a trained nurse, social worker, manager and educator, Trish has particular research, teaching and practice expertise in older people from marginalised communities and improving their experiences of care. Her main interests are in the engagement of service users, carers and the voluntary sector in the development and delivery of quality support services. She has published extensively across a range of interests.

Rebecca Johnson

Rebecca Johnson worked as a Research Assistant for the National Centre for Post-Qualifying Social Work and Professional Practice until 2016, focusing on scamming. Rebecca founded her research background with a Human and Physical Geography degree in which she was able to work with NASA's Environment and Energy team on research into the economic and environmental impact of launching the space shuttle. She has previously worked in both the public and private sectors in public consultation and communication roles.

Jane Lawson

Jane Lawson qualified as a social worker in 1983 and worked for local authorities in this role. She has managed a generic advocacy project and has undertaken safeguarding adults strategic roles. Her work on safeguarding adults and working with risk has been published as chapters in several textbooks on good practice. She has chaired several Safeguarding Adults Boards. Jane has chaired and authored a range of Serious Case Reviews/Safeguarding Adults Reviews, and facilitates learning and development across organisations and sectors involved in adult safeguarding. She worked on the LGA/ADASS Making Safeguarding Personal programme including as joint author of the reports from the 2013/14 pilot project and *Making Safeguarding Personal 2016 Temperature Check.*

Sally Lee

Dr Sally Lee is Post-Doctoral Research Fellow at the National Centre for Post-Qualifying Social Work and Professional Practice at Bournemouth University. She completed her doctoral research in 2016 exploring social work practice, physical disability and sexual wellbeing. She brings to her academic role extensive social work practice experience built up during more than 25 years of working in diverse practice settings and services. Her research interests focus on often-marginalised populations, and at present is investigating the experience of financial abuse and the detriment to individuals and society beyond financial loss.

Jill Manthorpe

Jill Manthorpe is Professor of Social Work at King's College London and Director of the Social Care Workforce Research Unit (SCWRU). She has a long history of researching adult safeguarding and has also chaired an Adult Safeguarding Board. She regularly undertakes training and continuing professional development activities with professionals on adult safeguarding using SCWRU research to link evidence to practice. She is a Trustee of a care home provider in the not-for-profit sector and a Fellow of Skills for Care.

Stephen Martineau

Stephen Martineau is a researcher at the Social Care Workforce Research Unit (SCWRU) in the Policy Institute at King's College London, working chiefly on adult safeguarding topics (e.g. disclosure and barring, Serious Case Reviews, and elder abuse policy), with a particular interest in legal aspects. He also manages social media at the Unit and its website, supporting the Unit's engagement with the Social Work History Network. He maintains the SCWRU collection of Adult Serious Care Reviews and Adult Safeguarding Reviews.

Nicki Norman

Nicki Norman has over 20 years' direct experience of delivering and developing domestic violence services, including survivor support groups, counselling, refuge, outreach, helplines, crisis and children's services. She has been an active member of local domestic violence partnerships, contributing to local multi-agency training and initiatives to improve responses to domestic violence. She has worked for Women's Aid Federation England since 2007, assisting with all aspects of the national charity's work to end violence against women, and has contributed to publications on this issue as well as working with national government to improve domestic violence policy and practice.

Caroline Norrie

Caroline Norrie is a researcher whose areas of interest include: adult safeguarding; gambling-related harm; care homes; inter-professional working; and professional migration. She is a Research Fellow at the Social Care Workforce Research Unit at King's College London. Caroline is currently working on three studies. The first is a study about adults at risk and gambling-related harm. The second study examines whether individuals are hindering safeguarding investigations and what helps practitioners in responding (the subject of her chapter in this volume). The third study is examining handovers at shift change in care homes. Caroline works closely with a local Healthwatch organisation.

Sean Olivier

Sean Olivier is the Safeguarding Coordinator for Adult Social Care in the London Borough of Croydon. He is the co-author of academic articles and has presented at several conferences. Sean has an interest in various aspects of adult safeguarding and safety including financial abuse and scam prevention, domestic violence prevention and responses to modern-day slavery. Sean qualified from the University of Cape Town in 2003 and holds a Masters degree in Social Policy and Management.

David Orr

Dr David Orr is Senior Lecturer in Social Work at the University of Sussex, where his principal research interests focus on adult safeguarding and self-neglect, dementia and transcultural mental health. He is co-editor of the *Palgrave Handbook of Sociocultural Perspectives on Global Mental Health* and has co-authored a number of knowledge reviews for the Social Care Institute for Excellence on topics including social work education, adult safeguarding and communication skills training. Before entering academia, he worked in Community Mental Health Teams in the areas of Adult Learning Disability and Older Adult Mental Health.

Lindsey Pike

Dr Lindsey Pike is a Senior Research and Development Officer for Research in Practice for Adults (RiPfA). She leads on developing RiPfA's resources on safeguarding adults. Before working at RiPfA she led a Knowledge Transfer Partnership about maximising the effectiveness of safeguarding adults training, which informed her PhD. Lindsey has published in the *Journal of Adult Protection*, updated the LGA guidance on safeguarding and domestic abuse (2014), and led the evaluation of Making Safeguarding Personal (2014/15). She recently co-led a project on coercive control and safeguarding with colleagues from Women's Aid and is part of the Housing and Safeguarding Alliance.

Michael Preston-Shoot

Michael Preston-Shoot is Professor Emeritus (Social Work) and was Executive Dean of the Faculty of Health and Social Sciences at the University of Bedfordshire, England. He is a Fellow of the Academy of Social Sciences. He was Chair of the Joint University Council Social Work Education Committee (2005–2009), Editor of *Social Work Education* (1993–2006), Managing Editor of the *European Journal of Social Work* (2003–2007) and a Founding Editor of the journal *Ethics and Social Welfare*. His publications have concentrated on law and social work practice, most recently focused on adult safeguarding, and adults who self-neglect. He is Independent Chair of two Safeguarding Adults Boards.

Tony Stanley

Dr Tony Stanley is the Chief Social Worker for Birmingham City Council as the professional lead for quality social work and improving practice. Tony was the Principal Social Worker at Tower Hamlets for children, families and adults. Recent publications include problematising the role of statutory services for cases of suspected radicalisation risk, and looking at organisational cultures and the effects for practice. He promotes 'child-centred and family-focused' social work, the importance of seeing children and adults with care and support needs relationally, and supporting their connections with family and relational networks.

Martin Stevens

Martin Stevens is a Senior Research Fellow at the Social Care Workforce Research Unit at King's College London. He has conducted a series of important studies of personalisation and of safeguarding and has a particular interest in services supporting people with learning disabilities, having worked in this area of social care. His current research focuses on access to adults thought to be at risk of harm. He has a long-standing interest in research ethics and governance and has assisted the Department of Health in developing this framework. Martin is Chair of the Health Research Authority Social Care Ethics Committee and also Chair of the Social Services Research Group.

Linda Tapper

Linda Tapper is an independent Family Group Conferencing (FGC) trainer and consultant, specialising in adult safeguarding. Previously she worked for Daybreak FGC pioneering the use of family group conferences for elder abuse, and expanding their use for adults of any age who may be at risk of harm. Linda developed the first accredited training specifically for coordinators providing adult FGC and has delivered training across the UK and in Europe. Linda has ten years' experience as a FGC coordinator, working especially with families experiencing domestic abuse, and is also an experienced advocate. Previously she has worked in the statutory and voluntary sectors.

Marilyn Taylor

Marilyn Taylor is the co-founder and CEO of Daybreak Family Group Conferences (FGC). She has worked in social work and probation, as a practitioner, manager and trainer, in both the statutory and voluntary sectors, in England and in Canada. Daybreak remains the only charity in England to focus entirely on FGC. It values innovative and reflective practice, including using FGC to address issues for adults with care and support needs and domestic violence. She leads Daybreak's provision of a FGC social franchise as well as expanding its training and consultancy programmes. Marilyn has presented at a range of national and international conferences.

Emily White

Emily White is a social worker with a range of experience across adult social care, including services for older people, learning disability, physical disability and drugs and alcohol. She has worked for the Audit Commission in performance assessment, the Care Quality Commission as a regulatory inspector and as an advisor to the Local Government Association (LGA) on Making Safeguarding Personal. She wrote the fourth edition of *Making Safeguarding Personal: A Toolkit for Responses* (LGA 2015). She is currently working as Principal Social Worker and Head of Quality Improvement and Safeguarding for Central Bedfordshire Council.

Subject Index

Author Index